QuickTime for .NET and COM Developers

QuickTime Developer Series

Apple's QuickTime is a way to deliver multimedia—video, sound, styled text, MIDI, Flash, virtual reality, 3D models, sprites, and more—wrapped in a package that will play on Windows or Macintosh computers, on a DVD or CD-ROM, over the Internet, in a browser window, a PDF document, a PowerPoint presentation, a Word document, or all by itself. The **QuickTime Developer Series**, developed in close cooperation with Apple, is devoted to exploring all of the capabilities of this powerful industry standard. Books in the series are written by experienced developers, including engineers from within the development team at Apple. All of the books feature a practical, hands-on approach and are prepared according to the latest developments in QuickTime technology.

QuickTime for .NET and COM Developers
John Cromie

QuickTime Toolkit Volume One:
Basic Movie Playback and Media Types
Tim Monroe

QuickTime Toolkit Volume Two:
Advanced Movie Playback and Media Types
Tim Monroe

Interactive QuickTime: Authoring Wired Media
Matthew Peterson

Related title

Programming with Quartz:
2D and PDF Graphics in Mac OS X
David Gelphman and Bunny Laden

QuickTime for .NET and COM Developers

John Cromie

AMSTERDAM • BOSTON • HEIDELBERG • LONDON
NEW YORK • OXFORD • PARIS • SAN DIEGO
SAN FRANCISCO • SINGAPORE • SYDNEY • TOKYO

Morgan Kaufmann Publishers is an imprint of Elsevier

MORGAN KAUFMANN PUBLISHERS

Senior Editor	Tim Cox
Publishing Services Manager	Simon Crump
Project Manager	Elisabeth Beller
Assistant Editor	Rick Camp
Editorial Assistant	Jessica Evans
Cover Design	Laurie Anderson
Cover Image	© Getty Images (photographer, Eastcott Momatiuk)
Text Design	Rebecca Evans
Composition	Nancy Logan
Technical Illustration	Dartmouth Publishing Inc.
Copyeditor	Yonie Overton
Proofreader	Jennifer McClain
Indexer	Steve Rath
Interior printer	The Maple-Vail Book Manufacturing Group
Cover printer	Phoenix Color Corporation

Apple, the Apple Logo, QuickTime, iDVD, iLife, iMovie, iPhoto, iPod, and iTunes are trademarks of Apple Computer, Inc., registered in the United States and other countries, used by Morgan Kaufmann with permission.

The QuickTime logo is a trademark of Apple Computer, Inc., used by Morgan Kaufmann with permission.

Designations used by companies to distinguish their products are often claimed as trademarks or registered trademarks. In all instances in which Morgan Kaufmann Publishers is aware of a claim, the product names appear in initial capital or all capital letters. Readers, however, should contact the appropriate companies for more complete information regarding trademarks and registration.

Morgan Kaufmann Publishers is an imprint of Elsevier.
500 Sansome Street, Suite 400, San Francisco, CA 94111

Library of Congress Cataloging-in-Publication Data
Application submitted.

ISBN 13: 978-0-12-774575-6
ISBN 10: 0-12-774575-0

For information on all Morgan Kaufmann publications,
visit our website at *www.mkp.com* or *www.books.elsevier.com*.

Transferred to Digital Printing 2009

Working together to grow
libraries in developing countries

www.elsevier.com | www.bookaid.org | www.sabre.org

ELSEVIER   BOOK AID International   Sabre Foundation

Contents

About the Author x

Preface xi

Acknowledgments xv

Chapter 1 **Introduction** **1**

Introduction 1
 Why QuickTime? 2
Why .NET and COM? 3
 COM 4
 .NET 5
 COM Interop 6
QuickTime Meets COM and .NET 7
Who Is This Book For? 8
What Should I Know Before Reading This Book? 10
Code Samples 10
Additional Resources 12
 .NET, Visual Basic, and C# 12
 Windows Scripting 13
 QuickTime 13

Chapter 2 **Getting Started with the QuickTime Control** **15**

Introduction 15
Hello World! 15
Simple Player—The Basics 23
 Initialization 24
 Opening and Closing Movies 26
 Controlling the Movie 28
 Getting Information about the Movie 30
 Scaling the Movie 32
 Full-Screen Movies 33
 Automatically Sizing the Form 34
 About... 35
Summary 36

Chapter 3   **Using the QuickTime Control**   **37**

Introduction 37

The Apple QuickTime Control 38

  Get the Big Picture 39

Movies 40

  Loading a Movie 41

  Movie Scaling and Sizing 42

  A Resizeable Window for Simple Player 46

  Background and Border 49

  Movie Controller 51

  Auto Play 52

  Control over Full-Screen Display 52

Initializing QuickTime 55

  Is QuickTime Available? 58

Probing Deeper 58

Summary 59

Chapter 4   **The QuickTime Object Model**   **61**

Introduction 61

Object Models 62

The QuickTime Object Model 64

  QTMovie and Its Offspring 66

  QTQuickTime and Its Offspring 83

Summary 94

Chapter 5   **Diving Deeper**   **95**
                 Essential Topics for Serious QuickTime Development

Introduction 95

QuickTime Events 95

  Registering for QuickTime Events 96

  Handling QuickTime Events 96

  Sample: QuickTime Events Demo 105

QuickTime Metadata 114

  Annotations 115

CFObject and Its Uses 122

  CFObject Collection 124

  The Annotations CFDictionary 128

Complex CFObject Data Structures   132
Persistent CFObject   140
Error Handling   144
Summary   153

Chapter 6   **Create and Edit**   **155**
Creating and Editing QuickTime Content
Introduction   155
The Joy of Cut, Copy, and Paste   156
    Implementing the Edit Menu   156
    Saving the Movie   158
    Creating a New Movie   159
Movie Builder   160
    Assembling a Movie   161
    Adding an Overlay   171
    Subtitling the Movie   175
Summary of the Edit Capabilities of QTMovie   181
Creating a Movie from Images   181
SMIL the Movie   183
Creating a Movie Using GDI   189
Saving a New Movie   193
Summary   194

Chapter 7   **Browsing the Media**   **195**
Design and Build a Complete QuickTime Application
For the Birds   195
    Design Decisions   196
Implementation   200
    Picking the Components   200
    Building the Bare Bones   201
    Directory Browsing   204
    Media Display   208
    Wiring Up the Connections   218
    Adding the QuickTime Control   221
    Media Inspector   225
    A Tooltip   235
Summary   237

Chapter 8   **Scripting QuickTime Player**   **239**

Introduction   239

Scripting QuickTime on the Mac   239

Windows Scripting Host   241

   COM (Automation) Server   243

QuickTime Player: A COM Server   245

   Opening and Playing a Movie   245

   The QuickTime Player Object Model   246

   Working with Players   248

   A Movie Builder Script   250

   Batch Export from the Command Line   254

   Event Handlers   258

   Script Droplets   263

   Windows Scripting File (.wsf) Format   265

Summary   267

Chapter 9   **QuickTime Meets Office**   **269**
QuickTime Development in Microsoft Excel and Access

Introduction   269

Excel   270

   Adding the QuickTime Control   271

   ActiveX and Macro Security   272

   Adding a Play/Stop Cell   274

   Movie Inspector   275

   Movie Inspector with Annotation Editing   283

   Batch Processing: Movie Annotator   285

Access   288

   Movie Display   288

   QuickTime Event Handling   291

Summary   293

Appendix A   **QuickTime COM Library Reference**   **295**

QuickTime Control (QTOControlLib)   295

QuickTime Object Library (QTOLibrary)   296

Appendix B Additional COM Host Environments   **299**
QuickTime Control Basics in Other COM Hosts

Visual Basic 6   299

Getting Started   299
Adding a Load Button   300
Adding a Play/Stop Button   300
Resizing the Form to Fit the Control   303
Responding to Manual Resize of the Form   304
Porting Code Samples to Visual Basic 6 or
    Visual Basic for Applications (VBA)   305

Delphi   306

Getting Started   306
Loading a Movie   307
Playing the Movie   308
Handling QuickTime Events   309

ATL/WTL   311

Getting Started   311
Adding the QuickTime Control   314
Adding a Play/Stop Button   316
Handling Events from the QuickTime Control   317
QuickTime Events   318

Appendix C QuickTime Exporter Types   **321**
Exporter Types   321

Index   **325**

About the Author

John Cromie is one of the architects of Apple's QuickTime ActiveX/COM control for Windows and is the principal at the software development and consulting company, Skylark Associates. Skylark specializes in software design, website architecture, and interface design, and has clients in both Europe and the United States. With a strong portfolio of successful projects, many of which feature QuickTime, Skylark has established a reputation for innovative software development of interactive and web applications on both Windows and Mac platforms.

Having worked with QuickTime for over 12 years, John is a long-time QuickTime developer, first using HyperCard on the Mac and then moving on to Windows with the advent of QuickTime for Windows. An experienced developer, John has successfully delivered numerous CD/DVD-ROM titles, websites, and interactive applications using RAD tools, C++, and the Quick-Time API. Skylark is also responsible for the cross-platform software behind the award-winning *BirdGuides* range of CD/DVD-ROM titles for birdwatchers—again largely QuickTime based. John has overseen the development of *birdguides.com* into the leading bird information website in Europe. Consulting clients include Cambridge University, Esat/BT, The International Post Corporation, and Apple Computer.

Whenever the fickle weather in the northwest of Ireland permits, John gets out and about birding or walking in the mountains, and he is actively involved in nature conservation.

Preface

A gadget freak I am not—let's be clear about that from the outset—but in the past couple of weeks our postman (a.k.a. the mailman) has arrived not once, but twice, with a package containing one of the most ingeniously compact bundles of consumer technology that exists today. The first was a long-overdue necessity: a cell phone to replace the battered but trusty companion that had been bounced off a few too many rocks and hard floors. Actually it still worked fine—the necessity had more to do with sparing the blushes of my off-spring when such a three-year-old "dinosaur" was taken out in public. OK, I'll be honest: I was seduced by the upgrade model—a 3G "smartphone" with built-in browser, cameras (yes, plural: one front and one back, believe it or not!), MP3 player, FM radio, and the list goes on. It could also make and receive calls, which was a relief.

Even avowed nongadget types admit a frisson of anticipation when unpacking such a marvel. Sadly, the initial excitement soon evaporated to be replaced by disappointment and mounting frustration—before long I was looking around for a convenient rock. Yes, the phone certainly did all the things that it claimed to do, but it excelled at none of them. I may be particularly slow, but even making a call necessitated a quick glance at page 10 of the manual. The much-trumpeted accompanying software "suite" turned out to be a confusing hodgepodge of applications each with its own unique and inscrutable user interface. To top it all, the software was only for Windows—no mention of the Mac: it didn't exist so far as this major manufacturer was concerned. Ruefully, I stuffed the lot back into its fancy box and returned it, having duly made my peace with my old phone.

A week or so later, and that feeling of anticipation is back as I'm extricating an entirely different gadget from its packaging. No built-in camera this time; no browser, no FM radio, no Bluetooth—it can't even make a phone call. But—as I soon discover—the few things that this device *can* do are executed so superbly that it totally blows away my (already high) expectations. The accompanying software is fully integrated and works seamlessly with the device. It can be installed on both Mac and Windows and works exactly the same on both. I'm talking about the latest video iPod, of course, and its companion software—iTunes 6.

And the moral of this tale of two gadgets? Well, it should be obvious: if you nurture big ambitions for your gadget—or application or software tool—be sure to focus your efforts on its core function and usability: make that outstanding first and foremost—make it really shine.

QuickTime

QuickTime is the success that it is today precisely because Apple has focused its efforts on making sure that QuickTime continues to deliver the very best media playback and creation technology, even as standards, platforms, and hardware all evolve. And shine QuickTime does, not only on the Mac—where one would hardly expect less of Apple—but equally on the Windows platform, a fact that is often not fully appreciated nor admitted by Windows-oriented developers. It is no exaggeration to suggest that this unique cross-platform capability of QuickTime has, in no small way, helped to underpin the whole iPod/iTunes success story for Apple. A case in point is the way in which Apple was able to introduce into QuickTime a specific iPod export option in support of the fifth-generation video-capable iPod, thanks to the component-based nature of QuickTime. Suddenly anyone with QuickTime 7 Pro could create video podcasts or export existing content for the new iPod—on both Mac and Windows.

For readers of this book, the exciting thing is that this very same enabling technology is available to us—developers with a focus on the Windows platform. Not only that, but with the advent of QuickTime 7 on Windows it is now possible to develop with QuickTime using most of the popular RAD and scripting tools that Windows developers enjoy including, of course, the .NET environment. And with much of the complexity of QuickTime having been assiduously bundled up into a collection of easy-to-use components, even the feeble excuse of having to learn a new and complex API no longer washes.

What's in This Book?

This book specifically addresses QuickTime development on Windows using the QuickTime COM components that were released by Apple with Quick-Time 7. An introductory chapter sets the scene with useful background information on QuickTime as well as on .NET and COM development. The initial chapters then cover the basics of using the QuickTime COM/ActiveX Control to open a movie as well as to control its playback and display within the host application. As a key concept, the QuickTime Object Model is central to the material in this book, and it is presented next. Each of its constituent QuickTime objects is systematically examined, often in the context of a practical application. Subsequent chapters deal with specific topics, such as event handling, export, and metadata, in considerable depth and also delve into some of the more advanced aspects of QuickTime development. The culmination of all this is a chapter devoted to the design and development of a complete object-oriented QuickTime application in Visual Basic .NET. Broadening the focus somewhat, later chapters look at scripting with Quick-Time in both Windows Scripting Host and Microsoft Office applications.

The specifics of using QuickTime in other popular COM development environments, such as Visual Basic 6, Delphi, and ATL, are covered in an appendix. While much of this book inevitably focuses on using QuickTime in Visual Basic .NET and C#, the principles and even the code samples should be readily transferable to other component-based development tools and languages.

Code snippets are liberally scattered throughout the book and are specifically designed to support the explanation of each topic: for a developer, a few lines of code will often illuminate what any amount of careful explanation cannot. Longer code samples address the kind of real-world issues and applications that you are likely to encounter in your own projects. All of the code samples, scripts, and a few sample media files are available from the website associated with this book:

www.skylark.ie/qt4.net

Discovering QuickTime

QuickTime entered my world well over a decade ago when I serendipitously happened upon QuickTime and HyperCard on the Mac at more or less the same time. A revolutionary technology that could play videos and sounds in conjunction with a unique scripting language was an intoxicating mix for interactive developers at the time—but, sadly, not on the then-mushrooming Windows platform. Apple's farsighted release of QuickTime for Windows offered half the solution, but unfortunately there was no HyperCard equivalent on Windows. Or was there? The more I looked at Microsoft's Visual Basic, the more I liked it: it had all the immediacy and productivity of HyperCard and yet was clearly a serious development tool—but how to put the two together? Initially this necessitated the development of a 16-bit QuickTime VBX control (or VB plug-in) written in C. In time I rewrote this in C++ as a 32-bit QuickTime ActiveX control, eventually to be released in its own right as a commercial component (and still available*). Pairing Visual Basic with QuickTime turned out to be a hugely productive development platform for efficient delivery of CD/DVD-ROM titles and other interactive applications.

Remarkably, this is even more the case today when you consider the latest developments in QuickTime, the advent of next-generation RAD tools, such as Visual Basic .NET and C#, and now, at last, the authoritative components from Apple to put the two together effectively.

You may be entirely new to QuickTime or perhaps you are about to embark on developing with QuickTime on the Windows platform for the first time. Whatever the case, you may be forgiven for feeling a scintilla of anticipation at this point—as I often do when about to delve into some new and potentially exciting piece of technology. As you unwrap and discover the capabilities of QuickTime and the QuickTime COM components and as you apply them in your own applications, I hope that, with the aid of this book, your experience will be both rewarding and enjoyable

---

* *www.skylark.ie/skylight*

Acknowledgments

Having had the pleasure of working with the QuickTime engineering team at Apple, I can personally attest to the creative energy, skill, and sheer commitment that is the human driving force behind QuickTime. Eric Carlson, with whom I worked closely on the QuickTime for COM project at Apple, epitomizes this. Not only did Eric have the vision for opening up QuickTime to the COM and .NET developer community, he also brought to bear a deep understanding of QuickTime itself, which, combined with his technical acumen and pursuit of excellence, ensured that the subject of this book became a reality. As the content of this book gradually took shape, Eric's input and comments have been invaluable and very much appreciated.

Many others on the QuickTime engineering team at Apple have provided assistance and encouragement. The solidity and robustness of the QuickTime for COM technology are testimony to the efforts of Paul Zemanek. Paul has been generous with his help, spot-checking code samples, commenting on drafts, and providing an all-important reader's perspective. Respected authors of other books in the *QuickTime Developer Series*, Steve Gulie and Tim Monroe have both contributed constructive and detailed reviews of draft chapters. Without their encouragement and enthusiastic feedback, this book might well have foundered. Comments from Jeremy Jones and Thai Wey Then have also been helpful in shaping the style of the book at an early stage and in weeding out one or two decidedly shaky analogies.

I am grateful to Tim Cox of Morgan Kaufmann and Michael Hinkson at Apple who together made this book possible. Tim's gentle prodding has given this developer the impetus to leave aside coding (fun) and keep up with the writing (hard work). Thanks also to Jessie Evans and Richard Camp at Morgan Kaufmann.

Not having written a book before, I was never entirely sure what an editor actually did. Well, now I know—and I admire her. Elisabeth Beller has helped to inject clarity and consistency, while all the time fighting an uphill battle to Americanise (or should that be "Americanize") my spelling, grammar, (comma here—I'm learning!) and punctuation. I have greatly appreciated her efficiency and organization in pulling this book together in the face of a tight deadline and the vagaries of a first-time author.

The illustrations and code samples in this book have been enlivened with video clips and images from the extensive *BirdGuides* archive. My thanks are due to Max Whitby and Dave Gosney, my fellow directors at *BirdGuides,* for allowing me to use this material. David Suttle of suttledesign kindly created the funky *Hello World* movie that features in early chapters.

Jan has been a constant support as I have been writing. If she has sometimes wondered why technical writing requires sustained periods gazing out of the window at the birds on the feeders, or how come the end result of a full day's "writing" can amount to no more than a few measly paragraphs or a single anemic-looking code sample, she has had the graciousness never to let on. Robert, Mary-Lynn, Joel, and Simon have treated Dad's book project with the light-hearted good humor that it deserved, helping to keep me sane and (usually) good-humored in the process.

Introduction

Introduction

It's a fair bet that since you bothered to beg, borrow, or perhaps even buy this book, you will have some idea, however vague, of the capabilities of QuickTime. Some of you will be intimately acquainted with the QuickTime C/C++ application programming interface (API) in all its savage glory; others will have used QuickTime in various scripting environments on the Mac or on Windows—perhaps in Macromedia Director or via AppleScript— maybe even in HyperCard if you've been around long enough. Or your QuickTime experience may amount to nothing more than fiddling around with the Pro edition of QuickTime Player.

Nor is it unreasonable to assume that you may already have worked with Visual Basic or with one of the many other Rapid Application Development, or RAD, tools. If so, you will not need to be convinced of the productivity, efficiency, and plain old ease of use that has characterized such tools, from the humble beginnings of Visual Basic over a decade ago to those heavyweights of today: Visual Basic .NET and C#.

Underpinning the success of these tools has been the component-based architecture—first in COM (the Component Object Model) and later in its now fully fledged .NET incarnation. Millions—literally—of developers have grown to love these tools for no other reason than the fact that should their application demand, say, a Kanji editor or a simulated aircraft instrument panel or maybe a calendar with psychedelic dates, all they have to do is source the appropriate component, drop it into their toolbox, and away they go.

QuickTime has not entirely been left out of this party: a few third-party developers have been supplying useful QuickTime components for quite a number of years. But none of these components has been anywhere near comprehensive in its exposure of the QuickTime API nor, critically, has Apple itself gotten involved. The release in 2005 of the official *Apple Quick-Time Control* changes all this.

The Apple QuickTime Control delivers a substantial chunk of QuickTime technology—at least in playback and editing—to the toolboxes of component-based developers. Using Visual Basic, C#, Delphi, and other component-based tools, developers can now have access to the unique capabilities of QuickTime in their Windows applications, with the blessing and support of Apple.

Why QuickTime?

For many Windows developers, QuickTime is perceived as nothing more than a media playback technology, vying with the likes of Microsoft Windows Media Player and Real Player for the right to handle the multiplicity of video and audio files that litter their disks. This does QuickTime a grave injustice: QuickTime is about a whole lot more than just video playback. What is often not understood is that QuickTime can also be used for audio and video capture, for media creation and editing, for combining media from various online and off-line sources, for importing and exporting media in a host of different formats, for display and manipulation of images, for creating sophisticated interactive applications, for exploring interactive 3D environments—and so the list goes on. In short, QuickTime is a complete media architecture and, as such, it is unique.

None of the competing playback technologies—not even Windows Media Player—can sustain such a claim. Launched way back in 1991, the Quick-Time architecture has managed to embrace a succession of emerging media technologies and standards. Today, QuickTime is more successful than at any point in its history, and this is testimony to the robustness of its enduring architecture and its cross-platform appeal.

Another common misconception amongst Windows developers is worth scotching at the earliest opportunity. This is that QuickTime is essentially a Mac (slight pejorative inflexion here) technology, a few essential bits of which have been ported, somewhat hastily, over to Windows. The fact, of course, is that QuickTime for Windows is every bit as feature-laden and performance-oriented as its twin sibling on the Mac. Just as QuickTime on OS X builds on the powerful video, audio, and graphics services of that operating system, so QuickTime for Windows takes maximum advantage of the equivalent services in Windows. True, new QuickTime features often first see the light of day on the Mac—that's inevitable—but, more often than not, they soon make an appearance in QuickTime for Windows.

From the developer perspective, QuickTime is best thought of as an enabling technology. It enables us, as developers, to include capabilities in our applications that would otherwise be beyond our capacity (either technically or due to limited resources). In some cases, entire applications are made possible only with the underlying capabilities of QuickTime. Some of the useful capabilities that QuickTime might bring to our applications include

- Playback of media in many different video, audio, and animation formats
- Streaming media playback
- Video and audio editing
- Frame-by-frame video creation
- Video and audio capture
- Conversion of video and audio between a whole range of popular formats
- Addition of close captioning and graphic overlays to video
- Ability to view and navigate around panoramic VR scenes and 3D objects

Why .NET and COM?

Visual Basic 1.0 was released in 1991—about seven months before Quick-Time 1.0—bringing together the ease of use of the familiar BASIC programming language with an interactive graphical user interface (GUI) design environment. Suddenly anyone with a smattering of BASIC and the ability to drag and drop could try their hand at creating GUI applications for Windows. And they certainly did: within the space of a few years, Visual Basic was to become the most popular programming language of all time.

Professional developers, meanwhile, working with traditional programming languages such as C, and the emerging C++, gazed out disdainfully at this upstart from the safety of their curly brackets. With its evil GOTO statement, BASIC had always been an object of scorn for proponents of structured programming languages. In 1975, Edsger W. Dijkstra famously declared of students who had some prior exposure to BASIC: "as potential programmers they are mentally mutilated beyond hope of regeneration." Sadly this attitude has a tendency to live on in the mindset of many software professionals, tarring Visual Basic with the same brush.

But, while such prejudiced engineers grew old on their endless edit-compile-link-test treadmills, less-blinkered developers began to realize that using Visual Basic allowed them to develop GUI applications and, more important, get them to market much quicker than traditional programming languages. And all this could be achieved without abandoning good design and structured programming techniques: it was possible to use Basic without polluting your code with GOTO statements. The RAD era had begun.

COM

Efficiency and ease of development were not the only reasons why Visual Basic thrived. Its support for the Component Object Model, or COM, standard provided a ready means of accessing software libraries and user interface (UI) components, often developed by third parties. RAD benefited enormously, and still does, from a huge and diverse range of available software components. Everything from small specialized UI controls to a full working spreadsheet could simply be dropped into your application.

COM is an application and vendor-independent standard, and a COM component such as the QuickTime Control can be used in a variety of different development tools and even desktop applications as long as they respect the requisite COM containment standards. The popularity of Visual Basic, and the resulting proliferation of useful COM components, prompted other development tool vendors to introduce COM support. The best example is Borland's Delphi, offering a very similar—and many would argue, superior—development environment to that of Visual Basic, but using Object Pascal[1] instead of Basic.

In Depth: COM

Component-based development would simply not be possible without rigorous and well-defined standards that ensure that a component from vendor X will work smoothly alongside a component from vendor Y or Z. The Component Object Model (COM) is by far the most successful standard, with hundreds of vendors supplying an incredible array of components to meet every conceivable developer need.

Much of the success of COM as a basis for software components is due to its rigorous insistence on well-defined component *interfaces*—the collections of properties and functions exposed by an object.

---

1 This was rechristened as the Delphi programming language in recent versions of Delphi.

The COM standard (amongst many other details):

■ Defines the way in which the interface(s) of a component are made available to its host.

■ Defines a set of standardized data types that can be used to pass data back and forth between components.

■ Defines how the component can notify its host of interesting events.

A COM *control* is distinguished from COM components in general by the fact that it has a visual representation of some kind (often managing its own window) and can only be placed on a visual container such as a form or dialog. Standards ensure that both the COM control and its container can communicate with each other through a set of mutually respected interfaces.

When it comes to desktop applications, the most comprehensive COM support is, not surprisingly, to be found in the Microsoft Office suite of applications, any of which can host COM controls, with scripting support available through Visual Basic for Applications (VBA). As we will see later in this book, the judicious use of COM components in an Excel spreadsheet or Access database can open up interesting and productive avenues in that twilight zone between off-the-shelf and fully custom applications.

So carried away did Microsoft become with the potential of COM that not only did they add COM support to their desktop applications, they decided to add it to the desktop itself in the form of Windows Script Host—an operating system–level environment for running scripts written in either Visual Basic Scripting Edition (VBScript) or Microsoft's version of JavaScript (JScript). Such scripts can directly create COM objects and can also be used to script any application that exposes its functionality through COM interfaces: a potent tool (as we will discover in Chapter 8) but one that has, unfortunately, been ruthlessly hijacked by darker forces ever since.

.NET

Visual Basic .NET and C# are the next-generation RAD tools, building upon the success of Visual Basic 6.0. Both languages depend entirely on the underlying .NET Framework for their execution environment and for system services. At the very heart of the .NET Framework is the Common Language Runtime, or CLR. All code in the .NET environment, whether written in Visual Basic or C# (or any other .NET language, for that matter), is compiled to Intermediate Language (IL)—a kind of assembly language for .NET. The IL is then, in turn, compiled to native code by the CLR just prior to execution.

Code that runs under the CLR is known as *managed code*: its execution is tightly monitored and controlled by the CLR, which can check on such things as array indexes and type safety, as well as provide exception handling, garbage collection, and security services. Contrast this with traditional compiled or *unmanaged* code, which once loaded into memory, essentially has a free hand to do its worst.

The CLR also replaces the older COM environment, except that instead of managing COM objects, the CLR is tasked with the management of .NET objects. The .NET Framework takes the object-based environment pioneered by COM to an entirely new level: even operating system components, such as a file or folder, or the display screen, are full-fledged .NET objects. Indeed, much of what was once the preserve of the Win32 API is now wrapped by the extensive and unified suite of classes known as the .NET Framework class library.

User interface development is also enhanced: in place of the motley collection of UI controls provided with Visual Basic 6.0, RAD developers can draw on the services of *Windows Forms*—a collection of UI controls whose usefulness belies its uninspiring name.

To the RAD enthusiast, Visual Basic .NET and C# hold out the promise of even more productive and efficient development, dispensing with many of the idiosyncrasies and shortcomings of Visual Basic 6.0 and Delphi. None of this comes without a flip side: .NET applications require the .NET runtime, which weighs in at a whopping 20+ megabytes and must be installed before even the most simple application can run.

Many would argue too, with some justification, that the .NET Framework—with its extra layer between operating system and application code—adds significantly to execution overhead. In time, though, as Windows XP gives way to Vista (formerly Longhorn), the .NET Framework becomes more closely intertwined with the operating system itself, and with faster hardware, these considerations will inevitably become less relevant.

COM Interop

While COM has been eclipsed by .NET's new component architecture, COM components are still very much accommodated within the .NET Framework through its *COM Interop* services. COM Interop wraps a COM component with a .NET wrapper; in this way it can be used as if it were a native .NET object. Almost invariably, this Interop wrapper works seamlessly behind the scenes so that using COM components with Visual Basic .NET and C# is no different from using native .NET components.

◖ QuickTime Meets COM and .NET

Serious QuickTime development, on both Mac and Windows, has tradition-ally been the preserve of developers working directly with the QuickTime API in languages such as C or C++. For those lacking the requisite resources or inclination to use the QuickTime API, the alternative was to use authoring tools that supported QuickTime, such as Macromedia Director. Both the QuickTime API and the major authoring tools were available cross-platform, so QuickTime developers on Windows tended to fall into either the API or authoring camps. RAD tools, such as Visual Basic, were largely ignored for want of QuickTime support.

An irony, not lost on Mac developers of a certain vintage, is that many of the concepts that have made Visual Basic such a resounding success—graph-ical UI design, event-driven scripts, drop-in components—originated in HyperCard: a ground-breaking programming environment for the Mac re-leased by Apple in 1987. When QuickTime appeared on the scene, it was logical for Apple to include QuickTime support in HyperCard, and it wasn't long before the HyperCard/QuickTime combination became the platform of choice for pioneer interactive multimedia developers. Unfortunately, Apple rather lost the plot with HyperCard, and it faded from the scene by the mid-1990s.

Apple's farsighted decision to port QuickTime to the Windows platform left some developers wondering if perhaps the HyperCard/QuickTime com-bination on the Mac could be replicated on Windows with Visual Basic and QuickTime for Windows. A number of third-party ActiveX controls appeared that exposed a basic QuickTime feature-set for use in Visual Basic and other COM-aware environments. These components enjoyed a limited degree of success, particularly with developers producing CD-ROM and DVD-ROM products for the consumer and educational markets. But, inevita-bly, without the direct support of Apple, QuickTime adoption within the ever-growing COM and .NET sector was never going to be significant. Mean-while, Mac developers on OS X were reaping the benefits of the comprehen-sive and easy-to-use QuickTime support included in the Cocoa framework with QuickTime Kit (QTKit), not to mention the powerful QuickTime Player scripting/automation capabilities provided by AppleScript. Nothing like this existed for Windows developers.

Aware of the need to promote QuickTime development with the popular COM- and .NET-based Windows tools, Apple released the QuickTime COM Control and Object Library in 2005. Exposing a similar view of QuickTime to that offered by QTKit on the Mac, the new QuickTime Control opens up the possibilities for using QuickTime in any application or scripting environment that supports the hosting of COM controls.

Suddenly it becomes possible to use QuickTime in all sorts of unexpected places: in an Excel spreadsheet, on a database form, or in more specialist applications such as LabVIEW (National Instruments: *www.ni.com*). But, exciting as it might be to have movie trailers brightening up that cash flow, it is the ability to deploy QuickTime in any of the mainstream RAD development tools that really gets developers excited. Visual Basic, C#, and Delphi (Borland) are the big-hitters of course, but there are also less well-known but still popular tools such as ToolBook (SumTotal: *www.toolbook.com*).

If you're familiar with the component-based development scene, you may be wondering why Apple has gone to all this trouble to release a COM control and not a 100 percent native .NET control. Well, the answer is that a native .NET control must, by definition, run entirely within the Common Language Runtime (CLR)—the mandatory runtime environment for .NET. QuickTime has been running on Windows since long before .NET was ever conceived of, so all of the code within QuickTime is, rather pejoratively, classed as *unmanaged* code and regarded as untouchable by a native .NET control. This is why the QuickTime Control is delivered as a COM control with an Interop wrapper so that it can be used in the .NET environment.

Porting QuickTime itself to run under the CLR would in any case be a mammoth task, and given that the outstanding performance of QuickTime depends heavily on carefully tuned access to low-level system facilities, it's difficult to see how adding an extra layer would not impact performance. Interestingly, Microsoft currently adopts the same approach with their competing Windows Media Player technology: if you want to use Media Player in your .NET application, then you use the Media Player COM Control with its Interop wrapper.

▶ Who Is This Book For?

When a book purports to cover the intersection between two such wide-reaching topics as QuickTime and COM/.NET development, it inevitably attracts a diverse readership. There is no such thing as a typical reader for whom this book has been fine-tuned. Nevertheless, I have presumed to identify several groups of potential readers to whom this book should appeal:

- You are a Windows developer, with reasonable competency in Visual Basic 6.0, Visual Basic .NET, C#, Delphi, or perhaps other RAD or component-based development tools. You have some basic understanding of what QuickTime is and what it can do, and you are keen to find out more.

  You will learn how to use QuickTime in your Visual Basic 6.0, Visual Basic .NET, or C# applications. In the process, you will inevitably learn more about QuickTime and especially about how to get the most out of the QuickTime Control and Object Library. For a more in-depth understanding of QuickTime itself, you may occasionally need to refer to Apple's QuickTime documentation or other resources.

- Already familiar with QuickTime, you have developed QuickTime applications either on the Mac or on Windows. While you may or may not be conversant with the QuickTime API, you will certainly have a good grasp of the principal concepts of the QuickTime architecture. Your development experience with RAD tools such as Visual Basic, on the other hand, is still at the steep part of the learning curve.

  You will very quickly learn how to include basic QuickTime functionality in the Visual Basic .NET or C# applications that you are learning to develop. As you learn how to exploit some of the more advanced Quick-Time features, the code samples become more intricate, and you may find that you need to refer to your Visual Basic .NET or C# learning material or documentation from time to time. By the end, you should be confident to deploy your expanding skills in pursuit of more sophisticated Quick-Time applications.

- You are, or are about to be, involved in QuickTime content production on the Windows platform. You are anxious to discover how much, if any, of your workflow can be automated using COM or .NET scripting. You may already be familiar with what can be achieved using Apple-Script on the Mac and are wondering whether something similar might be possible on Windows.

  You will discover that QuickTime Player on Windows can be scripted (or automated) in a very similar way to what is possible with QuickTime Player on the Mac. You will learn that once a movie is loaded in Quick-Time Player, the entire QuickTime Object Model is exposed and available for you to script from JScript, VBScript, or even from applications such as

Microsoft Excel. Depending on your specific workflow requirements, various techniques will be available for creating and manipulating Quick-Time content in a variety of formats.

- As a battle-hardened C or C++ developer with the QuickTime API, there is very little that you don't already know about QuickTime. You already create advanced QuickTime applications on the Mac directly with the QuickTime API or with Cocoa and QTKit, or on Windows using Visual C++ with the QuickTime API. Nevertheless, curiosity impels you to find out more about what can (and can't) be achieved developing with Quick-Time in a RAD or scripting environment.

  You may be pleasantly surprised.

If you've gotten as far as this and you don't even faintly recognize yourself in any of the cameos above, what can I say? Thank you for buying this book: I do hope you enjoy it and learn something, even if you bought it to look at the pictures or to impress your manager!

What Should I Know Before Reading This Book?

Since this book deals with the convergence of QuickTime with RAD technologies such as Visual Basic and C#, it clearly helps to know a little about both. At the very least, you should be comfortable with creating a simple Windows Forms (the .NET UI platform) application in either Visual Basic or C#. Fortunately, this is very easy to learn, and there are innumerable books out there that purport to introduce you to Visual Basic in 21 days, 21 hours, or perhaps even in your sleep for all I know.

Experienced Visual Basic 6.0 developers who haven't yet made the leap to .NET will find most of the code samples to be readily comprehensible, although a short foray into Visual Basic .NET is highly recommended.

If, however, you're coming to this book completely new to QuickTime, you may well find the learning curve more of a challenge. There is no getting around the fact that there is a lot to QuickTime. A good starting point would be to purchase QuickTime Pro ($29.99 at the time of writing) and familiarize yourself with the basics of movie playback and editing.

Code Samples

While the majority of code samples in this book are in Visual Basic .NET, translating these into C# is often a trivial exercise and should not present a major obstacle to anyone familiar with C#. That said, there are a few cases where C# examples are used, either explicitly to demonstrate techniques that might differ significantly from Visual Basic or, more likely, because I happened to get out of the C# side of the bed that day. Developers coming to this book from a C++ or Java background will undoubtedly be more comfortable working with C#, and I would encourage you to stick with this: C# is a superb language.

Many of the code samples shown in the text are simply fragments. While these fragments should be correct and functional in themselves, they will, of course, only work within the context of a complete application. In quite a few cases, however, we go beyond code fragments to a complete working sample application. In order not to pad this book unnecessarily with irrelevant code, I have often omitted boilerplate code that has no particular relevance to the topic under consideration, especially when it comes to the sample applications.

One specific point should be drawn to your attention in case it causes confusion. Visual Basic .NET and C# event handlers tend to have rather long-winded and repetitive event handler parameters. Here's the Play menu item handler, for example

```
Private Sub mnuPlay_Click(ByVal sender As System.Object,
          ByVal e As System.EventArgs) Handles mnuPlay.Click

  If AxQTControl1.Movie Is Nothing Then Exit Sub
  AxQTControl1.Movie.Play()

End Sub
```

The event handler parameters (ByVal sender As System.Object, ByVal e As System.EventArgs) tend to distract from the simplicity of the implementation code, so I took the rash decision to get rid of them in the text, replacing them with an ellipsis instead as shown here:

```
Private Sub mnuPlay_Click(...) Handles mnuPlay.Click

  If AxQTControl1.Movie Is Nothing Then Exit Sub
  AxQTControl1.Movie.Play()

End Sub
```

I hope you will forgive such unilateral tinkering with linguistic syntax and remember to add the standard event arguments back in should you ever transcribe such handlers into your own code. Better still, just copy the event handler implementation into the prototype that Visual Studio will invariably have generated for you.

Most of the sample code fragments and complete sample applications, together with specific media samples, are available to download from the website associated with this book:

www.skylark.ie/qt4.net

Additional information and code samples may also be found on this website, together with any errata.

Additional Resources

It is not difficult to find useful learning and reference material online covering many of the technologies and tools that we will be discussing later in this book. Often, though, the sheer volume of available information can make the process of finding what you want rather exasperating. To aid you, here are some of the more useful and authoritative online resources.

.NET, Visual Basic, and C#

When it comes to .NET, Visual Basic, and C#, there is no shortage of books catering to everyone from the absolute beginner to the experienced professional developer. As with many things in life, don't be deceived by size. Take the extra time to research the table of contents and perhaps a sample chapter, and you are more likely to end up with a book that is appropriate to your needs and level of experience.

For comprehensive online information on developing for .NET, the Microsoft Developer Centers are usually a good starting point:

- .NET Developer Center: *http://msdn.microsoft.com/netframework/*
- Visual Basic Developer Center: *http://msdn.microsoft.com/vbasic/*
- C# Developer Center: *http://msdn.microsoft.com/vcsharp/*

Amongst a plethora of independent developer sites, the Code Project holds a substantial repository of useful code samples in Visual Basic .NET and C#, as well as instructive tutorials and "How To" guides:

www.codeproject.com

Windows Scripting

Definitive information and sample code for scripting on Windows, using VBScript or JScript, is available from Microsoft at their Script Center and Scripting Developer Center:

www.microsoft.com/technet/scriptcenter/

http://msdn.microsoft.com/scripting/

QuickTime

If you're serious about QuickTime development, it will be well worth your while investing in the two-volume *QuickTime Toolkit* (Morgan Kaufmann, 2004) also in the QuickTime Developer Series. This is the definitive work on development with QuickTime and, while oriented towards the Quick-Time API, covers a vast amount of invaluable background and conceptual material.

Useful online resources from Apple include

- General QuickTime resources including QuickTime User Guide:

    www.apple.com/quicktime/resources/

- Apple QuickTime API documentation:

    http://developer.apple.com/documentation/QuickTime/

- For general QuickTime articles, tutorials, and other resources:

    www.quicktiming.org

2

Getting Started with the QuickTime Control

Introduction

In a nutshell, the Apple QuickTime COM Control is a component that provides us as developers with facilities to load, view, edit and even create digital media within our applications. All of this powerful functionality is of course provided by QuickTime but, in the well-established tradition of good COM components, the complexity of the underlying technology is distilled into a set of easy-to-master COM interfaces.

Component-oriented developers are not the type to waste hours (or even precious minutes!) poring over documentation—not when it's so easy to drop an unfamiliar component onto an empty form and see how far we can get. The goal is usually to figure out as quickly as possible whether or not the new component meets our expectations. That's really all this chapter is about: uncovering the basics of the QuickTime COM Control as painlessly as possible. Later chapters follow with more systematic and in-depth information on QuickTime and the QuickTime Control.

Hello World!

No self-respecting book on practical software development would be complete without the de rigueur Hello World! application to kick things off. But since we're dealing here with an exciting media technology rather than a dull programming language, perhaps our starting point (Figure 2.1) should be a minimal application to load and play a Hello World! movie—complete with backing sound track!

Figure 2.1 Hello World! movie. (See `HelloWorld.mov` at *www.skylark.ie/qt4.net.*)

Since we don't want to lose anybody before we even get started, let's first make sure that you have indeed installed QuickTime 7.0.2—the first version of QuickTime to include the QuickTime COM Control—or a later version. If in doubt, check the version in the QuickTime Control Panel or QuickTime Preferences (Figure 2.2).

Figure 2.2 About QuickTime dialog showing QuickTime version.

If you're an experienced Visual Basic .NET hack, feel free to just skip right ahead and create a new Visual Basic application called *QTHelloWorld*. However, if Visual Studio .NET is not your second home:

- Launch Visual Studio .NET and choose File | New | Project....
- Select Visual Basic Projects in the left-hand panel and Windows Application in the right-hand panel.
- Give your application a name—*QTHelloWorld*.
- Choose a folder where all the application files will be kept.
- Now click OK.

Completely New to Visual Basic and Visual Studio .NET?

If you have never used Visual Basic (VB) before, I would highly recommend that you don't proceed too much farther without investing just a little time familiarizing yourself with VB and the Visual Studio .NET development environment. This book is not intended to teach you VB, and some prior knowledge will be assumed as we progress. The good news, of course, is that learning VB is a piece of cake! Visual Basic itself comes with some excellent getting-started tutorials or, if you collect dead forests, most book outlets will oblige with a bewildering array of VB titles to satisfy your every whim.

You should end up with a freshly created Windows application consisting of one form and not much else. If you are new to Visual Basic .NET and overcome with excitement at having created your first Windows application without touching a line of code, then I suggest you press F5 to build and run your application. This will create and run an executable called *QTHelloWorld.exe* in the *bin* folder, which you'll find buried deep in your *QTHelloWorld* project folder.

What do we need to add to this shell application so that we can open a movie? Not much, it turns out: just one Apple QuickTime Control. But first we must add the QuickTime Control to the Visual Studio Toolbox so that it is available for us to use in our applications. To do this, find the Visual Studio Toolbox from which controls of all shapes and sizes are available for use on our application forms. The Toolbox is usually on the left-hand side of the screen; if not visible, choose View | Toolbox. Select the General tab in the Toolbox. Right-click anywhere in the tab area and choose Add/Remove Items... to bring up the *Customize Toolbox* dialog as shown in Figure 2.3. Choose the COM Components tab and scroll down until you find *Apple QuickTime Control 2.0*. Tick the checkbox opposite and then click the OK button: the Apple QuickTime Control should now appear in the Toolbox.

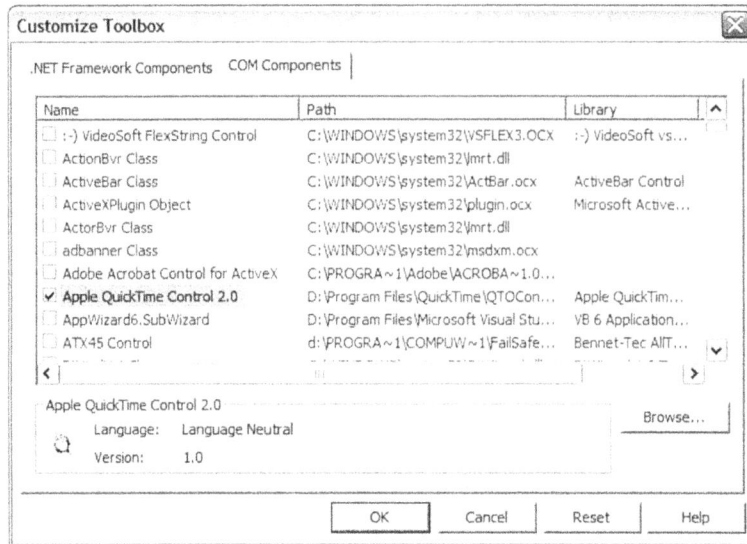

Figure 2.3 Adding the QuickTime Control to the Toolbox in Visual Studio .NET.

Note If *Apple QuickTime Control 2.0* does not appear in the COM Components tab, then you should quit Visual Studio and install/reinstall QuickTime 7.0.2 or later.

Now that the QuickTime Control is sitting in the Toolbox, you can easily add an instance of the control to your empty form—the window with Form1 in the caption bar. Select the Apple QuickTime Control in the toolbox and move the cursor over the form; you'll notice that the cursor has changed to the QuickTime logo. Click and drag to position a new instance of the Apple QuickTime Control on your form. You should see a box with a black outline and the QuickTime logo nestled reassuringly in the center.

Next make sure the QuickTime control is selected on the form and choose View | Properties Window to bring up the standard Visual Studio Properties window as shown in Figure 2.4. Skimming down through the list of properties, you'll immediately notice some of the standard properties that you would expect any visual control to have, such as Location, Size, and Visible. Near the top, you'll also notice the important Name property, which you can use to give a control its own unique identifier. In this case we'll allow it to keep its default name assigned by VisualBasic—AxQTControl1.

Why AxQTControl1?

The *Ax* prefix signifies that the control is in fact an ActiveX or COM control, rather than a native .NET control.

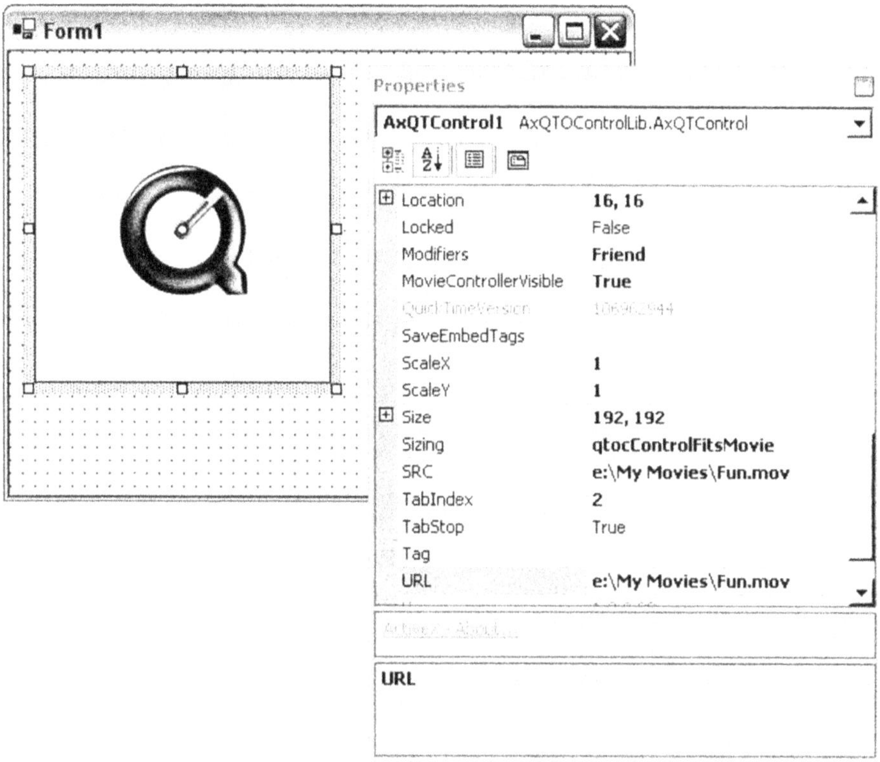

Figure 2.4 Apple QuickTime Control with its properties.

Sprinkled in amongst the standard properties, however, you'll notice such things as MovieControllerVisible, AutoPlay, and URL, which are clearly specific properties of the QuickTime Control. Setting the URL property to point to a movie somewhere on the hard disk is as simple as entering a full path and file name for the URL property, for example, *e:\My Movies\Fun.mov,* as shown in Figure 2.4.

However, since we've rather lazily avoided typing anything so far, let's see how far we can get before having to resort to the keyboard. Many controls support a handy feature known as *Property Pages.* This is a dialog, often with several "tabbed" pages, that provides a custom user interface for setting key properties of the control. Sure enough, the QuickTime Control has a simple property page that we can bring up by clicking on the Property Pages button, the fourth button in the toolbar on the Properties window shown in Figure 2.5.

As we see in Figure 2.6, only a small subset of properties is exposed here but, as we might expect, they include some of the most useful ones. For now

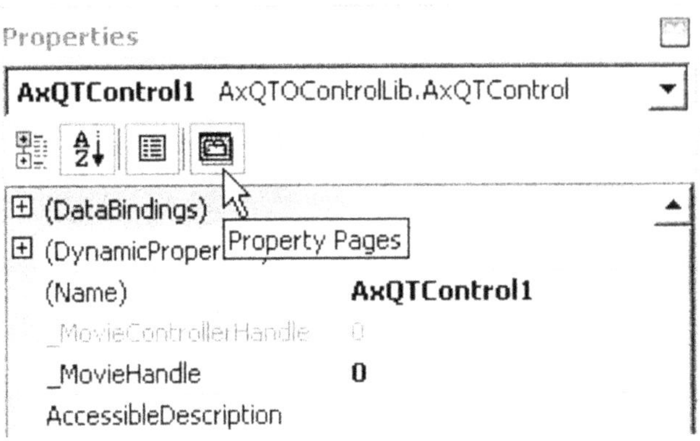

Figure 2.5 Accessing the Property Pages from the Properties window.

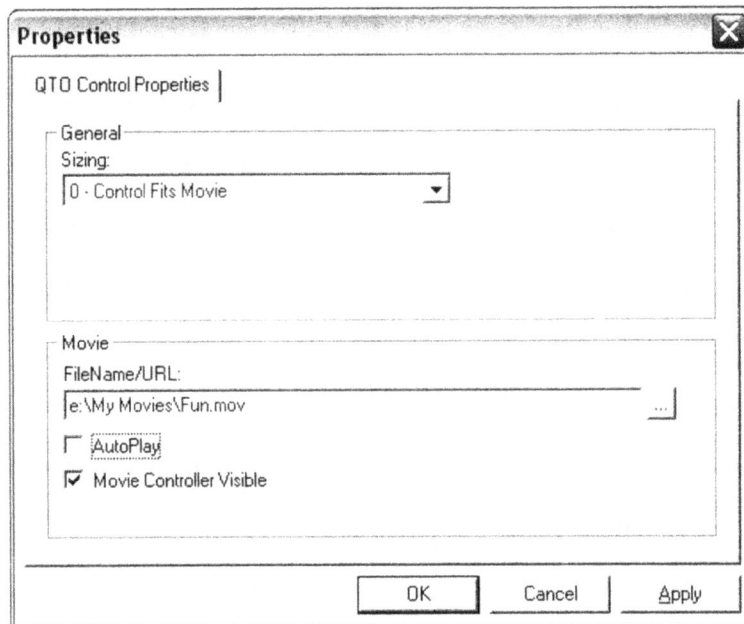

Figure 2.6 The QuickTime Control Property Page.

let's just set the URL by clicking on the Browse button at the end of the File-Name/URL entry field and choosing a movie from the Open dialog that pops up: perhaps `Movies\HelloWorld.mov`. Close the Property Page dialog by clicking OK, and you should notice that the path to the movie you selected now appears in the URL property entry field in the Properties windows. If you're a stickler for neatness, expand the Location property and set both X and Y to zero: the control should snap into the top-left corner of the form.

Now press F5 to build and run the application again. This time things take a little longer as QuickTime is being loaded, but in a few seconds you should see your first QuickTime movie opening up in a VB.NET application—and all without a line of code so far. Click the Play button on the left-hand side of the playback control bar under the movie (the movie controller) if you're not convinced! Check out *QTHelloWorld.exe* in the *bin* folder and you'll find that it's tiny—under 20k. All the QuickTime services required to load and play a movie are provided by the QuickTime Control installed on your computer, which is simply referenced by your VB application.

Before we move on to things more complicated (and indeed more useful), let's briefly dip our toes in a little deeper and add our own Play button. Make sure you are back in Design mode by quitting your running application, and then select the Windows Forms tab in the Toolbox. Select Button and place a button somewhere on your form. In the Properties window, set its Text property to "Play." Double-click on your new Play button and you will land in the code editor, with the cursor blinking in the middle of a skeleton Button1_Click handler routine that VB has thoughtfully created for you.

At the cursor, start typing the name given to our QuickTime control, AxQTControl1, and then type a dot or period:

```
Private Sub Button1_Click(ByVal sender As System.Object,
    AxQTControl1.|
End Sub           Left                              ▲
                  Location
                  ModifierKeys
                  MouseButtons
                  MousePosition
                  Movie                             ⌐
                  MovieControllerVisible
                  Name
                  NewMovie
                  NewMovieFromImages                ▼
```

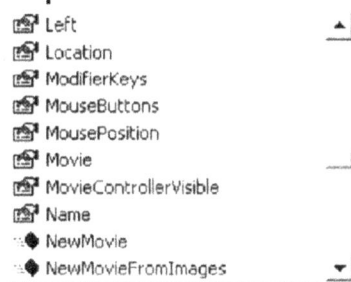

If you're new to coding in the Visual Studio environment, you might be pleasantly surprised by what happens next: a drop-down list appears containing the names of all the possible properties and methods (functions) available in the QuickTime Control. This list combines both standard properties and methods applicable to all visual controls (e.g., Size, Location), together with those that are specific to the QuickTime Control.

Let's keep typing, continuing with the `Movie` property followed by a second dot:

```
Private Sub Button1_Click(ByVal sender As System.Object,
    AxQTControl1.Movie.|
End Sub        ☞ Rate                        ▲
               ☞ Rectangle
               ◆ Replace
               ◆ Reverse
               ◆ Rewind
               ☞ right
               ◆ Rotate
               ◆ Save
               ☞ SeeAllFrames
               ◆ SelectAll                   ▼
```

Hitting the dot again, we are presented with another list, this time of all the properties and methods of the Movie within the QuickTime Control. You'll notice that properties (values that you can set or get such as `Width` or `Duration`) are distinguished from methods (commands like `Hide` or `Play`) by the small icons.

Intellisense

These drop-down lists of properties and methods that appear just when you need them are part of the cool Intellisense technology built into Visual Studio. Intellisense is one of the reasons why developing with VB.NET or C# can be so productive: it can often save unnecessary trips to the documentation since a quick scan up and down the list of what's available is often enough to intelligently guess which particular property or method you're after, even if you're unfamiliar with the component concerned.

It turns out that `Movie` isn't just a plain and simple property like URL with a single value, but in fact exposes a fully fledged child object with its own rather intriguing set of properties and methods, but more about this anon. For now just select its `Play` method:

```
Private Sub Button1_Click(...) Handles Button1.Click[1]

    AxQTControl1.Movie.Play()

End Sub
```

---

1 Event-handler parameters omitted for clarity.

Build and run your application again and you should notice that the Play button works.

C#

Everything I've just described works almost identically in C# with a few minor syntactical differences:

```
private void button1_Click(object sender, System.EventArgs e)

{
  axQTControl1.Movie.Play(1.0);
}
```

Note that we must pass a Rate parameter to the Play method. In VB.NET this is an optional parameter, but C# does not support optional parameters, so we must give it a value.

So far we've found out how easy it is to use the QuickTime Control in Visual Basic to create a Windows application that loads a movie and plays it. In the next section we build on what we've discovered so far to create a handy little utility application: Simple Player.

Simple Player—The Basics

As I said in the Introduction, this book is really all about bringing those amazing technologies that are available in QuickTime into such powerful and productive development environments as Visual Basic .NET or C#. As we've discovered in the previous section, the Apple QuickTime Control makes this possible in a very straightforward and accessible way. Indeed, one can develop a QuickTime application without really needing to know too much about QuickTime at all, let alone about the somewhat daunting QuickTime API (Application Programming Interface).

In the rest of this chapter, we're going to put together a very simple but useful movie player (Figure 2.7). Think of it as a bare-bones version of the QuickTime Player application that comes with QuickTime. In later chapters we will extend the functionality of this application as we bring in additional

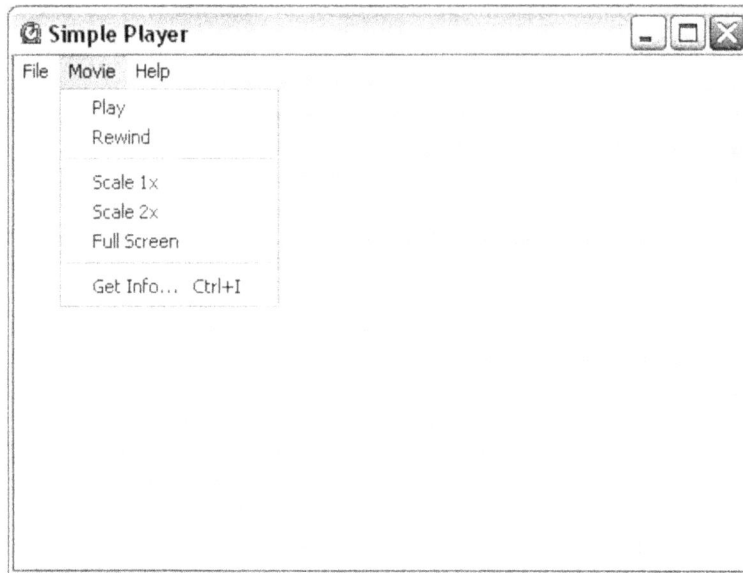

Figure 2.7 Simple Player.

features of QuickTime. In the process you should pick up useful concepts and sample code to deploy in your own applications.

As a starting point, I have put together a skeleton Visual Basic application comprising a resizeable window with a few simple menus. You will find this project on the website in `Samples\SimplePlayer\SimplePlayer A`. Build and run this application, and then skim through the menus: this should give you a good overview of what we're about to do.

Initialization

If you've looked at the Simple Player skeleton application in Design mode, you'll have noticed that `Form1` is completely devoid of any controls. The first thing we must do is to add a QuickTime Control to the form from the Toolbox. This time, instead of setting properties via the Properties window or Property Page, we'll set them in some initialization code. This is generally better practice since it's all too easy to set properties manually via the Properties window and then forget that we've actually set them.

The usual place to carry out any initialization of controls on the form is in the Form1_Load subroutine, which gets called just after the form and all its controls are loaded. Double-click on the form to edit the code behind the form: we'll add a few lines to the Form1_Load handler to anchor the control in the top-left corner of the form, turn off its border, and make the movie controller visible by default.

```
Private Sub Form1_Load(...) Handles MyBase.Load

   AxQTControl1.Location = New System.Drawing.Point(0, 0)
   AxQTControl1.BorderStyle = QTOControlLib.BorderStylesEnum.bsNone
   AxQTControl1.MovieControllerVisible = True

End Sub
```

In Depth: Enumerations

If you're not very familiar with Visual Basic, COM, or .NET, you may be wondering what's going on in the middle line in the preceding code in which the BorderStyle property is set. Well, the explanation is that certain properties of the control, such as BorderStyle or Sizing, can only be set to one of a fixed set of predefined numeric values, each representing a legal option for that property. The valid options for BorderStyle are 0, 1, or 2, representing no border, plain border, or 3D border, respectively. So we could equally have written

```
AxQTControl1.BorderStyle = 0
```

and it would have happily done the same thing. But it's not easy to remember what arbitrary numeric values stand for. So COM and .NET (along with many serious programming languages) allow such sets of values to be grouped together into an *enumeration* where each value is assigned an easier-to-remember name that you can use in your code instead of the value itself.

In this case the enumeration is called BorderStylesEnum and it contains the following set of values:

0 = bsNone   (no border)

1 = bsPlain   (plain border)

2 = bs3D   (3D border)

The name of the enumeration is prefixed by the name of the library or namespace to which it belongs: in this case QTOControlLib, which is the namespace for everything relating to the QuickTime Control.

Opening and Closing Movies

At the start of this chapter, we saw that we could open a movie by setting the URL property of the QuickTime Control to the full path and file name of a movie:

```
AxQTControl1.URL = "d:\My Movies\KidsPicnic.mov"
```

In Simple Player we'd like to be able to browse for any movie anywhere on our computer—or even on our network for that matter—and then open it. Windows Forms provides a convenient file browsing dialog in the shape of the OpenFileDialog control, which can be found on the Windows Forms tab in the VS.NET Toolbox (you might need to scroll well down the long list of Windows Forms controls to find it). Just pop one of these controls on the form, where it will be given the default name OpenFileDialog1. Now select the File | Open Movie... menu item in our Form1 design view, double-click to get into code view, and you can implement the menu item handler as follows:

```
Private Sub mnuOpen_Click(...) Handles mnuOpen.Click

  If OpenFileDialog1.ShowDialog() = DialogResult.OK Then
    AxQTControl1.URL = OpenFileDialog1.FileName()
  End If

End Sub
```

So we have a single line of code to show the standard File Open dialog and check that a file was indeed selected, plus a second line to set the control's URL property to the file we've selected—that's it! With just a handful of lines of code we can select and load any movie (or, indeed, sound file or image). Before you try it, let's make sure we can properly close any file that we might open by setting URL to an empty string in the mnuClose_Click handler:

```
Private Sub mnuClose_Click(...) Handles mnuClose.Click

  AxQTControl1.URL = ""

End Sub
```

Also, for completeness, let's make sure that when someone closes the form, the movie gets closed. We can do this in the handler for the form's Closed event:

```
Private Sub Form1_Closed(...) Handles MyBase.Closed

  AxQTControl1.URL = ""

End Sub
```

Now you can experiment with opening and closing a few movies.

You may have noticed that OpenFileDialog is not selective and will allow you to open any type of file irrespective of its file extension, leaving Quick-Time with the unenviable task of trying to figure out what to do with it. A little polish would be appropriate here, such as the ability to choose the type of file we would like to open: *Movies, Audio files,* or *All files.* This turns out to be quite easy to achieve with the Filter property of the OpenFile-Dialog control:

```
Private Sub mnuOpen_Click(...) Handles mnuOpen.Click

  Dim filter As String
  filter = "Movies|*.mov;*.mpg;*.avi;*.dv|"
  filter += "Audio files|*.wav;*.aif;*.mp3;*.m4a;*.m4p|"
  filter += "All files (*.*)|*.*"
  OpenFileDialog1.Filter = filter

  If OpenFileDialog1.ShowDialog() = DialogResult.OK Then
    AxQTControl1.URL = OpenFileDialog1.FileName()
  End If

End Sub
```

Note the pipe characters (|) that delimit the filter fields and the fact that there is a pair of fields for each filter option. The first field in each pair is purely descriptive, for example,

```
Audio files
```

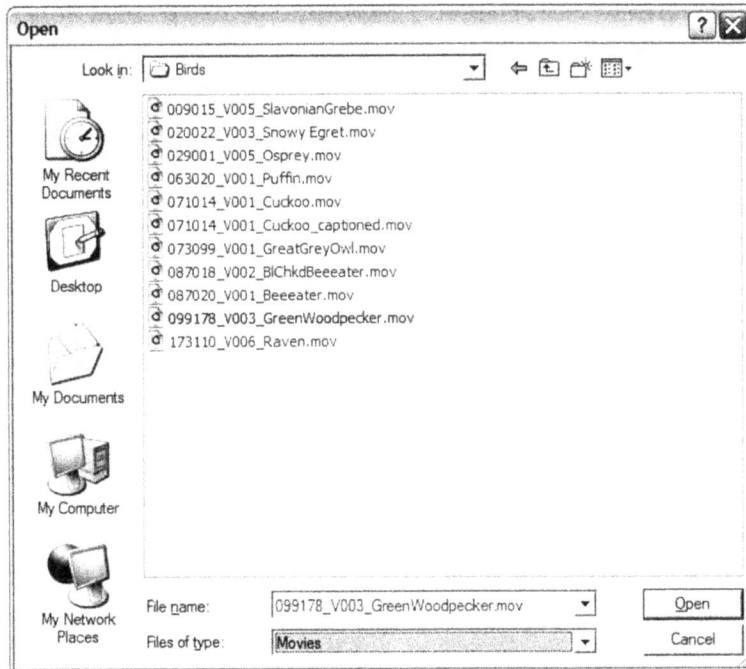

Figure 2.8 Open Movie dialog for Simple Player.

while the corresponding second field comprises a list of wildcard file specifications delimited by *semicolons,* for example,

```
*.wav;*.aif;*.mp3;*.m4a;*.m4p
```

Now—Figure 2.8—we have an Open Movie dialog to be proud of!

Controlling the Movie

Now that Simple Player is capable of opening and closing movies, we can shift our attention to the Movie menu that's lurking in our menu bar and, more specifically, to some of the basic functionality required to work with movies.

You will recall from the *QTHelloWorld* example earlier in this chapter that the properties and methods associated with a movie are all accessed through the QuickTime Control's Movie property. As we discovered, this property returns a child object representing the movie itself. This makes the first two items in the Movie menu rather trivial to implement:

```
Private Sub mnuPlay_Click(...) Handles mnuPlay.Click

  AxQTControl1.Movie.Play()

End Sub


Private Sub mnuRewind_Click(...) Handles mnuRewind.Click

  AxQTControl1.Movie.Rewind()

End Sub
```

Build and run Simple Player again and load a movie—you'll notice that these two menu items work as advertised.

But, as it turns out, we have been a little too simplistic especially if our application is to be professionally robust. Try running the application again, but this time DON'T load a movie and select Movie | Play. Dumb? Of course! But someone is sure to try it and the resulting error message is rather alarming:

> *An unhandled exception of type 'System.NullReferenceException' occurred in SimplePlayer.exe.*

While *unhandled exception* (loosely translated: Oh dear me! Something untoward occurred!) may feature vaguely in the lexicon of the seasoned computer user, *System.NullReferenceException* is just plain baffling whatever way you look at it. Clearly, we need a more meaningful message, but you might well ask, Why the error in the first place?

The additional information that .NET supplies in the error message hints at the reason:

> *Additional information: Object reference not set to an instance of an object.*

Translated from .NET-speak, the entire error message simply reads

> *You tried to tell a Movie object that doesn't exist to Play—I just can't handle it!*

Remember that AxQTControl1.Movie is in fact a reference to a movie *object*. However, if we haven't loaded a movie, then no movie object exists and .NET is perfectly entitled to protest with a *System.NullReferenceException* when you attempt to invoke the Play method on a nonexistent object!

Exception

An exception occurs when something out of the ordinary, or *exceptional*, occurs outside of the normal program flow—often an error of some kind, but sometimes simply a notification that something has happened that we should know about. Fortunately, it is not difficult to catch exceptions and manage them gracefully, as we'll see in Chapter 5 when we discuss exception handling in more detail.

Experienced developers will recognize that there are two ways we can handle this more gracefully: we can put in place an exception handler to trap the error condition, or we can fend off the error by preventing its occurrence in the first place. In this case, we will add a simple check that the Movie object does in fact exist before attempting to access its Play method:

```
Private Sub mnuPlay_Click(...) Handles mnuPlay.Click

    If AxQTControl1.Movie Is Nothing Then Exit Sub
    AxQTControl1.Movie.Play()

End Sub


Private Sub mnuRewind_Click(...) Handles mnuRewind.Click

    If AxQTControl1.Movie Is Nothing Then Exit Sub
    AxQTControl1.Movie.Rewind()

End Sub
```

More sophisticated UI design, of course, would dictate that we should disable or gray-out the Play and Rewind menu items until such time as we have a loaded movie. Notwithstanding, battle-hardened developers will always cater for the unexpected error even if it "should never occur."

Getting Information about the Movie

Having gone to the trouble of opening a half-forgotten movie buried somewhere in the bowels of our hard disk, it would be useful if we could easily view some basic information about the movie such as its title or perhaps its length. Such information is usually referred to as *metadata* (more to come in Chapter 5) and can be viewed through the Annotations tab in the Properties window in QuickTime Player (Window | Show Movie Properties). Happily, our Movie object provides easy access to metadata about the movie through its Annotation property: we must specify which annotation we want with an annotation ID from QTAnnotationsEnum.

In Simple Player, the last item in our Movie menu is Movie Info.... Selecting this should display a dialog with some key information about the movie:

```
Private Sub mnuGetInfo_Click(...) Handles mnuGetInfo.Click

Dim s As String
If AxQTControl1.Movie Is Nothing Then Exit Sub

  s = ""
  With AxQTControl1.Movie
    s += s + "Full Name    : "
    s += .Annotation(QTAnnotationsEnum.qtAnnotationFullName) + vbCrLf
    s += "Duration     : "
    s += CStr(.Duration) + vbCrLf
    s += "Copyright    : "
    s += .Annotation(QTAnnotationsEnum.qtAnnotationCopyright) + vbCrLf
  End With
  MsgBox(s, MsgBoxStyle.Information, "Movie Info")

End Sub
```

Note the use of the With AxQTControl1.Movie syntax to simplify coding: within the With construct, properties and methods of the Movie object are referenced with a leading period to represent the object. Notice also that Duration, being an integer property, is converted to a string using the CStr function.

For simplicity each piece of information is appended to a string, which is then displayed in a humble MsgBox dialog, as shown in Figure 2.9.

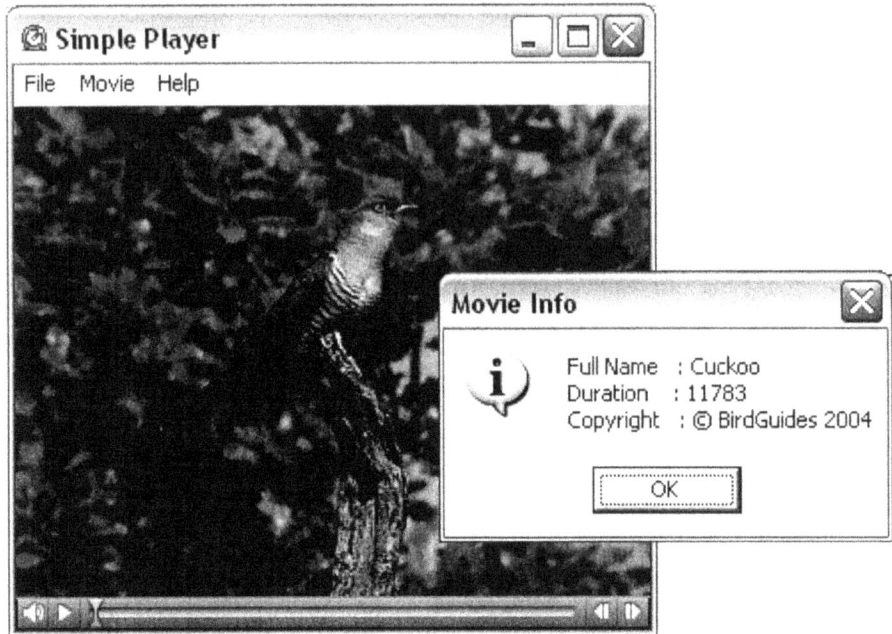

Figure 2.9 Information about the movie.

Scaling the Movie

In many applications you will want to change the scale at which the movie is displayed on the screen, say, to double size or half size or perhaps even to fill the screen. Our Movie menu has two scale options—1X and 2X—and these are easily implemented using the SetScale method of the QuickTime Control:

```
Private Sub mnuScale1x_Click(...) Handles mnuScale1x.Click

    AxQTControl1.SetScale(1)     '1X

End Sub

Private Sub mnuScale2x_Click(...) Handles mnuScale2x.Click

    AxQTControl1.SetScale(2)     '2X

End Sub
```

SetScale can take either a single floating-point value that is applied to both X and Y axes, or two floating-point values for independent X and Y scaling:

```
AxQTControl1.SetScale(0.5, 5.75)    'Tall and thin
AxQTControl1.SetScale(10.2, 1.75)   'Short and fat
```

The default behavior of the control is to scale its own size to that of the movie it contains. In many cases, as with our Simple Player, this is exactly the behavior we want, but there are other options that we will touch on in more detail in the next chapter.

Full-Screen Movies

Anyone who has shelled out for the Pro version of QuickTime will be familiar with the Present Movie... option in QuickTime Player, which allows you to play your movies at stunning full-screen resolution. Irritatingly fond of this feature are owners of 30" flat-screen displays and other such decadent visual real estate!

You may be surprised to learn that this is not in fact a unique feature of the Pro QuickTime Player application but is available via the QuickTime API to anyone with QuickTime installed, even if they have never paid Apple a penny. As you should come to expect by now, the QuickTime Control exposes this functionality very simply using its Boolean FullScreen property:

```
Private Sub mnuFullScreen_Click(...) Handles mnuFullScreen.Click

  AxQTControl1.FullScreen = True

End Sub
```

OK, so we can get our movie to display full screen, but why hasn't our Movie menu got an option to TURN OFF full screen? Stop and think for a moment...

Got it yet? Well, full screen implies just that: our movie fills the entire screen obliterating everything else, our application and menus included. The only means of escape—for now, anyway—is the (default) Escape key.

Automatically Sizing the Form

Up to now we have been concerned with dispatching commands to our QuickTime Control to do this and that, and occasionally asking it for some piece of information. But there will often be occasions when we would like the QuickTime Control to take the initiative and tell us when something happens so that we can respond to it—an essential requirement for any serious, event-driven application.

For example, we might like to be informed whenever the movie changes size. This will occur when the movie is first loaded or if its scale is changed: some movies may even change size dynamically as they play. If the Sizing property of the control is set to its default option (qtControlFitsMovie), then anytime the movie changes size, the control will change size in sympathy so that it always wraps itself snugly around the movie.

And anytime the *control* changes size, it *fires* a SizeChanged event to tell anyone who's listening that it is now a different size. The form on which the control is placed can intercept this event in a code routine known as an *event handler* (Figure 2.10).

Knowing that the movie has changed size is clearly very useful especially in a user interface (UI) context. For instance, we might wish to reposition controls on our form so that they line up neatly with the movie irrespective of its size. In our Simple Player application, however, we can put the SizeChanged event to good use in automatically sizing our form to fit the control, which in turn fits the movie—a bit like tightly packed Russian dolls—all with a single line of code. Here's the event handler on Form1:

```
Private Sub AxQTControl1_SizeChanged(ByVal sender As Object,
   ByVal e As System.EventArgs) Handles AxQTControl1.SizeChanged

   Me.ClientSize = AxQTControl1.Size

End Sub
```

Notice we are setting the ClientSize, or the *inside* dimensions, of the form to which this event handler belongs (Me) to match the size of the control. The overall size of the form including caption bar and frame will automatically change to accommodate this.

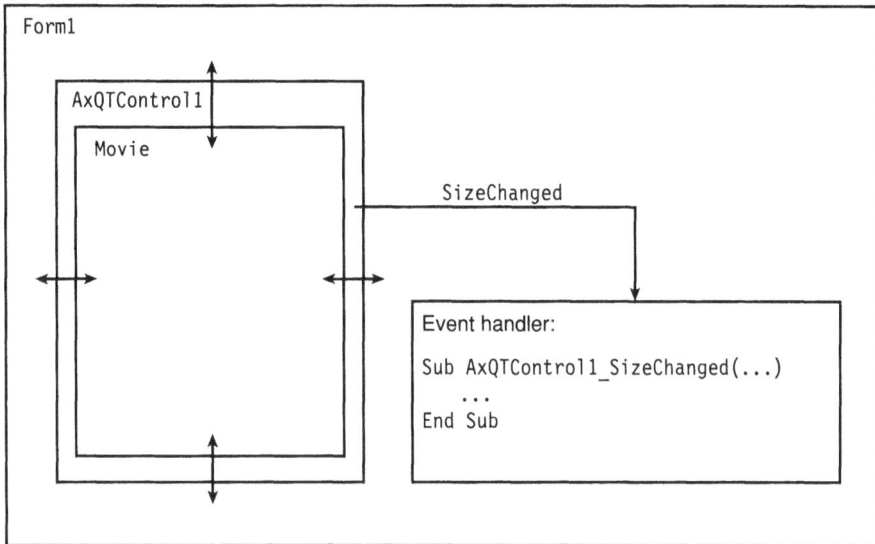

Figure 2.10 Event handler on the form handles `SizeChanged` event fired by the QuickTime Control.

About...

Every application should have an About screen and Simple Player is no exception. In fact, it has two: the Help | About... menu item displays information about the application, while Help | About QuickTime Control... displays information about the QuickTime Control and about QuickTime itself. *AboutForm.vb* is a standard application About box populated with key attributes of the .NET assembly using the `AssemblyInfo` helper class as defined in `AssemblyInfo.vb`.

More interesting is the menu handler that displays information about the QuickTime Control:

```
Private Sub mnuAboutQTControl_Click(...) Handles mnuAboutQTControl.Click

    AxQTControl1.ShowAboutBox()

End Sub
```

All this does is call the `ShowAboutBox` method of the control, which in turn displays some useful version information about both the control and Quick-Time, as we see in Figure 2.11.

Figure 2.11 QuickTime Control About box.

Summary

Rather than burdening you with pages of tedious introduction, we have deliberately jumped straight in, dropped a QuickTime Control on a Visual Basic form, and quickly discovered what we could do with it. If my ploy worked, you should by now have a feel for just how useful and productive this combination of the QuickTime Control with the .NET environment can be. We managed to rapidly create a useful and nontrivial little QuickTime application using remarkably few lines of code. Significantly, the code we *did* have to write was almost all genuine application code: the .NET Framework, Windows Forms, and the QuickTime Control all combined forces to relieve us of a lot of the drudgery.

3

Using the QuickTime Control

Introduction

Flinging together the odd sample application—such as our Simple Player—to demonstrate a new software component is one thing; applying that component in the creation of real-world, professional-grade applications is quite another. The challenge is even greater when the technology involves digital media such as video, sounds, and images, where lofty user expectations often extend to smart visual design, sophisticated user interfaces, and smooth interaction, not to mention stability and performance.

With this in mind, the last chapter was sort of a tantalizing antipasti course designed to whet the appetite for what *might* be possible, while leaving ample room for what's to come. The next two chapters are more main course—solid and chunky, with the odd interesting accompaniment on the side. We take a more considered and in-depth look at the QuickTime Control itself, at the object model that it exposes, and at the essential concepts needed to get the most out of both in your own applications. Just so things don't get too abstract, we will revisit Simple Player every now and again whenever we spot something useful that could enhance its feature set or performance.

Review the detail in these next two chapters, study its application in the code samples, and convince yourself that the QuickTime Control really does merit serious attention if you are developing with QuickTime on the Windows platform. And if you are already developing with a competing technology such as Windows Media Player, you will be in an excellent position to assess the relative merits.

The Apple QuickTime Control

The best way to think of the QuickTime Control is as a wrapper component that encapsulates QuickTime and exposes much of its functionality in a standardized and easy-to-use format. Or, if you want to be more precise, you can describe the QuickTime Control as a COM control that encapsulates QuickTime functionality inside a COM container such as the form or dialog box (i.e., window) in your own application.

COM/ActiveX?

Q: I've heard the QuickTime COM Control also referred to as an ActiveX control. What's the difference?

A: *COM control* is the more up-to-date name for what was once known, and is frequently still referred to, as an *ActiveX control.*

Q: But I thought there already was a QuickTime ActiveX Control used as the QuickTime plug-in in Internet Explorer?

A: Correct. Apple released the QuickTime Plug-in ActiveX Control way back when Microsoft suddenly dropped support for Netscape-style plug-ins in Internet Explorer (IE) 5.5. However, this ActiveX control was specifically designed just to replace the QuickTime plug-in in IE and lacked support for embedding in other COM/ActiveX hosts such as Visual Basic.

So the starting point for developing QuickTime-based applications in the .NET and COM environments is the QuickTime Control. As we will discover in the next chapter, the QuickTime Control is really just the root of an extensive QuickTime Object Model that becomes available to us, obviating any need to go near the traditional C/C++ QuickTime API.

Beginning with QuickTime 7.0.2, the Apple QuickTime Control is installed and registered with QuickTime itself, so there is nothing additional to install. It comprises two dynamic link libraries (DLLs): *QTOControl.dll,* which is the QuickTime COM Control, and *QTOLibrary.dll,* which is the COM library of QuickTime Objects. You will find these DLLs in the *Program Files\QuickTime* folder or wherever you happen to have installed QuickTime.

A COM Control in .NET?

The QuickTime Control is not a native managed code .NET control, nor could it ever really be since QuickTime itself does not run on the Common Language Runtime (CLR). However, the .NET Framework has excellent support for COM through its COM Interop services. In order to use a COM control or library in .NET, you must have what's known as an Interop Assembly—essentially a .NET wrapper for the COM object. Visual Studio .NET will automatically generate these Interop Assemblies when you add a COM control to a project, and they will appear as Interop DLLs in the project bin folder.

To avoid the need for each project to hold its own private Interop wrappers for a COM component, a Primary Interop Assembly (PIA) is often supplied with the component and can be registered with the system. While not available at the time of writing, it is likely that Apple will provide PIAs for the QuickTime Control and associated QuickTime Objects Library as part of the QuickTime 7 SDK.

Get the Big Picture

In common with all COM controls, the QuickTime Control is incapable of survival on its own and must reside within a host window known as its container—normally the form, dialog box, or other window that you provide as part of your application (Figure 3.1). When embedded in its container window, the QuickTime Control is allocated its own visual real estate as a child window of its host, or parent window.

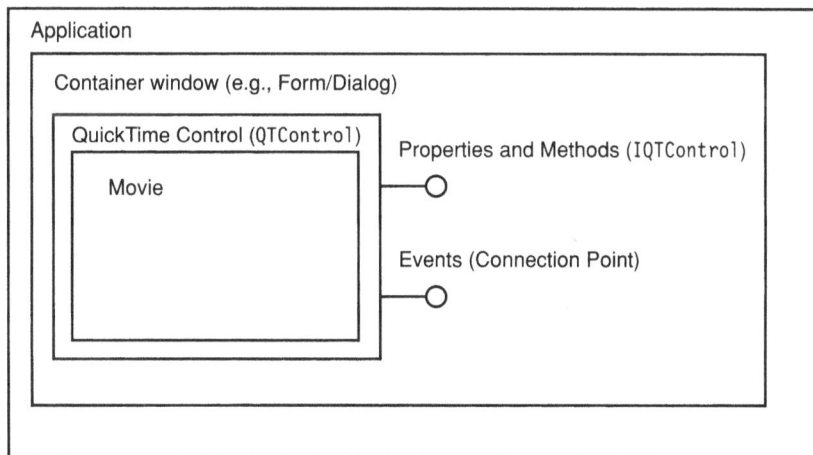

Figure 3.1 The QuickTime Control hosted in its container window.

Like most children, many aspects of the control's existence are out of its own hands: its size, position, and visibility are all under control of the parent. However, within the confines of its own window, the QuickTime Control becomes fief of its own mini-QuickTime domain: virtually anything you could conceivably open with the QuickTime Player application can also be opened, played, viewed, edited, and generally mucked about with inside the QuickTime Control, and all under the control of your application.

Recall the extensive collection of media and interactive formats that QuickTime can handle and you'll quickly grasp the potential: video clips, sounds, music, animations, interactive (wired) movies, Flash movies, virtual reality (VR) scenes, and images, in a bewildering variety of formats and all capable of being embedded, controlled, and in many cases even edited within your application.

Whenever your form is loaded—at start-up for example—the QuickTime Control on that form gets loaded along with all the other controls you might have on the form. The control is allocated as an object in memory and is now referred to as an *instance* of the QuickTime Control. Whatever name you gave the control at design time (the default is *AxQTControl1*) now refers to this instance of the control.

In Depth

In COM terminology, the loaded QuickTime Control in memory becomes an instance of the QTControl class and it exposes the IQTControl interface to its host.

As we saw in the previous chapter, the QuickTime Control exposes a COM interface (IQTControl) providing its host—your application—with a comprehensive set of properties and methods that you can use to communicate with the control. And, so that you are kept up to date with everything that is going on in the control, it also provides your application with a set of useful events via its Connection Point interface (see Figure 3.1).

Movies

For anyone not familiar with QuickTime, a little digression on terminology is appropriate. Way back in the mists of time (1992 to be precise), QuickTime was released as an intriguing, novel technology targeted primarily at the playback of digital video, albeit at postage stamp size. It made sense to refer to the files that QuickTime could open as "movies," and the .mov extension was born. In the intervening decade or so, QuickTime has evolved to handle a diverse array of digital media formats. Once opened, each of these formats—whether a sound file, an MPEG movie, a VR scene, or even a text file—is treated democratically within QuickTime as a movie. The fact that this is possible at all speaks volumes for the farsighted extensibility built into QuickTime by its original architects. And so the *movie* name sticks.

In order to simplify the forthcoming discussion, I shall use the term *movie* rather loosely to refer to anything that the QuickTime Control can sensibly open. With all this in mind let's take a closer look at the facilities provided by the QuickTime Control for loading a movie and controlling the essential visual aspects of movie presentation.

Loading a Movie

Our gateway to the world of movies is, not altogether surprisingly, the QuickTime Control's URL property. Setting this property tells the control which particular movie we wish to load and from where. A movie is, more often than not, simply a discrete file somewhere, say, on your hard disk or on a DVD-ROM. It can be fully specified by a local path to which the URL property may be set:

```
AxQTControl1.URL = "C:\My Movies\KidsPicnic.mov"        'Movie

AxQTControl1.URL = "D:\My Music\Blues.mp3"              'Sound

AxQTControl1.URL = "D:\My Pictures\Stawberries.jpg"     'Image

AxQTControl1.URL = "G:\Flash\PingPong.swf"             'Flash movie
```

However, in our networked world, nothing says the file has to be on a local disk. The control will cope just as well with a UNC (Universal Naming Convention) path to a network share

```
AxQTControl1.URL = "\\Eeyore\D\My Movies\KidsRemotePicnic.mov"
```

or indeed with a URL to a file way out there somewhere on a server:

```
AxQTControl1.URL = "http://www.blueplanet.com/movies/hello_world.mov"

AxQTControl1.URL = "http://mww.redplanet.com/movies/hello_mars.mov"
```

And of course, the URL property is not restricted to discrete files. Those 24x7 news junkies and Internet radio fans can point the URL at their favorite streaming channels:

```
AxQTControl1.URL = "http://stream.qtv.apple.com/channels/wcpe/
            sprites/wcp_sprite.mov"
```

The URL property opens the door to digital media of all sorts, from local sources or remote servers, and embeds it right where we want it in our applications.

Movie Scaling and Sizing

Once a movie is loaded, we invariably want some control over its size and position within the control. The QuickTime Control obliges with a number of useful properties and methods. Understanding how these work and interact together is essential if you want to ensure that your application copes well with movies of different shapes and sizes. Both scale and aspect ratio are important factors to take into account.

Scale is the ratio of the movie's normal size (width and height) to the size at which we wish to view the movie in our control. If the movie is very big, we may wish to view it at a reduced scale or, rather like QuickTime Player, we may wish to offer our users the ability to view a movie at Half Size, Normal Size, or Double Size. Different screen resolutions may also mean that the usable area available to our application can vary enormously, and we therefore need to scale the movie appropriately (Figure 3.2).

Scale can be applied independently to the X and Y axes using the ScaleX and ScaleY properties, both of which take floating-point values:

```
AxQTControl1.ScaleX = 2.5
AxQTControl1.ScaleY = 4.956
```

Alternatively, as we saw in the last chapter, the SetScale method can take either a single value applied to both X and Y axes, or separate X and Y values:

```
AxQTControl1.SetScale(3.5)
AxQTControl1.SetScale(2.5, 4.956)
```

Aspect ratio is the ratio of the width of a movie to its height. Computer screen resolutions have traditionally settled on a 4:3 aspect ratio (e.g., 640 x 480 pixels or 1400 x 1050 pixels), while movie-goers have become accus-

Figure 3.2 Scaling the movie.

Figure 3.3 Movie captured at 4:3 aspect ratio (left) and stretched to 16:9 (right). Result: peculiar-looking horse and fatter kids!

tomed to a (wide-screen) 16:9 aspect ratio on the big screen. Depending on its source, digital content is liable to come in a variety of aspect ratios: consumer DV cameras typically churn out movies at 4:3, whereas movie trailers will usually reflect their 16:9 origins. Panoramic VR movies are often very wide indeed relative to their height.

Unlike scale, if we alter the aspect ratio, we usually end up introducing undesirable geometric distortion. If you have ever watched an old big-screen movie that has been converted to video format for television, you may have noticed the effect (Figure 3.3).

Aspect ratio and scale are intimately related: changing the aspect ratio is in fact just scaling the width differently from the height. In most situations we will want to avoid changes to the aspect ratio even if we choose to scale the movie.

The Sizing property of the control determines how it handles both size and aspect ratio. There are several options to which it may be set as enumerated in QTSizingModeEnum and illustrated in Figures 3.4 and 3.5.

1. qtControlFitsMovie: The control resizes itself to fit the natural size of the movie, taking into account any applied X and Y scaling. Aspect ratio is preserved, unless of course you deliberately force it to change by applying different scale values to the width and height.

   Use this option if you need to display a movie at its natural size, or if you need to be able to apply manual scaling. While this sizing option might appear to be an automatic choice, your carefully laid-out user interface is

Figure 3.4 Sizing options: (left) qtControlFitsMovie, (center) qtMovieFitsControl, (right) qtMovie-FitsControlMaintainAspectRatio.

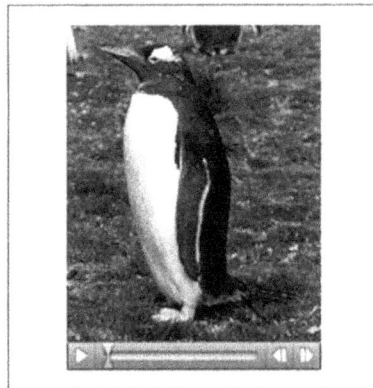

Figure 3.5 Sizing option: qtMovieCenteredInControl.

at the mercy of whatever movies—large or small, fat or thin—that your user might choose to load. This is the default sizing option for the Quick-Time Control.

2. `qtMovieFitsControl`: The movie is automatically sized to fit within the bounds of the control—in effect, the logical opposite of option 1, `qtControlFitsMovie`. Both scale and aspect ratio are no longer at your discretion since they are slavishly driven by the control as it keeps the movie corralled.

   The use of this sizing option is limited to cases where you simply must ensure that the control remains a fixed size and where you couldn't give a toss about aspect ratio. Either that or all your movies are of a known aspect ratio (e.g., 4:3) and you deliberately preset the size of the control to accommodate them.

3. `qtMovieFitsControlMaintainAspectRatio`: As you might guess from the name, this is essentially a smarter variation on option 2, `qtMovieFitsControl`. Instead of blindly filling the entire control, this option seeks to display as much as possible of the movie in the available space while *preserving* its aspect ratio. Depending on whether the aspect ratio of the movie is greater than or less than that of the control, the result is a movie centered vertically in the available space with gaps above and below, or centered horizontally with gaps to each side. Either way the movie is scaled to fit into the available space without geometrical distortion, and any resulting gaps are filled with the control's background color.

   If your carefully laid-out form has a well-defined space in which the control should sit and display movies irrespective of their natural size (e.g., a preview window for movies), this is the sizing option to go for.

4. `qtMovieCenteredInControl`: The movie is positioned so that the center of the movie is in the center of the control, irrespective of the size of the control or the size of the movie (Figure 3.5). The control size never changes, and no attempt is made to constrain the movie within the bounds of the control: (1) if the movie is too big for the control, we see only part of it; (2) if the movie is too small, the control background color will fill any space surrounding the movie. Both aspect ratio and scale are retained; changes to scale simply determine how much or how little of the movie is visible. This option can be useful where the control fills an area that is much larger than the movie and where you want to position the movie centrally in that area.

5. `qtManualSizing`: Here, the control absolves itself of all responsibility for sizing and leaves it entirely up to you. Not a lot of use, and presumably here just for completeness.

A Resizeable Window for Simple Player[1]

Our Simple Player as developed in the last chapter implicitly used sizing option 1, the default qtControlFitsMovie, and we arranged for the application window size to be dictated by the control size. Imagine now that we want our application window to be resizeable so that, once a movie is loaded and displayed at its natural size, the movie can then be scaled simply by dragging the window's resize handle (Figure 3.6).

To achieve this, we must switch from the default situation we had in the last chapter, where the movie dictates the size of the control and hence the size of the window, to essentially the reverse; that is, the size of the resizeable window now governs the size of the control, which in turn scales the movie. However, in order to have the movie display *initially* at its default size, we have to start off with Sizing set to qtControlFitsMovie. Then as soon as we've loaded the movie, we change Sizing to qtMovieFitsControl:

```
'Initially resize control to fit movie
AxQTControl1.Sizing = QTSizingModeEnum.qtControlFitsMovie

If OpenFileDialog1.ShowDialog() = DialogResult.OK Then

  AxQTControl1.URL = OpenFileDialog1.FileName()

  'Once we've loaded movie, its size is determined by control size
  AxQTControl1.Sizing = QTSizingModeEnum.qtMovieFitsControl

End If
```

But there's more to it than that. The control will not resize unless we tie it into the parent's form's SizeChanged event, which is fired whenever we drag its resize handle:

```
Private Sub Form1_SizeChanged(...) Handles MyBase.SizeChanged

  AxQTControl1.Size = Me.ClientSize

End Sub
```

---

1 This sample is available on the website at *www.skylark.ie/qt4.net/Samples/SimplePlayer.*

Figure 3.6 Resizing the Simple Player window.

Astute readers may spot a potential problem here. Consider this: the user resizes the form, which then resizes the control in Form1_SizeChanged. The control in turn fires its own SizeChanged event, for which you'll recall we have a handler AxQTControl1_SizeChanged that resizes the form once again. And so it proceeds around in circles potentially *ad infinitum,* a classic race condition. The simplest way to put a stop to this nonsense is to set a flag in Form1_SizeChanged that politely tells AxQTControl1_SizeChanged to ignore SizeChanged events if the window is being resized. First, we declare a member variable in our Form1 class to act as the flag:

```
Private m_bExternalSizeChange As Boolean
```

Then we set the flag to True while we change the size of the control:

```
Private Sub Form1_SizeChanged(...) Handles MyBase.SizeChanged

  m_bExternalSizeChange = True
  AxQTControl1.Size = Me.ClientSize
  m_bExternalSizeChange = False


End Sub
```

Finally, we ignore SizeChanged events if the flag is set:

```
Private Sub AxQTControl1_SizeChanged(...) Handles
          AxQTControl1.SizeChanged

  'Ignore events triggered by Form1_SizeChanged
  If m_bExternalSizeChange Then Exit Sub

  Me.ClientSize = AxQTControl1.Size

End Sub
```

One further detail remains to be tidied up in our resizeable Simple Player. If we want the Scale 1X and Scale 2X menu items to work as before, we need to force the Sizing property temporarily back to qtControlFitsMovie, otherwise our scale changes will have no effect. Remember qtMovieFitsControl ignores attempts to change scale:

```
Private Sub mnuScale1x_Click(...) Handles mnuScale1x.Click

  AxQTControl1.Sizing = QTSizingModeEnum.qtControlFitsMovie
  AxQTControl1.SetScale(1)    '1X
  AxQTControl1.Sizing = QTSizingModeEnum.qtMovieFitsControl

End Sub

Private Sub mnuScale2x_Click(...) Handles mnuScale2x.Click

  AxQTControl1.Sizing = QTSizingModeEnum.qtControlFitsMovie
  AxQTControl1.SetScale(2)    '2X
  AxQTControl1.Sizing = QTSizingModeEnum.qtMovieFitsControl

End Sub
```

Incidentally, this illustrates how sometimes Sizing can be usefully changed on the fly and not just set before a movie is loaded.

The QTOControlLib Namespace

If you try some of the preceding code examples, you may be perturbed to find that your code throws up build errors:

Name QTSizingModeEnum is not declared.

Before you accuse me of not bothering to check my code samples, let me hasten to point out that I have simplified the code by importing the QuickTime Control's namespace at the top of the *Form1.vb* code module, giving all code in the form access to all the members of QTOControlLib, including its various enumerations:

```
Imports QTOControlLib

Public Class Form1
  Inherits System.Windows.Forms.Form
```

This means that I can use code like

```
AxQTControl1.Sizing = QTSizingModeEnum.qtControlFitsMovie
```

instead of the considerably more unwieldy

```
AxQTControl1.Sizing =
          QTOControlLib.QTSizingModeEnum.qtControlFitsMovie
```

In C#, reference the namespace with the using directive at the top of *Form1.cs:*

```
using QTOControlLib;

namespace QTHelloWorld
{
  public class Form1 : System.Windows.Forms.Form
```

Background and Border

Visual controls such as the QuickTime Control traditionally offer control over background color and a facility to have a border drawn around the control.

You could be forgiven for wondering why background color is relevant once a movie is loaded: in many cases it isn't relevant since the movie fills the control completely but, as we saw in the discussion of sizing options, there are situations where the movie does not completely fill the bounds of the control, leaving gaps that will be painted with the background color. There will also be situations where the control is visible but has no movie loaded. The BackColor property allows us to set this background to any standard color or indeed any arbitrary ARGB (alpha, red, green, blue) value:

```
AxQTControl1.BackColor = Color.Aquamarine
AxQTControl1.BackColor = Color.FromArgb(120, 255, 0, 0)

// C#
AxQTControl1.BackColor = Color.FromArgb(0x49,0x99,0xFF);
```

In practice we often want to set the background color of the control to that of its parent form so that it blends in whenever no movie is loaded or when there are gaps around the movie. You may already have discovered that whenever you drop a QuickTime Control on a form, its background color is automatically set to that of the form.

The BorderStyle property offers three options (Figure 3.7) that are pretty much self-explanatory:

- bsNone: No border—useful with background color set to match that of the form so that your movie blends into the form.
- bsPlain: A single-pixel border—often set to a subdued color to set off your movies.
- bs3D: A sunken, beveled border for that genuine Windows look.

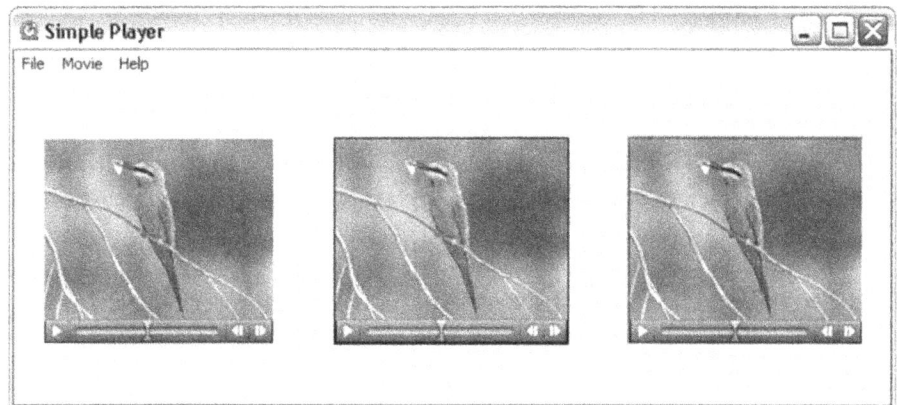

Figure 3.7 The QuickTime Control's border options: bsNone, bsPlain, and bs3D.

The BorderColor property only applies when BorderStyle is bsPlain and can be set to any System.Drawing.Color value as with BackColor.

```
AxQTControl1.BorderColor = Color.DarkGoldenrod
AxQTControl1.BorderStyle = BorderStylesEnum.bsPlain
```

Movie Controller

A critical design decision in any application involving QuickTime movies is whether or not to display the movie controller bar, or just plain "movie controller" as it's commonly called. Unless you are providing your own custom playback controls, the movie controller will be essential if your users are going to be able to start, stop, rewind, or step frame-by-frame forward or backward through the movie. Sometimes, of course, all you want is to play the movie without any user interaction, in which case the movie controller is irrelevant.

But What Is a Movie Controller?

If you are new to QuickTime, then you may wonder what exactly a movie controller is and why anyone would want to hide one! Well, the movie controller is simply the little control/progress bar that QuickTime displays immediately underneath a movie, as shown in Figure 3.8. As well as indicating progress, it provides basic facilities for controlling playback: start, stop, step forward, step back, plus the ability to slide the playback position forward or back or, in the jargon, to *scrub* the movie. If your movie has a sound track, you'll find that the movie controller also sports a volume control.

The movie controller bar may in fact appear quite different depending on the type of media loaded into the control. For example, load a QuickTime VR movie and you will get a very different movie controller with all the controls you need to navigate inside a virtual environment.

Figure 3.8 Examples of movie controller bars.

Fortunately, turning the movie controller on and off is a dawdle using the `MovieControllerVisible` Boolean property. You can toggle the movie controller at any time or ensure that it is off prior to loading a movie if you don't need it:

```
AxQTControl1.MovieControllerVisible = False
AxQTControl1.URL = "D:\My Movies\TitanFlyby.mov"
```

One fact worth mentioning at this point is that the movie controller is always exactly 16 pixels tall. This is taken into account by the control whenever it sizes itself to fit the movie in the `qtControlFitsMovie` sizing mode. You can easily verify this by adding the following line after the movie is loaded:

```
Dim mcHeight = AxQTControl1.Height - AxQTControl1.Movie.Height
Debug.WriteLine(CStr(mcHeight))
```

The value of `mcHeight` is the difference between the control's height and the height of the movie that it contains.

Auto Play

In many situations the obvious next step after loading a movie is to play it. In keeping with its tradition of saving developers from superfluous typing, the QuickTime Control provides an `AutoPlay` property that, when set to `True`, will automatically start playing the movie once it is loaded. This is especially convenient if you need sounds or music in your application: just place a QuickTime Control on your form (even a hidden control will do), set `AutoPlay = True`, load any audio file, and it will proceed to play immediately.

Control over Full-Screen Display

In the last chapter we saw how easy it is to flick the control into eye-popping full-screen display mode using the `FullScreen` property:

```
AxQTControl1.FullScreen = True
```

Finer control over this display mode is provided by a number of additional properties of the control.

By default, you exit full-screen mode by hitting the Escape (Esc) key, which seems logical enough. However, your application might use the Esc key for some other purpose or you may prefer to use a function key instead. As its name suggests, the FullScreenEndKeyCode property allows us to define any key code we like as the means of escape:

```
AxQTControl1.FullScreenEndKeyCode = Keys.F2
```

```
AxQTControl1.FullScreenEndKeyCode = Keys.Space
```

Full-screen mode has its own sizing property FullScreenSizing that is independent of the sizing mode the control exerts. In most cases you will want to set FullScreenSizing to preserve the movie aspect ratio:

```
AxQTControl1.FullScreenSizing = QTFullScreenSizingModeEnum.
        qtFullScreenMovieFitsControlMaintainAspectRatio
```

Given that all you probably want to do in full-screen mode is just watch the movie, the cursor can be an irritating distraction. We can easily get rid of it by setting a flag in the FullScreenFlags property:

```
AxQTControl1.FullScreenFlags = QTFullScreenFlagsEnum.
        qtFullScreenFlagHideCursor
```

If your system supports multiple monitors as many now do, it's even possible to direct the full-screen output to a monitor of your choice:

```
AxQTControl1.FullScreenMonitorNumber = 2
```

This property can be set to any number from 1 to the number of active monitors on your system, but setting it will fail if the monitor number does not exist. Since it's not uncommon for additional monitors to be unplugged or otherwise unavailable, it's worth using SystemInformation to do a quick check on the actual number of monitors before setting this property:

```
If (monitorNumber > 0) And (monitorNumber <=
            SystemInformation.MonitorCount) Then
   AxQTControl1.FullScreenMonitorNumber = monitorNumber
Else
   AxQTControl1.FullScreenMonitorNumber = 1
End If
```

One thing to beware of with full-screen display is the effect it may have on the scale of the movie. When entering full-screen mode, the QuickTime Control scales the movie to fit the screen according to the sizing mode specified in the `FullScreenSizing` property. On leaving full-screen mode, however, the original movie scale is not explicitly restored. If the `Sizing` mode of the control is set to `qtMovieFitsControl` or `qtMovieFitsControlMaintain-AspectRatio`, then this is not a problem since the movie will immediately be scaled to fit the control, which, of course, is the same size as it was before the full-screen interlude. But if the control `Sizing` is set to `qtControlFits-Movie` or `qtMovieCenteredInControl`, then you're in for a shock when you drop out of full-screen mode: the movie scale will remain exactly as it was in full-screen mode.

One solution to this problem would be to restore the movie scale after leaving full-screen mode, but how might we know when this has happened? We can't use the `SizeChanged` event of the control since the control hasn't changed size. Fortunately, another event comes to our rescue: the `StatusUp-date` event of the QuickTime Control. This event is triggered for a variety of reasons including entering and leaving full-screen mode. The available `Sta-tusUpdate` codes are found in `QTStatusCodesEnum`, and the pair we are interested in is `qtStatusFullScreenBegin` and `qtStatusFullScreenEnd`. Below is a `StatusUpdate` event handler showing how the X and Y scales are saved upon entering full-screen mode and then restored on exit:

```
Private Sub AxQTControl1_StatusUpdate(...) Handles
        AxQTControl1.StatusUpdate

  Static scaleX As Single, scaleY As Single

  Select Case e.statusCode

    Case QTStatusCodesEnum.qtStatusFullScreenBegin
      scaleX = AxQTControl1.ScaleX
      scaleY = AxQTControl1.ScaleY

    Case QTStatusCodesEnum.qtStatusFullScreenEnd
      AxQTControl1.SetScale(scaleX, scaleY)

  End Select

End Sub
```

Initializing QuickTime

One of the first things that traditional QuickTime developers using the C API often learn the hard way is that QuickTime must be *initialized,* or loaded, before you can expect it to do anything useful. If you are already familiar with this concept, you may be wondering how we seem to have gotten so far without ever mentioning this! Well, the good news is that QuickTime *is* being initialized for us by the QuickTime Control just at the right time so that we never have to worry about it, and it is unloaded behind the scenes as well. This is component technology at its best: ease of use is preeminent and the intricacies of a particular technology are not allowed to get in the way.

If you happen to have sneakily jumped way ahead and looked more closely at the QuickTime Control interface, say, in Object Browser, you might interrupt at this point: If the QuickTime Control really is so smart as to load and unload QuickTime when it needs to, how come it has `Quick-TimeInitialize` and `QuickTimeTerminate` methods?

That's a good question, and to answer it we have to look a little more closely at how the QuickTime Control manages its relationship with Quick-Time itself. Three key points to bear in mind are

1. QuickTime need be initialized only *once* by your application, or strictly speaking by any process, irrespective of how many movies the application might have open.

2. The QuickTime Control can be loaded by your application without having to load QuickTime itself, for example, when the control's container form gets loaded. The QuickTime Control should not be confused with Quick-Time itself—the control just *loads* QuickTime whenever it needs to. This is important to grasp.

3. Once loaded by a process, QuickTime maintains an internal reference count on the number of times that it is initialized and terminated. This means that we shouldn't be shy about calling `QuickTimeInitialize` and `QuickTimeTerminate` multiple times within our applications: only the very first call to `QuickTimeInitialize` and the very last call to `QuickTimeTermi-nate` will have any effect.

When the QuickTime Control is loaded as part of your form, it doesn't need QuickTime until such time as you tell it to do something that involves QuickTime. So you can happily change the border style or the background color and the control doesn't have to trouble with QuickTime since these are incidental properties of the control that do not require QuickTime. However, the moment you go to load a movie, the control suddenly has to do some heavy lifting, and so it invokes QuickTime.

There are good reasons, however, for why we might wish to be more in control of when and how QuickTime gets loaded and unloaded. Here are three:

1. **Disguising load time:** Most users will tolerate a reasonable start-up delay when an application launches. Just throw up the hourglass cursor and they will contentedly wait. However, the very same users will curse any irritating delays that occur once the application is up and running. Loading QuickTime for the first time does take a few seconds, especially on slower systems, and it is often easiest to bury this in with the general application loading overhead. This is where `QuickTimeInitialize` comes in: we can call this method to initialize QuickTime within our start-up code. In simple Visual Basic applications, a handy place to do this is in the form `Load` event handler of the main application window:

```
Private Sub Form1_Load(...) Handles MyBase.Load

  Cursor.Current = Cursors.WaitCursor

  AxQTControl1.Location = New System.Drawing.Point(0, 0)
  AxQTControl1.BorderStyle = BorderStylesEnum.bsNone
  AxQTControl1.MovieControllerVisible = True

  AxQTControl1.QuickTimeInitialize()        'Load QuickTime

  Cursor.Current = Cursors.Default

End Sub
```

Whenever our application quits and the process is killed, QuickTime will get unloaded anyhow. However, it is still good practice to do this explicitly using `QuickTimeTerminate` as part of an orderly shut-down sequence, for example, in our form's `Closed` event handler:

```
Private Sub Form1_Closed(...) Handles MyBase.Closed

  AxQTControl1.URL = ""

  AxQTControl1.QuickTimeTerminate()        'Unload QuickTime

End Sub
```

2. **Handling load errors:** It is unlikely, but not inconceivable, that Quick-Time may fail to load for some reason. Perhaps the version is too old and not compatible with the QuickTime Control or the installation may be corrupt or damaged. If our application depends heavily on QuickTime, this could be catastrophic and we would be well advised to break the bad news during start-up checks. Fortunately, `QuickTimeInitialize` returns an integer error code that we can check, and any failure can be intelligently reported back to the user:

```
Private Sub Form1_Load(...) Handles MyBase.Load

  Dim loadError as Integer

  Cursor.Current = Cursors.WaitCursor

  AxQTControl1.Location = New System.Drawing.Point(0, 0)
  AxQTControl1.BorderStyle = BorderStylesEnum.bsNone
  AxQTControl1.MovieControllerVisible = True

  'Load QuickTime
  loadError = AxQTControl1.QuickTimeInitialize()
  Cursor.Current = Cursors.Default

  'Check for error: report and exit if failed
  If loadError <> 0 Then
    MsgBox("Unable to load QuickTime! Error: " + CStr(loadError),
          MsgBoxStyle.Critical)
    Application.Exit()   'Abort
  End If

End Sub
```

3. **Configuring QuickTime:** You may have noticed that `QuickTimeInitialize` has a couple of optional parameters. We can safely ignore `InitOptions` (just pass zero), but `InitFlags` allows us to configure QuickTime in ways that may be useful under certain circumstances by passing one or more flags as defined in `QTInitializeQTMLFlagsEnum`. For example, if for some reason we wish to completely disable sound output from QuickTime we could call

```
AxQTControl1.QuickTimeInitialize(0,
          QTInitializeQTMLFlagsEnum.qtInitializeQTMLFlagNoSound)
```

In general, you shouldn't need to concern yourself with these initialization flags, but every now and again they can be very useful, especially during development.

Is QuickTime Available?

Whenever a user launches your application, the mere presence of the Quick-Time Control (*QTOControl.dll*) is no real guarantee that QuickTime itself is necessarily installed on the system. The IsQuickTimeAvailable property checks for the presence of QuickTime and returns True if available. You must pass a howToCheck parameter with this property, which determines how thorough the check for QuickTime will be:

0:   does not attempt to initialize QuickTime but merely checks for the presence of *QuickTime.qts*.

1:   a more thorough check for QuickTime involving an attempt to initialize it

IsQuickTimeAvailable(0) is clearly the more useful option in this context, and should generally precede any attempt to call QuickTimeInitialize.

Note   While IsQuickTimeAvailable is a property, it is a parameterized property, and as such is not available in C#. Instead, it can be accessed through property accessor method get_IsQuickTimeAvailable.

Probing Deeper

In Simple Player we already touched briefly on the Movie property of the control. We saw that this property exposes an object that represents the movie that we have currently loaded into the control. As we have seen so far in this chapter, the control takes care of loading and presentation of the movie. If we want to obtain information about the movie itself or to manipulate it, then we must work through the Movie object, a child object of the control:

```
movieLength = AxQTControl1.Movie.Duration
```

```
AxQTControl1.Movie.Time = 2000
```

Similarly, if we want to check the QuickTime version or twiddle with QuickTime settings, then we turn to the `QuickTime` property of the control:

```
qtVersion = AxQTControl1.QuickTime.Version
```

This should be enough to convince you that the QuickTime Control warrants a lot more exploration beneath the surface. The extensive object model exposed via the `Movie` and `QuickTime` properties is the subject of the next chapter.

Summary

Whatever way you choose to integrate QuickTime into your application, you will want the user experience to be smooth and seamless. Achieving this in any nontrivial application will depend very much on how thoroughly you understand the various presentation options available within the QuickTime Control and how these interact with your application. This is especially true if your user has free reign to load media of arbitrary size and type. Once you master the intricacies, though, you should be able to achieve very tight integration, with the added bonus of some sophisticated features such as full-screen playback.

4

The QuickTime Object Model

○ Introduction

In 1976 Tim Severin set out from Ireland with some doughty companions in a leather-covered boat to sail—or rather, hoping to be driven by wind and current—across the North Atlantic. His objective was to inject some reality into the intriguing legends of the sixth-century Irish monk St. Brendan, who was supposed to have visited America hundreds of years before Columbus. Amongst many adventures before their eventual landfall in Newfoundland, Severin recounts several thrilling encounters with ice: deceptively small and benign-looking above the water but deadly below, especially when all that separates you from the cold sea is a quarter-inch-thick skin of cowhide.[1]

So far in the last two chapters we have been paddling around carefully studying the most obvious features of the QuickTime Control—the bits above the water. But every now and again, we've stumbled across something like the Movie object, hinting at greater things below. In this chapter we get to grips with the underlying library of QuickTime objects that lies beneath the surface.

Before getting down to the detail, we should pause to acquaint—or perhaps reacquaint—ourselves with the concept of an object model. If you are already familiar with object models, such as the Document Object Model (DOM), you may choose to skip over the next section.

---

1 *The Brendan Voyage,* Tim Severin. London: Arrow, 1979.

◉ Object Models

One of the most useful concepts to come out of the object-oriented programming paradigm is that of the object model. An object model is essentially a conceptual representation of a system in terms of its constituent objects and their relationships: a rather terse theoretical definition for what is in fact a very straightforward and eminently practical concept that can be applied to any system.

The compact bundle of flesh and bones writing this book is as good an example as any.

Our bodies comprise a torso, a collection of limbs (usually four), and a head (usually one). Applying the object model terminology (Figure 4.1), we can treat the head and torso as simple child objects of the body. If we can regard our collection of limbs as an object, then we can say that our Limbs collection has four child objects, each of which is a Limb. Notice that the Limb object comes in two flavors: *arm* Limb objects and *leg* Limb objects, but notwithstanding, they are all limbs.

Now if we take any Limb object, either arm or leg, we know that it contains a number of joints and a number of bones. Let's call them the Joints collection and the Bones collection. In the Joints collection we have elbows, wrists, knees, and ankles—all Joint objects of various kinds. Rattling around in our Bones collection are Bone objects such as the femur, tibia, humerus, and other reminders of high school biology.

This skeletal example illustrates the key concepts of the object model:

- The system is broken down into subobjects.
- Some subobjects can be conveniently grouped into collections of objects that share certain characteristics.
- Collection objects contain a number of child objects all of the same type.
- Subobjects themselves may be further broken down.

An object model could conceivably be extended down almost to the nth degree as each object is in turn decomposed into its subobjects. Imagine taking our human body model down to the cellular level!

The Component Object Model (COM) standard is specifically designed to facilitate the implementation of abstract object models such as the one just described. Each object that we have identified in our model can be implemented as a COM object. A COM collection, as the name implies, is itself a COM object that defines a collection of other COM objects. A COM collection has a mandatory Count property that returns the number of items in the

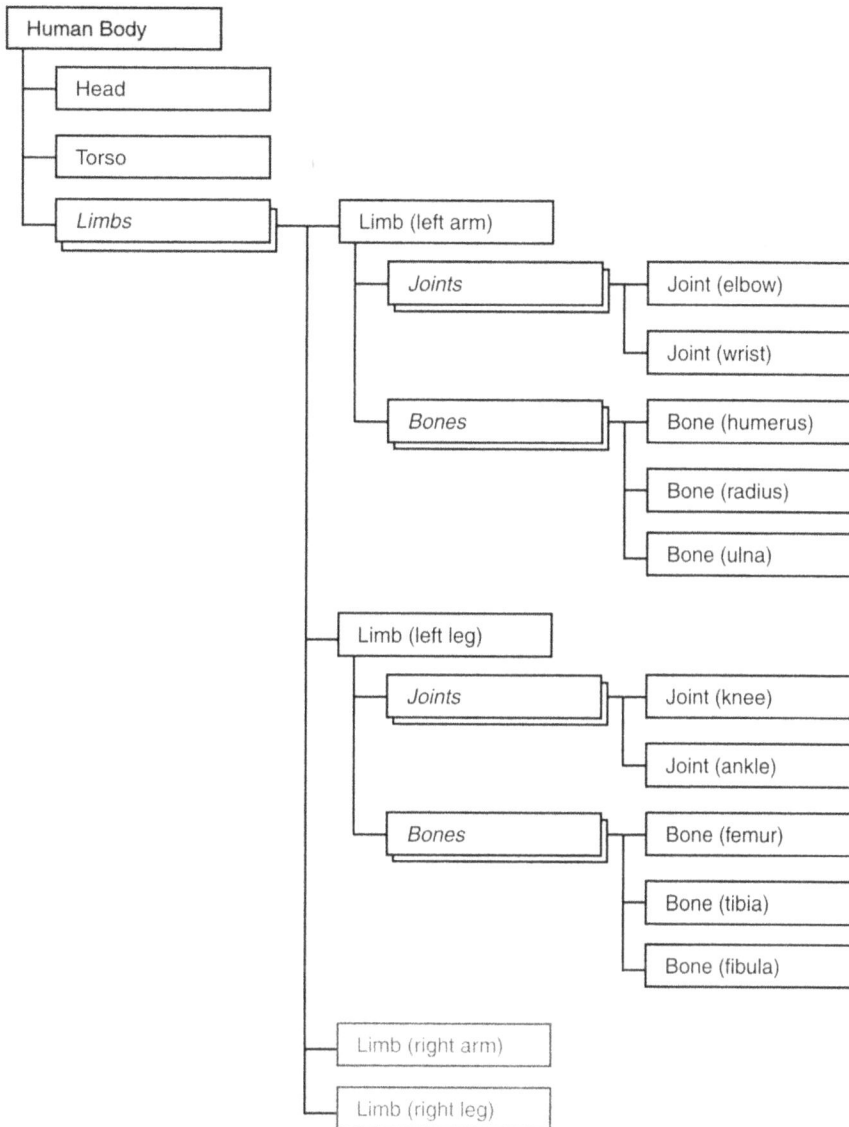

Figure 4.1 The Human Body object model.

collection, together with a mandatory Item method that returns a specified item of the collection—usually by index or by name.

Pre .NET versions of Visual Basic were based entirely on COM: even the built-in objects are part of the VB object model, as you will readily see if you use the Object Browser (View | Object Browser, or F2). The .NET environment builds on the success of COM: the entire .NET Framework is in fact one giant object model, exposing much of the Windows API in the form of a hierarchy of .NET objects and collections of objects. Just bring up the .NET Object Browser (View | Object Browser, or Ctrl-Alt-J), choose any of the System assemblies, and you'll see what I mean.

It's only to be expected then that both Visual Basic and C# facilitate the creation of a set of objects and collections that implement an object model, allowing us to write code such as

```
Dim myBody As New HumanBody
Dim myLimb As Limb

For Each myLimb In myBody.Limbs
  If (Not myLimb.Joints(1).Sprained) Then
    myLimb.PutIn
    myLimb.PutOut
    myLimb.PutIn
    myLimb.ShakeItAllAbout
    myBody.DoHokeyPokey
    myBody.Rotate
  End If
End If
```

As we can see from this hypothetical code, a well-designed object model allows us to represent the structure of an object-oriented system in a convenient and intuitive form.

Since many types of documents are comprised of hierarchies of objects, they can often be modeled using a document object model. By far the best-known of these is the World Wide Web Consortium (W3C) Document Object Model (DOM) that describes an HTML page, starting with the document itself as the root object and extending through a hierarchy of child objects to every individual HTML element on the page. If you have ever used JavaScript on a web page, you have encountered the DOM.

The QuickTime Object Model

QuickTime has long boasted a component-based architecture that lends itself to being expressed in an object model format. The QuickTime COM Control and its associated library of QuickTime COM objects exposes this underlying structure in the .NET and COM environment through the QuickTime Object Model as depicted in Figure 4.2.

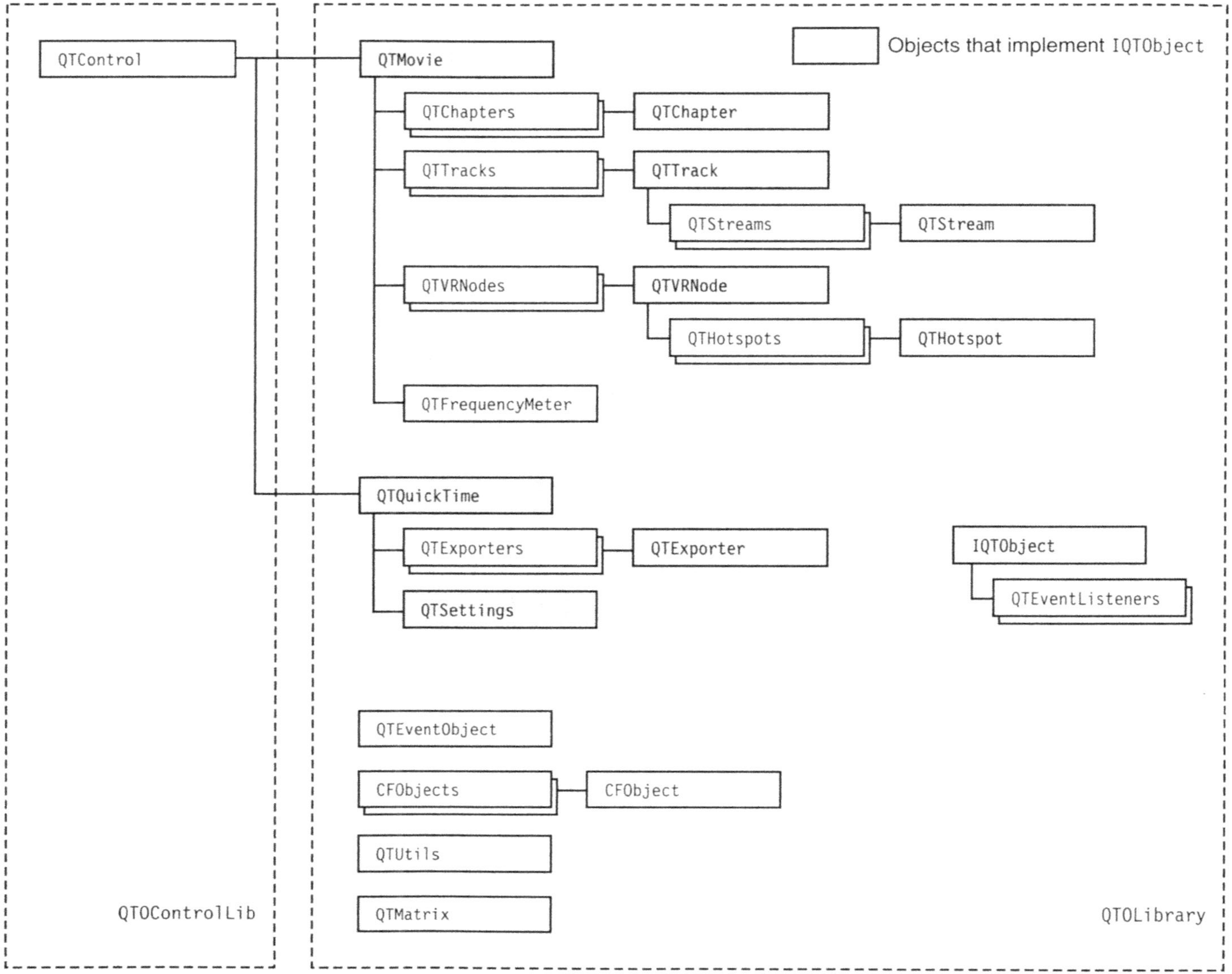

Figure 4.2 The QuickTime Object Model as exposed by the QuickTime Control and Object Library.

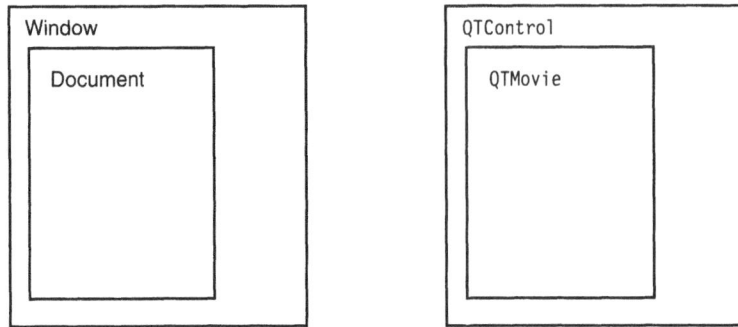

Figure 4.3   DOM Window/Document model analogous to `QTControl`/`QTMovie`.

Every hierarchical object model grows out of one or more root objects. In our anatomical example, the Human Body object is the root object, and we can only get at Limbs and Joints by starting with the root object. Similarly, in the W3C Document Object Model (DOM) the Document object is at the root of the entire hierarchical object model: we can only get at individual elements of an HTML form by starting with the Document itself.

Referring to the QuickTime Object Model as shown in Figure 4.2, and applying the DOM analogy, it is obvious that the QuickTime Control, or `QTControl`, is the equivalent of the Window object, while `QTMovie`, which wraps the movie that was opened in the control, is essentially equivalent to the Document root object (Figure 4.3).

`QTQuickTime` is the root object that enshrines QuickTime itself. Both `QTMovie` and `QTQuickTime` expose a hierarchy of underlying objects. We will devote the remainder of this chapter to exploring these two objects in detail.

QTMovie and Its Offspring

The Movie: QTMovie

In the last two chapters we saw how the QuickTime Control COM object— or, more precisely, the `QTControl` object—manages the opening of a Quick-Time movie and its visual presentation within the container form or window. Once a movie has been successfully opened by the `QTControl` object, the `Movie` property of `QTControl` can be used to gain access to the `QTMovie` child object that represents the movie itself:

```
Dim myMovie as QTMovie

myMovie = AxQTControl1.Movie
```

The properties and methods of `QTMovie` provide us with powerful control over many aspects of the movie. Let's have a look at a few.

Playback Control

Playing a movie couldn't be simpler:

```
AxQTControl1.Movie.Play()
```

as is stopping the movie:

```
AxQTControl1.Movie.Stop()
```

and rewinding the movie when we're done:

```
AxQTControl1.Movie.Rewind()
```

There are sometimes cases where we might wish to speed up or slow down playback. The `Play` method takes an optional floating-point `movieRate` parameter that can be used to play the movie forwards (or even backwards!) at any speed:

```
AxQTControl1.Movie.Play(2.0)      'Play at twice normal speed
AxQTControl1.Movie.Play(0.5)      'Play at half normal speed
AxQTControl1.Movie.Play(-1.0)     'Play backwards
AxQTControl1.Movie.Play(-0.25)    'Play backwards at quarter speed
```

Your users may need frame-by-frame control to reach a particular frame in a movie. For example, you might be using a QuickTime movie as a convenient means of storing a collection of still images and wish to be able to step between them. This is where the `Step` methods come in handy:

```
Dim myMovie as QTMovie
myMovie = AxQTControl1.Movie

myMovie.StepFwd()     'Step forward one frame
myMovie.StepRev()     'Step back one frame
myMovie.Step(6)       'Step forward 6 frames
myMovie.Step(-16)     'Step back 16 frames
```

Precise control over movie playback position may be achieved using the Time property:

```
Dim nSaveTime as Long

nSaveTime = myMovie.Time          'Save current location
myMovie.Time = 5000               'Jump to time 5000
```

The Duration property provides the overall length of the movie so, for example, to go to the end of the movie, all we have to do is set the Time property equal to the Duration:

```
myMovie.Time = myMovie.Duration   'Jump to end of movie
```

Movie Time and Movie Time Scale

The value obtained from time-based properties of QTMovie and other Quick-Time objects, such as Time or Duration, can often be puzzling when you first start using QuickTime. You would naturally expect these to be in units of seconds or perhaps frames.

All of the time-based properties of a movie or a track are, in fact, expressed in units of *movie time*. So what is movie time and how do I relate it to something concrete? Well, movie time is defined by an arbitrary *time scale* that is the number of units of movie time per second. The time scale is a property of the movie and may be obtained from the Movie.TimeScale property.

So converting any movie time to seconds is trivial:

$$\text{Time (seconds)} = \frac{\text{Time (units of movie time)}}{\text{Movie time scale}} = \frac{\text{Movie.Time}}{\text{Movie.TimeScale}}$$

Here it is in code:

```
Dim myTimeInSeconds As Single
myTimeInSeconds = myMovie.Time / myMovie.TimeScale
```

As an example, if a movie reported a duration of 1920 and a time scale of 600, then it would be 1920/600 = 3.2 seconds long.

The *time scale* of a movie can be any arbitrary number of units per second. In practice, the time scale is usually chosen for convenience in working with common video frame rates so that the number of units of movie time per frame is a whole number. The default is often 600 movie time units per second, which works well with a range of frame rates such as 30, 25, 24, 15, 12.5, 12, 10, and 8 frames per second (fps).

If a movie has a fixed frame rate, then the time per frame can easily be worked out:

$$\text{Movie time units per frame} = \frac{\text{Movie time scale}}{\text{Frames per second}}$$

For example, if a movie is 15 fps and has a time scale of 600, then advancing one frame is equivalent to advancing 40 units of movie time.

Tip   In general it is best to work in movie time rather than converting to and from seconds or milliseconds, unless you have a very definite reason to do so. Bear in mind that while many movies do indeed use the default time scale of 600, you should not depend on this: if you need the time scale then always explicitly load it from the movie in question.

Playing Selections

Cases often arise where you only want to play a part of a movie, perhaps one particular clip of a longer sequence or one verse of a song. One rather simple-minded way of doing this would be to jump to the desired start time, Play the movie, and then repeatedly check the Time property of the movie, calling Stop whenever the desired end point has been reached. Such a polling technique is clearly rather tedious, and latency could mean that we don't quite stop precisely where we want to.

This is one situation where the selection properties of the movie come into play: just set the SelectionStart and SelectionEnd properties to the start and end times, respectively, of the clip we wish to play and then set the movie's PlaySelectionOnly property to True.

```
myMovie.SelectionStart = 1500
myMovie.SelectionEnd = 2500
myMovie.PlaySelectionOnly = True
```

Alternatively, we can use the SetSelection method to set the start and *duration* of the selection:

```
myMovie.SetSelection(1500, 1000)        'Alternative – same effect
myMovie.PlaySelectionOnly = True
```

Now when we Play or Rewind the movie, all the action is confined to the selection. And if we were to set Looping to True, the selection would play over and over repeatedly.

This turns out to be a particularly useful facility in many interactive situations: imagine we have a movie that contains the full 123 minutes of the *Euro 2004* quarter-final (soccer, in case you don't know) between Portugal, playing at home, and England. With two goals during normal time, two in extra time, and a nail-biting penalty shoot-out to follow, there is no shortage of action, including a hilarious (or notorious if you're English!) penalty miss by England captain Beckham. We want to give our users the opportunity to pick any one of these highlights and view it. All we need to do is to create an array containing the start time and length of each of the highlights. When the user chooses a highlight, say, from a menu, we just use the SetSelection method to simultaneously set the start time and duration for the selected highlight from our array and then execute the Play method:

```
Sub PlayHighlight(ByVal n As Integer)

    myMovie.SetSelection(m_arrayHighlights(n, 0),
                         m_arrayHighlights(n, 1))
    myMovie.PlaySelectionOnly = True
    myMovie.Play()

End Sub
```

You may encounter similar situations where it is more convenient to keep many short clips in one single composite movie. Performance is improved by not having to load and unload discrete movies all the time: QuickTime is surprisingly adept at jumping around even within quite large movies. Production is also more efficient by avoiding the necessity to process large numbers of individual movies.

Movie Playback Settings

The QTMovie object has a number of properties that provide control over various aspects of movie playback. Say your movie comprises a collection of advertising clips: you probably want the movie to begin playing automatically when someone opens it, and you will also no doubt want to bore them to tears by looping the movie to play over and over again:

```
myMovie.AutoPlay = True
myMovie.Loop = True
```

Whenever AutoPlay is True, the movie will begin to play as soon as it is opened. This is really just a convenience property as you could easily call the

Play method to do the same thing once the movie is loaded. If Loop is True, as soon as the movie reaches the end, it will jump back to the beginning and start playing again.

If you sneakily embed subliminal messages in your advertising clips that only make sense when played backwards, then you might well opt for the LoopIsPalindrome property. If LoopIsPalindrome is set to True, as soon as the movie reaches the end, it will start to play in reverse towards the beginning again; and once it reaches the beginning, it plays forward again, constantly shuttling backwards and forwards. Palindrome looping can sometimes be useful for movies that contain animation sequences.

Both the Loop and LoopIsPalindrome properties also apply whenever a selection exists, except that in this case the specified behavior applies to the selection only. A children's game may involve short, repeated sequences of animated action—say, a character running away or falling through the air. Many such sequences can be included in the same movie; playing a sequence involves code something like the following:

```
Const kMonsterRunningStart = 4570
Const kMonsterRunningDuration = 3500

myMovie.PlaySelectionOnly = True
myMovie.Loop = True
myMovie.SetSelection(kMonsterRunningStart, kMonsterRunningDuration )
myMovie.Time = kMonsterRunningStart
myMovie.Play()       'Run away from the monster
```

AutoPlay, Loop, and LoopIsPalindrome are all *persistent* properties of the movie. This means that the state of these properties can be saved with the movie. So, for example, if we were to load a movie, set AutoPlay to True, and then call the movie's Save method, the next time the movie is opened, its AutoPlay property will already be True and it should start to play immediately. Both QuickTime Player and the QuickTime browser plug-in also respect these properties.

Tracks: QTTracks and QTTrack

If you have worked with QuickTime for any length of time, you soon become familiar with the concept of a *track*. In its most commonly understood form a track is usually a linear sequence of media samples, such as video frames or audio samples. A QuickTime movie is then comprised of one or more of these tracks or media sequences. So a very simple Charlie Chaplin silent movie might contain only a single video track, while the trailer for

Lord of the Rings is likely to contain two tracks: a video track and a separate audio track. As the movie plays, QuickTime cleverly combines the tracks and synchronizes them (Figure 4.4).

Movies can, of course, have multiple tracks, as shown in Figure 4.5. The tracks may be separated both spatially (in different locations within the movie's bounding area) and temporally (over different time periods within the movie).

In the QuickTime Object Model the tracks are represented as child objects of the movie and are made available through the QTTracks collection of the movie.

The Tracks property of the movie returns the QTTracks collection. Accessing the individual tracks is then syntactically straightforward:

```
'Let's have some peace
myMovie.Tracks.Item(3).Mute = True
```

Notice that Tracks.Item(n) returns the *n*th QTTrack object. Since this is a frequently used construct, some languages such as Visual Basic allow you to omit the Item property of the Tracks collection altogether:

```
'Let the music play
myMovie.Tracks(3).Mute = False
```

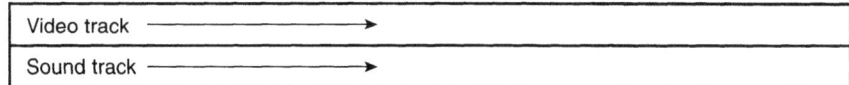

Figure 4.4 Movie with a video track and a sound track.

In Depth

Look up the QTTracks object in the Object Browser and you will notice that the Item property is defined as the *default* member of the QTTracks collection: if you leave out the name of the property, as in the preceding code, the default member is assumed.

Iterating over the Tracks

As with any collection, we will often want to retrieve some information about, or perhaps do something to, every item in the collection: in other words we want to *iterate* over the collection. For example, if we have a mixed bag of movies, it's often instructive to iterate over the tracks collection of any movie that we might open, so that we can extract useful data about each

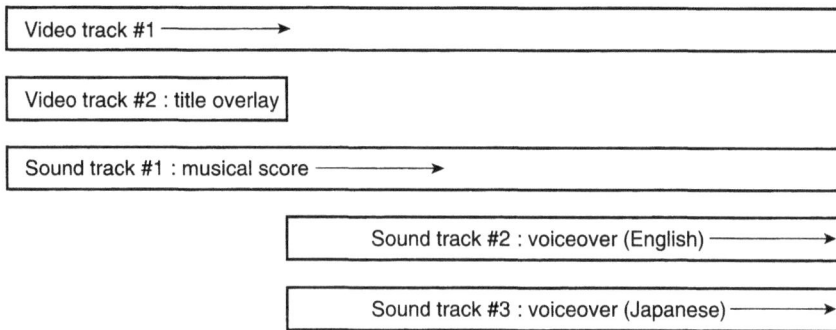

Figure 4.5 Movie with multiple tracks.

track. There are two ways that we can do this; the first makes use of the Count property, which every collection must have:

```
For i = 1 To myMovie.Tracks.Count

    t += "Track : " + CStr(i) + vbCrLf
    t += vbTab + "Type     : " + Hex(myMovie.Tracks(i).Type) + vbCrLf
    t += vbTab + "Format   : " + myMovie.Tracks(i).Format + vbCrLf
    t += vbTab + "Duration : " + CStr(myMovie.Tracks(i).Duration)
                            + vbCrLf
    t += vbTab + "StartTime: " + CStr(myMovie.Tracks(i).StartTime)
                            + vbCrLf

Next i
txtResults = t
```

Alternatively, at least in Visual Basic, we can use the For Each construct for improved readability:

```
Dim trk As QTTrack
For Each trk In myMovie.Tracks

    t += "Track : " + vbCrLf
    t += vbTab + "Type     : " + Hex(trk.Type) + vbCrLf
    t += vbTab + "Format   : " + trk.Format + vbCrLf
    t += vbTab + "Duration : " + CStr(trk.Duration) + vbCrLf
    t += vbTab + "StartTime: " + CStr(trk.StartTime) + vbCrLf

Next trk
txtResults = t
```

Having gotten our hands on a QTTrack object from the tracks collection of our movie, let's see what we can do with it.

Enabling and Disabling a Track

Imagine a training movie with instructional audio tracks in different languages, say, one in English, one in French, and one in Japanese. For obvious reasons, we only want one of these tracks to play at a time, so we use the Enabled property of the track to turn off all of the tracks except the one that we want to hear:

```
'Voiceover in English
myMovie.Tracks(2).Enabled = True
myMovie.Tracks(3).Enabled = False
myMovie.Tracks(4).Enabled = False

'Voiceover in French
myMovie.Tracks(2).Enabled = False
myMovie.Tracks(3).Enabled = True
myMovie.Tracks(4).Enabled = False

'Voiceover in Japanese
myMovie.Tracks(2).Enabled = False
myMovie.Tracks(3).Enabled = False
myMovie.Tracks(4).Enabled = True
```

A text track is often used to subtitle a movie: again we can easily toggle the subtitles on or off.

Positioning a Track

The QTTrack object also has a full suite of properties that allow you to dynamically position the track relative to the movie. This can be really useful in some applications. Taking an educational example, our application might have a collection of video clips of various natural habitats. Overlaid as a second track on each clip is an expert "talking head" who explains the interesting features of each habitat. As well as simply enabling or disabling the talking head, we could allow control of both the position and size of the talking head overlay.

Meet the FourCharCode

In the earlier code snippets that iterate over the tracks, rather than just converting the numeric Type property to a string, we used the Hex function to convert it to a string representing a hexadecimal number. The result still looks rather meaningless but you might notice a pattern: all video tracks will share the same Type value, as will all sound tracks. Here's the output from a movie with an H.263 video track and an IMA 4:1 sound track:

```
Track :
  Type      : 76696465
  Format    : H.263
  Duration  : 34505
  StartTime: 0
Track :
  Type      : 736F756E
  Format    : IMA 4:1
  Duration  : 34501
  StartTime: 0
```

Notice that the Type of any track is an 8-digit hex number that can be split into four 2-digit single-byte values. It so happens that each of these bytes is the ASCII hex code for a specific character:

```
Video Track Type = 76696465 = 76 69 64 65 = v i d e = vide

Sound Track Type = 736F756E = 73 6F 75 6E = s o u n = soun
```

So what appears initially to be a meaningless 32-bit numeric code turns out in fact to be a four-character sequence that represents the type of the track: a video track is of type *vide* and a sound track is of type *soun*. This is the four-character code or FourCharCode data type that you will encounter quite frequently when developing with QuickTime.

To facilitate working with FourCharCode values, the QTUtils object includes two handy functions that convert between numeric FourCharCode values and their string representations: FourCharCodeToString and StringToFourCharCode. To use these utilities, all we need is an instance of the QTUtils object:

```
Dim trk As QTTrack
Dim qtu As New QTUtils
For Each trk In myMovie.Tracks
  t += "Track : " + vbCrLf
  t += vbTab + "Type    : " + qtu.FourCharCodeToString(trk.Type)
                                + vbCrLf
  t += vbTab + "Format : " + trk.Format + vbCrLf
Next trk
txtResults = t
```

to produce an output like

```
Track :
  Type     : vide
  Format   : H.263
Track :
  Type     : soun
  Format   : IMA 4:1
```

In most cases the FourCharCode values that we need to use are all conveniently defined in enumerations in the QuickTime COM Control and Library. Occasionally, though, we will want to define our own FourCharCode values or to generate them automatically in some way. In such cases the starting point is a four-character string that can be converted to a FourCharCode using the StringToFourCharCode function of QTUtils as follows:

```
Dim trk As QTTrack
Dim qtu As New QTUtils
Dim soundTrackType As Long

soundTrackType = qtu.StringToFourCharCode("soun")

For Each trk In myMovie.Tracks
  If trk.Type = soundTrackType then
    t += vbTab + "Sound format    : " + trk.Format + vbCrLf
  End If
Next trk
txtResults = t
```

Notice that the FourCharCode that we create is simply stored in a Long: that's important to understand. There's nothing mysterious about a

FourCharCode—it's just a 32-bit unsigned integer whose 4 constituent bytes each represent a character.

Streams: QTStreams and QTStream (Advanced)

If you are playing a movie that is being streamed from a server, then instead of having separate tracks for audio and video, the movie will contain only a single streaming track of type *strm*. This streaming track contains one or more media streams from the server of different types: video, audio, text, and so on (Figure 4.6.)

The QTTrack object has a child QTStreams collection accessible via the Streams property of the track. Again, as with tracks, we can iterate through the streams and dump useful information about them:

```
For i = 1 To myTrack.Streams.Count
  t += "Stream " + CStr(i) + vbCrLf
  t += " Type : " + qtu.FourCharCodeToString(myTrack.
                      Streams(i).Type) + vbCrLf
  t += " Format : " + myTrack.Streams(i).Format + vbCrLf
Next i
txtResults = t
```

For a typical streaming movie with video and audio, this might produce an output like

```
Stream 1
  Type : vide
  Format : MPEG4 Video
Stream 2
  Type : soun
  Format : AAC
```

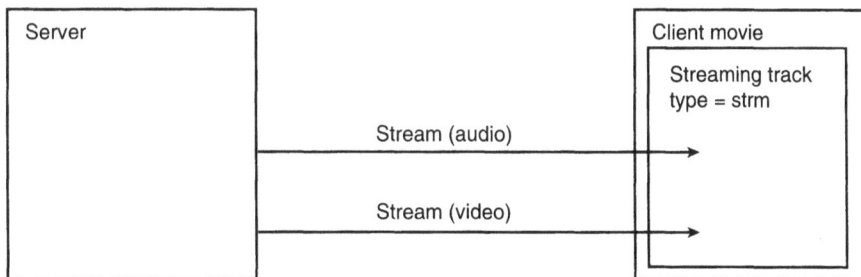

Figure 4.6 Streaming Movie with audio and video streams.

Of course, before attempting to iterate the streams of a track, it is important to establish that we have in fact got a streaming track; otherwise, we will just get an error when we attempt to access the Streams property of the track. First of all, we should use the HasCharacteristic property of the movie to check that the movie is indeed a streaming movie, and then we should check the Type of the track itself. So a more robust version of the streams iteration would be

```
If myMovie.HasCharacteristic(qtMovieCharacteristicIsStreaming) Then
   ...
   If myTrack.Type = qtu.StringToFourCharCode("strm") Then
     For i = 1 To myTrack.Streams.Count
       ...
     Next i
     txtResults = t
   End If
End If
```

As anyone who has ever watched much streaming video will be aware, the reality is often disappointing because bandwidth limitations, poor network connections, and server overload all take their toll. While the video we are watching might, in theory, be 25 frames per second, it may in fact drop so many frames that the end result is closer to 15 or 16 frames per second. QuickTime's streaming media handlers keep track of this kind of statistic as the movie is playing and, if we are concerned about measuring or logging performance, we can get at this useful information for any stream through several properties of the QTStream object. The difference between Average-FrameRate and ExpectedFrameRate tells us something about the video quality, while the underlying data stream performance is revealed by the various Chunks and Queue properties.

QuickTime VR Nodes and Hotspots: QTVRNodes, QTVRNode, QTHotspots, and QTHotspot

Most QuickTime movies comprise linear sequences of media samples that play one after the other in a sequence. These are known as linear movies and include sounds, video clips, and animation sequences. QuickTime can however handle other types of media such as VR panoramic scenes and three-dimensional (3D) objects, or interactive (wired) movies. In QuickTime jargon these are referred to as *nonlinear* movies—movies that don't have a timeline.

When dealing with a QuickTime VR movie, the word *movie* appears somewhat of a misnomer, as we are really talking about a 3D space that may be explored interactively. Technically, however, this VR experience is packaged up for us in the form of a QuickTime movie, complete with its own specialized tracks and a custom movie controller.

While a VR movie does contain tracks, and these tracks do contain all data about the environment we are exploring, they are of limited interest. Of far greater interest are the other conceptual entities such as the 3D scenes that make up the VR environment and the hotspots that can be used to link from one scene to the next or to carry out custom actions.

Nodes: QTVRNodes and QTVRNode

Each scene in a VR movie can be explored from a single viewpoint in space known as a node. A VR movie may have a collection of one or more nodes and so, in our QuickTime Object Model, a movie has a child QTVRNodes collection obtained through the VRNodes property of the movie. Clearly, only a VR movie will possess a QTVRNodes collection and so it makes sense to check this using the IsVRMovie property before we attempt to access the nodes collection:

```
If myMovie.IsVRMovie Then
   nodeCount = myMovie.VRNodes.Count
End If
```

The special QuickTime VR movie controller has interactive controls that allow you to explore the virtual environment, with a cameralike ability to pan and tilt around the scene or zoom in and out to points of interest. The QTMovie object (*not* the QTVRNode object) has a number of properties dedicated to controlling navigation around VR scenes, as summarized in Table 4.1.

Table 4.1 QTMovie Properties for VR Navigation

Property			Function in Current VR Node
Value	Min Value	Max Value	
PanAngle	PanAngleMin	PanAngleMax	Pan angle (side-to-side) (degrees)
TiltAngle	TiltAngleMin	TiltAngleMax	Tilt angle (up/down) (degrees)
FieldOfView	FieldOfViewMin	FieldOfViewMax	Zoom angle (in/out) (degrees)
PanTiltSpeed	1 (slowest)	10 (fastest)	Relative speed of panning and tilting default is 5.
ZoomRate	1 (slowest)	10 (fastest)	Relative speed of zooming in and out default is 5.

The following code iterates over all the nodes in a VR movie and prints out the values of the angular properties listed in Table 4.1. Notice the use of the movie's `CurrentNodeID` property to jump to a particular node under program control:

```
'Iterate over VR Nodes and Angles

Dim node As QTVRNode
Dim t As String
Const kFMT = "0.#°"

With myMovie

  For Each node In .VRNodes

    .CurrentNodeID = node.UniqueID

    t += "VR Node : " + CStr(node.UniqueID) + vbCrLf
    t += "  Pan Angle range : " + Format(.PanAngleMin, kFMT) + " to "
    t += Format(.PanAngleMax, kFMT) + vbCrLf
    t += "  Pan Angle : " + Format(.PanAngle, kFMT) + vbCrLf
    t += "  Tilt Angle range : " + Format(.TiltAngleMin, kFMT) + " to "
    t += Format(.TiltAngleMax, kFMT) + vbCrLf
    t += "  Tilt Angle : " + Format(.TiltAngle, kFMT) + vbCrLf
    t += "  FOV range : " + Format(.FieldOfViewMin, kFMT) + " to "
    t += Format(.FieldOfViewMax, kFMT) + vbCrLf
    t += "  FOV : " + Format(.FieldOfView, kFMT) + vbCrLf

  Next node

End With

tbResults.Text = t
```

Not only can you read these properties, setting them can place the entire navigational experience under program control. You may wish to jump to a specific viewpoint:

```
With myMovie

    .PanAngle = 125.0;
    .TiltAngle = 0.0;
    .FieldOfView = 40;

End With
```

There is no reason why your application couldn't store a whole set of these viewpoints and jump around between them—perhaps as part of game play.

Hotspots: QTHotspots and QTHotspot

A VR node may contain a number of hotspots. These can link to other nodes (for instance, a hotspot on a doorway), open a URL, or request some kind of application-specific action. In the QuickTime Object Model, the hotspots within a node are available as a QTHotspots collection from the Hotspots property of the node. So to fully explore a VR movie, we use a nested iteration, first over the nodes and then over the hotspots within each node:

```
'Iterate over VR Nodes and Hotspots

Dim node As QTVRNode
Dim hs As QTHotspot
Dim qtu As New QTUtils
Dim t As String

For Each node In myMovie.VRNodes

    t += "VR Node : " + CStr(node.UniqueID) + vbTab
    t += qtu.FourCharCodeToString(node.Type) + vbCrLf

    For Each hs In node.Hotspots

        t += vbTab + "HS : " + CStr(hs.UniqueID) + vbTab
        t += qtu.FourCharCodeToString(hs.Type) + vbCrLf

    Next hs

Next node
tbResults.Text = t
```

We use this to give us a concise dump of the structure of a multinode VR movie:

```
VR Node : 127      pano
   HS : 180        link
VR Node : 128      pano
   HS : 81         link
   HS : 100        url
VR Node : 129      pano
   HS : 16         link
```

We can see that this VR movie contains three nodes each with a link hotspot that presumably links to another node, and one node with a url hotspot.[2]

Chapters: QTChapters

QuickTime provides a useful index facility for creating an index to the sections or chapters within a movie. This comes into its own if you have a very long movie. Take, for example, a movie of a dramatic production such as Shakespeare's *Macbeth*. You could have a chapter for each act and scene, providing a means to rapidly navigate the entire movie.

Adding chapters to a movie is a somewhat tedious process in QuickTime Player, involving the pasting of a carefully crafted text file into a movie to create a special text track known as a chapter track. More detail on this topic is available at

www.apple.com/quicktime/tutorials/chaptertracks.html

Once created, however, getting at the chapters using the QuickTime Object Model couldn't be simpler using the QTChapters collection of the movie.

Here's a code snippet that iterates over the chapters in a movie and dumps the name and start time for each chapter:[3]

```
Dim myMovie As QTMovie = AxQTControl1.Movie
If AxQTControl1.Movie Is Nothing Then Exit Sub

Dim chptr As QTChapter
Dim t As String
```

---

2 Try these code samples (at the website) with *Media/Movies/VR/GolfCourse.mov.*

3 Try this with *Media/Movies/Chapters.mov.*

```
For Each chptr In myMovie.Chapters
  t += "Chapter " + CStr(chptr.Number) + " : "
  t += CStr(chptr.StartTime) + " "
  t += CStr(chptr.Name) + " " + vbCrLf
Next chptr
tbResults.Text = t
```

There isn't a whole lot that you can do with the QTChapter object other than extract some data about it as shown in the code. However, QTMovie has a GoToChapter method that will jump to any indexed chapter in the movie:

```
AxQTControl1.Movie.GoToChapter(4)
```

QTQuickTime and Its Offspring

In addition to the QTMovie child object, which, as we have seen allows us to delve deep into the movie itself, the QuickTime Control has another child object that exposes lots of useful information and features—but this time of QuickTime itself—QTQuickTime.

QTQuickTime

In the same way as we request the QTMovie object through the control's Movie property, the QTQuickTime object is available through the QuickTime property of the control:

```
Dim qt as QTQuickTime
qt = AxQTControl1.QuickTime
```

QuickTime Version

In our QuickTime-based applications, it is frequently useful to know the version of QuickTime that we are running on. We may simply wish to display this in an About box, or we may wish to alert the user that a later version of QuickTime is required. Here's how to display the version of QuickTime:

```
Dim ver As Long
ver = AxQTControl1.QuickTime.Version
MsgBox("QuickTime Version : " + CStr(ver))
```

The result is somewhat disconcerting—not quite what we expected:

SimplePlayer

QuickTime Version : 117579776

OK

The explanation is that `QuickTime.Version` returns the version as a long integer, but in a particular format known as a binary-coded decimal, or BCD, version. Fortunately, we are spared the gory details of how to convert this to something meaningful as Apple has thoughtfully provided us with a `Version-AsString` property:

```
Dim ver As String
ver = AxQTControl1.QuickTime.VersionAsString
MsgBox("QuickTime Version : " + ver)
```

This time things look much more meaningful:

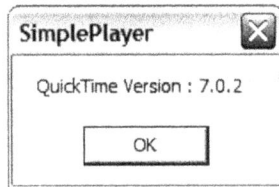

SimplePlayer

QuickTime Version : 7.0.2

OK

In Depth: BCD Version

The BCD version is a 32-bit integer split into 4 byte fields and designed to squeeze in far more information than is really good for it, as follows:

Byte #1	Major revision	2 BCD digits	Range 00–99
Byte #2	Minor and bug revision	1 BCD digit each	Range 0.0–9.9
Byte #3	Stage	develop, alpha, beta, or final stage	HEX 20, 40, 60 or 80
Byte #4	Nonreleased version	unsigned integer	Range 0–255

Version numbers like 7.0.2b101 can be packed into a single long value. Before dismissing the BCD version format as confusingly archaic, it should be pointed out that it does have one redeeming feature: when comparing versions using BCD values, later versions will always have a numerically greater value than older versions of the same stage. This is a much more robust means of comparing versions than just doing a string comparison between, say, "6.0.2" and "7.1".

QuickTime Settings: QTSettings

System-wide QuickTime settings may be adjusted through the QuickTime Control Panel (QuickTime Preferences). The QTQuickTime object provides programmatic access to a number of these settings through its QTSettings child object, which can be obtained from the Settings property. Most of these settings you should never need to go near, at least in your application, but one or two can be useful.

Language

It is possible to check or even change the QuickTime language setting:

```
Dim qt As QTQuickTime
qt = AxQTControl1.QuickTime
MsgBox("QuickTime Language : " + CStr(qt.Settings.Language))
```

The value returned is a standard localization code as defined in

http://developer.apple.com/documentation/QuickTime/APIREF/LocalizationCodes.htm

Media Keys

Certain codecs, such as Indeo and Sorenson, allow movies to be secured by a media key—effectively an unlock code—that is attached to the movie at the time it is compressed. A matching media key must be available to QuickTime if the movie is to be playable. Media keys may be permanently added to QuickTime using the Control Panel, or they may be added and removed at runtime using the QTSettings object. Each media key has a name, usually determined by the codec, and an associated value.

Try playing a movie[4] that is locked with a media key ("Indeo video4") with a value of "1234": you will see only blank frames. Now run the following, and then play the movie again:

---

4 Try loading the following movie: *Media/Movies/RTD_Indeo_Key = 1234.mov.*

```
Dim qt As QTQuickTime
qt = AxQTControl1.QuickTime

qt.Settings.MediaKey("IndeoVideo4") = "1234"
```

We have used a media key to unlock this movie. If you don't wish to add the media key permanently to QuickTime, you should remove it when you're done with it:

```
qt.Settings.DeleteMediaKey("IndeoVideo4")
```

Exporters: QTExporters and QTExporter

By far and away the most useful feature available through the QTQuickTime object is QuickTime's unrivalled export facility. Not only is QuickTime capable of *opening* a wide variety of media file formats, it can also *export* to a surprising number of formats as well. So, for example, we can open an AVI file with an Indeo video track and IMA 4:1 compressed sound track and export this as a 3GP video file with an AAC compressed sound track. Or, we can paste images frame by frame into an empty movie and then export our new composite movie using any of the standard codecs such as Sorenson. For anyone involved in digital media production and delivery, this export facility in itself has to be one of the compelling reasons for using QuickTime.

The QTQuickTime object has a QTExporters collection comprised of QTExporter objects. We access the collection of exporters through the Exporters property of QTQuickTime. A QTExporter is a QuickTime object that can perform an export function on a movie or even on an individual track within the movie, as shown in Figure 4.7. If you are familiar with the QuickTime API, the QTExporter is really a wrapper around one of the QuickTime exporter components.

Initially, the QTExporters collection is empty. The first thing we have to do before we can use an exporter is to add one to the collection and then retrieve the QTExporter object as follows:

```
Dim qt As QTQuickTime
Dim exp As QTExporter

qt = AxQTControl1.QuickTime
qt.Exporters.Add()
exp = qt.Exporters(1)
```

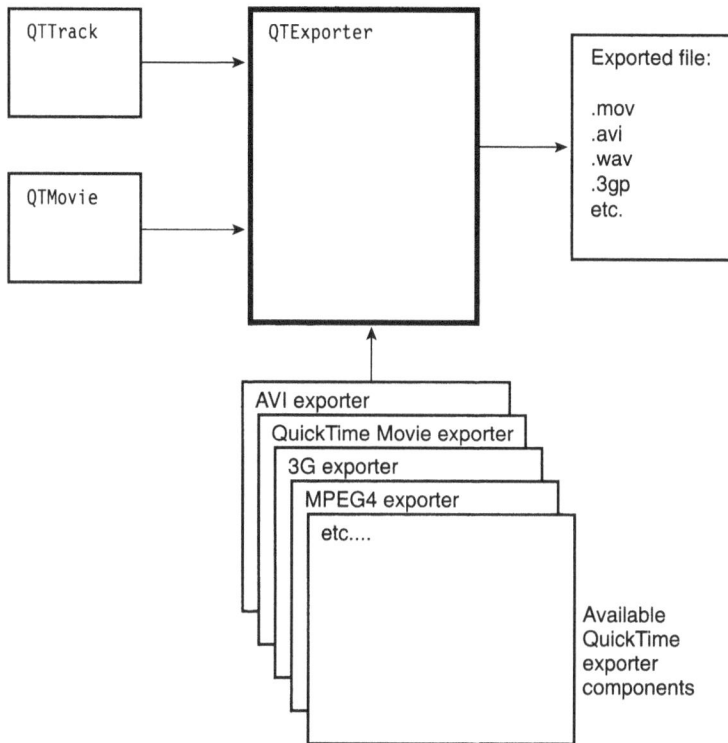

Figure 4.7 The QTExporter object can export a movie or a track.

Once we have an exporter, we can proceed to configure it to export whichever movie or track happens to be of interest. We do this by calling the SetDataSource method of QTExporter, passing the track or movie that we wish to export:

```
exp.SetDataSource (AxQTControl1.Movie)
```

```
exp.SetDataSource (AxQTControl1.Movie.Tracks(2))
```

So we now have an exporter and we have given it a track or movie that we would like to export. At this point you might reasonably ask why we have to go to all this trouble. Why don't the QTMovie and QTTrack objects simply have an Export method in the same way that QTMovie has a Save method? Well, the reason is mainly to do with efficiency. Once you have created and configured an exporter, which can be time consuming, especially if you have to allow its settings to be changed through the user interface, you can then use it over and over again with multiple movies or tracks.

Two further essentials are required before we can perform an export: (1) we must configure the exporter settings with the required file format, codecs, and settings that we wish to use; and (2) we must supply a file name and path for the exported file.

Export with Export Dialog

All of this can be accomplished in one go by presenting the user with a composite export file dialog using the ShowExportDialog method:

```
exp.ShowExportDialog()
```

The Export drop-down list can be used to select the type of exporter that we wish to use and the Options... button provides configuration settings for the selected format (Figure 4.8).

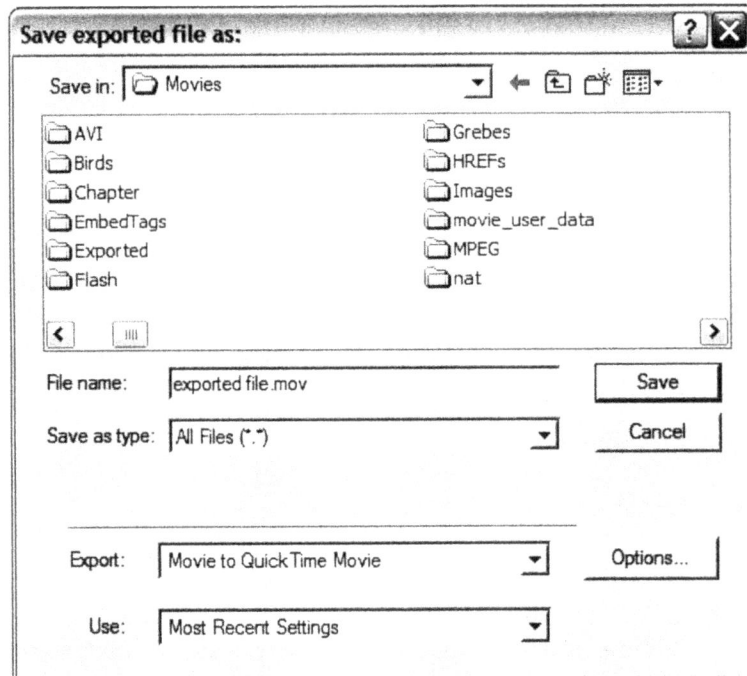

Figure 4.8 QTExporter's ShowExportDialog.

Once you have selected a file name and clicked Save, the export process will begin. Depending on the length of your movie and the compression settings selected, this export can take a significant length of time. A progress dialog keeps you informed of what's happening and you can of course abort the export by clicking the Stop button at any point (Figure 4.9).

Adding a sophisticated export movie feature to Simple Player[5] turns out to be surprisingly straightforward:

```
Private Sub mnuExport_Click(...) Handles mnuExport.Click

    Dim qt As QTQuickTime = AxQTControl1.QuickTime

    If AxQTControl1.Movie Is Nothing Then Exit Sub

    qt = AxQTControl1.QuickTime

    If qt.Exporters.Count = 0 Then qt.Exporters.Add()

    Dim exp As QTExporter = qt.Exporters(1)
    exp.SetDataSource(AxQTControl1.Movie)
    exp.ShowExportDialog()

End Sub
```

This proves to be yet another example of how much functionality can often be unlocked via a few apparently simple properties and methods of a QuickTime object. Anyone familiar with doing something similar in C++ using the QuickTime API will particularly appreciate this.

Figure 4.9 Export progress dialog.

5 See *www.skylark.ie/qt4.net/Samples/SimplePlayer* for this and subsequent code samples.

Export with Export Settings Dialog

In the preceding example, the user must first choose the particular *type of exporter* he wants to use from the Export drop-down list and then configure the *export settings* by clicking on the Options... button. In many cases we will already know the type of exporter that we wish to use (*AVI, MPEG, Quick-Time Movie,* etc.) and this can instead be set programmatically using the `TypeName` property of the `QTExporter` object.

```
exp.TypeName = "QuickTime Movie"
```

Once the exporter type has been set, we can call `ShowSettingsDialog`

```
exp.ShowSettingsDialog()
```

which displays the export settings dialog for the particular type of exporter that we have chosen. The example in Figure 4.10 shows the settings for the *QuickTime Movie* exporter. This is exactly the same settings dialog as we would get if we chose a particular exporter in the Export Dialog and clicked on the Options... button. Note that it may be quite different from exporter to exporter, as a comparison of Figures 4.10 and 4.11 will show.

Once the OK button is clicked, the `QTExporter` object is configured. All we have left to do is to supply a file name and path and initiate the export process:

```
exp.DestinationFileName = "D:\QuickTime\Movies\JustExported.mov"
exp.BeginExport()
```

Once an export process has begun, it is possible to cancel the process: you could of course click the Stop button on the export progress dialog or you can simply call the `CancelExport` method:

```
exp.CancelExport()
```

Batch Export

Once an exporter has been configured, either by exporting once with `ShowExportDialog` or by using `ShowSettingsDialog`, it can be reused as many times as you like with the same settings. Once configured, all you need do for each movie or track you want to export is

1. Use `SetDataSource` to set the data source of the exporter to the movie or track.

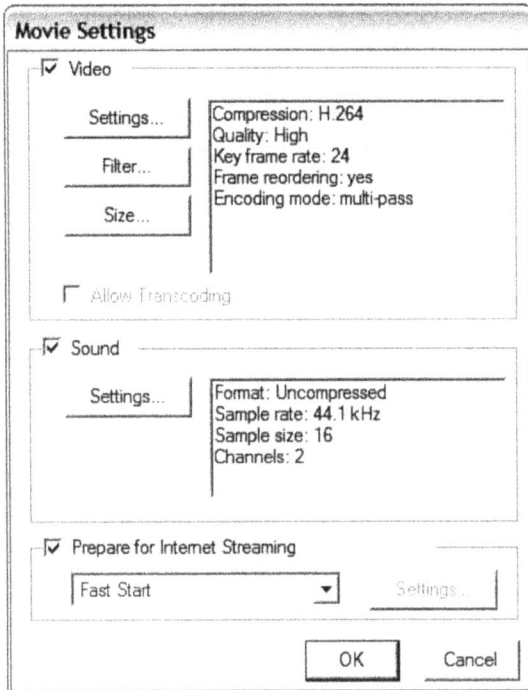

Figure 4.10 Export settings for *QuickTime Movie* exporter.

2. Set `DestinationFileName` to the path and file name for the exported file.

3. Call `BeginExport`.

Here is a useful function that takes a source folder of movies (`sourcePath`) and exports each movie in it to a destination folder (`destPath`) using the `exporterType` specified:

```
Private Sub BatchExport(ByVal exporterType As String,
                        ByVal sourcePath As String,
                        ByVal destPath As String,
                        ByVal destFileExtension As String)


    Dim srcFile As String
    Dim dstFile As String
    Dim log As String = ""
```

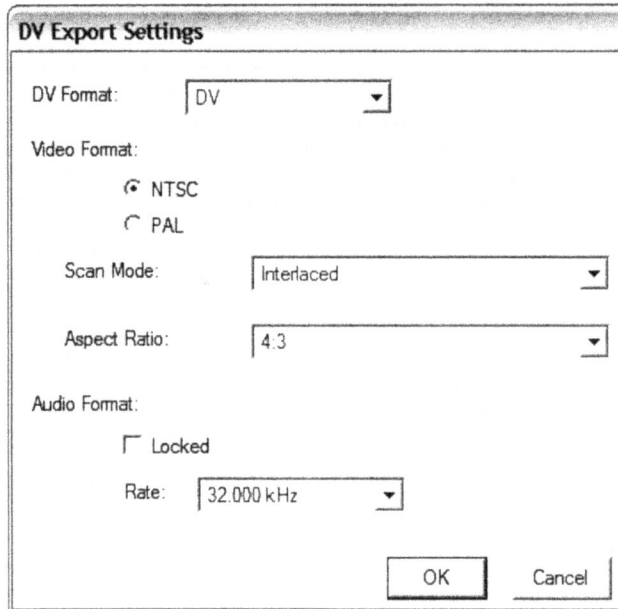

Figure 4.11 Export settings for *DV Stream* exporter.

```
If Not Directory.Exists(sourcePath) Then Exit Sub
If Not Directory.Exists(destPath) Then Exit Sub

Dim srcFiles As String() = Directory.GetFiles(sourcePath, "*.*")

If srcFiles.Length = 0 Then Exit Sub

Dim diDest As DirectoryInfo = New DirectoryInfo(destPath)

AxQTControl1.ErrorHandling =
         QTErrorHandlingOptionsEnum.qtErrorHandlingRaiseException

Dim qt As QTOLibrary.QTQuickTime = AxQTControl1.QuickTime
Dim qtu As New QTUtils

'Set up and configure the exporter
If qt.Exporters.Count = 0 Then qt.Exporters.Add()

Dim exp As QTOLibrary.QTExporter = qt.Exporters(1)
```

```
exp.TypeName = exporterType
exp.ShowSettingsDialog()


'Iterate through the files in the source folder exporting each one
For Each srcFile In srcFiles
  Dim fi = New FileInfo(srcFile)
  dstFile = diDest.ToString + "\"
  dstFile += Mid(fi.Name, 1, Len(fi.Name) - Len(fi.Extension))
  dstFile += destFileExtension
  log += "Exporting from : " + fi.FullName + vbCrLf
  log += "           to   : " + dstFile + vbCrLf

  Try
    AxQTControl1.URL = srcFile
    If Not AxQTControl1.Movie Is Nothing Then
         exp.SetDataSource(AxQTControl1.Movie)
         exp.DestinationFileName = dstFile
         exp.BeginExport()
    End If
  Catch e As COMException
    log += "**ERROR** : " + Hex(e.ErrorCode) + " "
    log += CStr(qtu.QTErrorFromErrorCode(e.ErrorCode)) + vbCrLf
  End Try

Next

AxQTControl1.URL = ""

tbResults.Text = log

End Sub
```

In a batch function such as this, repeatedly opening files and exporting them is inevitably prone to error. Since we may be processing thousands of files, we don't really want one or two errors or a single corrupt file to abort further processing. So we protect the critical code with a Try…Catch exception handler: if an exception occurs while opening a movie or exporting it, the COMException handler will trap the error, log it, and just move on to the next file. Note that we are catching a System.Runtime.InteropServices .COMException rather than a System.Exception. This allows us to extract the

COM error code (HRESULT) resulting from the failed COM call, which will be a help in identifying the cause of the exception. See Chapter 6 for a more detailed treatment of exception handling.

Potential Exporters

We've discovered that QuickTime allows us to export a movie or a track in a variety of different formats, but how can we find out what export formats are available for a particular movie or track? The list of potential exporters will vary depending on what type of movie or track we are dealing with. For example, we can't really expect to be able to export a video track to a sound format such as WAV or AIFF, or a sound-only movie as a sequence of PICT images. Also, since QuickTime exporters exist as components in the Quick-Time architecture, it is entirely possible that additional (perhaps third-party) exporters may, or may not, be installed.

This is where the `PotentialExporters` property of `QTMovie` and `QTTrack` comes to the rescue. This property returns a list of all the available exporters that could potentially be used to export that particular movie or track. Rather than just returning a delimited list in a string, `PotentialExporters` returns an array of all the exporter types packaged up in a `CFObject`. But what is a `CFObject`, and how do we extract the relevant data from it in a useful way? We'll find out in the next chapter.

◉ Summary

Most of the key objects in the QuickTime object library have been introduced in this chapter—some briefly and others in more detail. We have seen how these objects link together to form the QuickTime Object Model. Once a movie has been opened in the QuickTime Control, we've discovered that the `Movie` and `QuickTime` properties of the control become the gateways to the underlying objects in the hierarchy via the `QTMovie` and `QTQuickTime` objects. By this stage you should be able to confidently access and manipulate the various collections of objects together with the individual objects themselves.

Now that we have established a solid foundation, the next chapter is all about squeezing more out of QuickTime objects. We cover a number of key topics and techniques relating these to real-world examples.

5

Diving Deeper

Essential Topics for Serious QuickTime Development

Introduction

Dipping below the surface in the last chapter, we explored the QuickTime Object Model together with its principal constituent objects. We saw how these objects can be accessed through the QuickTime COM Control and looked at examples of how the objects can be used. Diving in somewhat deeper, this chapter moves on to tackle a number of more advanced topics. Master these and you will be well equipped to develop fully featured and professional-grade .NET applications using the QuickTime COM Control and associated library of QuickTime objects.

QuickTime Events

We can make considerable progress in the development of our QuickTime applications just by setting properties and calling methods of the various objects in the QuickTime Object Model. However, modern object-oriented applications more often than not employ an event-driven model: something happens—such as a mouse click—and we have an event handler to respond to it. A QuickTime application is no different except that, in addition to responding to user interface events, we can respond to events that are triggered by the QuickTime objects themselves. We touched on this briefly in Chapter 2 when we looked at the SizeChanged event of the QuickTime Control, which is fired whenever the control changes size.

Registering for QuickTime Events

As it turns out, there are so many events that the QuickTime objects can potentially notify us about that it would be impractical, not to mention grossly inefficient, for our application to receive and handle them all willy-nilly. So in order to be notified of events by an instance of a QuickTime object we must first specify the particular event(s) we are interested in. We do this by adding those events about which we want to be notified to the `EventListeners` collection of the object. Each type of event is specified by two constants: the *event class* and the *event ID*, as defined by two enumerations: `QTEventClassesEnum` and `QTEventIDsEnum`. By adding an event of a particular class and ID to the `EventListeners` collection, we are said to be *registering* to be *notified* of that event. Here's an example where we register to be notified when the play rate is about to change on a movie:

```
With AxQTControl1.Movie
  .EventListeners.Add(QTEventClassesEnum.qtEventClassStateChange,
          QTEventIDsEnum.qtEventRateWillChange)
End With
```

Looking through `QTEventClassesEnum` and `QTEventIDsEnum` in the Object Browser or in Table 5.2 (page 102) will give you some idea of the variety of QuickTime events that you can register to be notified about. You will notice that the events are grouped into a number of functional classes. The event constant names in `QTEventIDsEnum` are mostly self-explanatory, but note the careful wording that subtly conveys the precise meaning of the event:

DidChange : Something has already happened and we are being notified after the fact. The implication is that we can do nothing about it.

WillChange : Something is just about to happen and we are being notified beforehand. It may be possible to cancel it.

Request : A request is being made to allow something to happen. It may be possible to alter the behavior or cancel it.

Handling QuickTime Events

Now that we've registered for the `qtEventRateWillChange` event, how should our application *handle* the event when a notification comes through from the movie that the play rate is about to change? For convenience and efficiency, all event notifications originating from QuickTime objects are routed up through the object hierarchy and end up raising a QTEvent event from the QuickTime Control.

Before going any farther, let's pause briefly to clarify some potentially confusing terminology: it is important to distinguish between QuickTime events (as listed in the QTEventIDsEnum enumeration) and the QTEvent event of the QuickTime Control. The QTEvent event is the COM/.NET event that acts as the gateway for the QuickTime events that we register to be notified of.

In Depth

QTEvent is a connection-point–based event interface supplied by the QuickTime Control for COM clients. The COM Interop layer cleverly maps this connection-point event to the .NET delegate-based event model.

In most cases, the client that handles, or sinks, the QTEvent events is usually (but not always) the form that hosts the QuickTime Control, as shown in Figure 5.1. This is where we must add our code to handle any QuickTime events that we registered for.

Let's look at what it takes to add a QTEvent handler to our Visual Basic or C# form.

Thankfully, Visual Studio .NET takes the drudgery out of adding event handlers by generating a skeleton handler for us. Here's how we do this, first in Visual Basic and then in C#.

Adding a QTEvent Handler in Visual Basic .NET

- View Code on the form that contains the QuickTime Control.
- Select *AxQTControl1* from the left-hand Class Name drop-down list above the code window.
- In the right-hand drop-down list, you will now find a list of all the Events provided by the QuickTime Control. Select *QTEvent* and Visual Studio will generate a skeleton event handler.

Here's the skeleton Visual Basic QTEvent handler that Visual Studio generates for us:

```
Private Sub AxQTControl1_QTEvent(ByVal sender As Object,
         ByVal e As AxQTOControlLib._IQTControlEvents_QTEventEvent)
         Handles AxQTControl1.QTEvent


End Sub
```

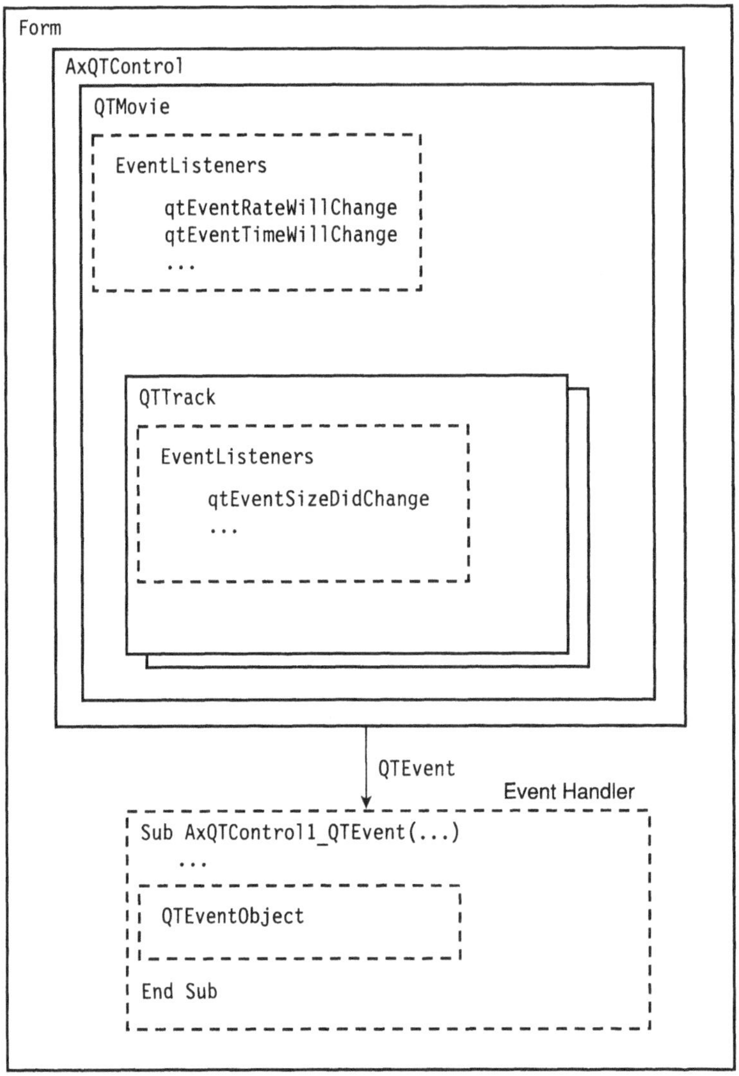

Figure 5.1 Event model for QuickTime events.

Adding a QTEvent Handler in C#

- Open the form that contains the QuickTime Control in Design view.
- Select the QuickTime Control and choose View | Properties Window.

- Click on the Events button in the toolbar at the top of the Properties Window.

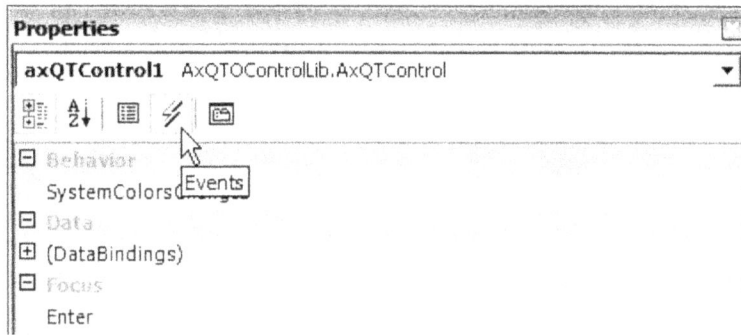

- Locate QTEvent in the list of events and enter a name for the event handler (e.g., OnQTEvent) in the space provided.

You will end up with a skeleton event handler like this:

```
private void OnQTEvent(object sender,
          AxQTOControlLib._IQTControlEvents_QTEventEvent e)
{

}
```

This time, behind the scenes in the Windows Form Designer–generated code, you'll also find that this event handler has been added as a *delegate* to the QTEvent:

```
this.axQTControl1.QTEvent += new
          AxQTOControlLib._IQTControlEvents_QTEventEventHandler
  (this.OnQTEvent);
```

Event Parameters

If you're new to .NET events, you may find the parameters of this event handler somewhat intimidating at first glance, but they really are quite straightforward:

sender : the .NET object that originated the event—in this case always the QuickTime Control.

e   : this object contains the event parameters as summarized in Table 5.1.

In most nontrivial cases, we are likely to have to register for a number of different QuickTime events, possibly even on different objects:

```
With AxQTControl1.Movie

    .EventListeners.Add(QTEventClassesEnum.qtEventClassStateChange,
            QTEventIDsEnum.qtEventRateWillChange)

    .EventListeners.Add(QTEventClassesEnum.qtEventClassTemporal,
            QTEventIDsEnum.qtEventTimeWillChange)

    .EventListeners.Add(QTEventClassesEnum.qtEventClassAudio,
            QTEventIDsEnum.qtEventAudioVolumeDidChange)

    .Tracks(1).EventListeners.Add(QTEventClassesEnum.
            qtEventClassAudio, QTEventIDsEnum.
            qtEventAudioVolumeDidChange)

End With
```

Notifications of all these events end up in our QTEvent handler. Since e.eventID returns the ID of the QuickTime event that raised this QTEvent, we can easily use a Select Case statement in Visual Basic, or a switch state-

Table 5.1   QTEvent Parameters

Property	Description
eventClass	The class of the QuickTime event (e.g., qtEventClassStateChange)
eventID	The ID of the QuickTime event (e.g., qtEventRateWillChange)
phase	Not used—usually 0
eventObject	Object of type QTEventObject that contains event-specific parameters and other useful information about the QuickTime event
cancel	Set this property to True to cancel the change that triggered an event. Only applies to certain events.

ment in C#, to distinguish between the different events so that we can take
the appropriate action:

```
Private Sub AxQTControl1_QTEvent(ByVal sender As Object,
           ByVal e As AxQTOControlLib._IQTControlEvents_QTEventEvent)
           Handles AxQTControl1.QTEvent

  Select Case e.eventID

    Case QTEventIDsEnum.qtEventRateWillChange
      Debug.WriteLine("RateWillChange")

    Case QTEventIDsEnum.qtEventTimeWillChange
      Debug.WriteLine("TimeWillChange")

    Case QTEventIDsEnum.qtEventAudioVolumeDidChange
      Debug.WriteLine("AudioVolumeDidChange")

  End Select

End Sub
```

If you examine Table 5.2, you will see that many of the QuickTime events
have specific parameters that are returned with the event, and that supply
useful event-related data. For example, the qtEventRateWillChange always
has a qtEventParamMovieRate parameter, while qtEventLinkToURLRequest has
a qtEventParamURL parameter. These parameters can be accessed through
e.eventObject, which returns an object of type QTEventObject. This object is
packed with event-specific data (Table 5.3) including the event parameters
that we have just mentioned.

To get a particular parameter, we use the GetParam method with the appropriate constant from QTEventObjectParametersEnum. We can now easily
extend our event handler to display some of these parameters:

Table 5.2 QuickTime Events

Event Class and Event ID	Objects	Description	Can Be Canceled	Parameters
qtEventClassAudio				
qtEventAudioVolumeDidChange	QTMovie QTTrack	The audio volume of a movie or track has changed.		qtEventParamAudioVolume: volume (floating point)
qtEventAudioMuteDidChange	QTMovie QTTrack	The mute state of the movie audio mix or track audio has changed.		qtEventParamAudioMute: state (Boolean)
qtEventAudioBalanceDidChange	QTMovie QTTrack	The audio balance of a movie or track has changed.		qtEventParamAudioBalance: value (floating point)
qtEventClassSpatial				
qtEventSizeDidChange	QTMovie QTTrack	The size of a movie or track has changed.		'size': size (string) left, top, width, height
qtEventClassStateChange				
qtEventRateWillChange	QTMovie	The playback rate of the movie has changed.		qtEventParamMovieRate: playback rate (floating point)
qtEventChapterListDidChange	QTMovie	The chapter list associated with a movie has changed.		
qtEventCurrentChapterDidChange	QTMovie	The current chapter has changed in a movie.		qtEventParamChapterIndex: chapter index (integer)
qtEventLoadStateDidChange	QTMovie	The load state of the movie has changed.		qtEventParamLoadState: state
qtEventMovieDidEnd	QTMovie	The movie has been played to the end of the movie or to the end of the current selection if PlaySelectionOnly is True.		
qtEventMovieSelectionDidChange	QTMovie	The current selection of the movie has changed.		qtEventParamSelectionStart start time of selection (integer) qtEventParamSelectionDuration: duration of selection (integer)

continued

Event	Object	Description	Sendable	Parameters
qtEventMovieWasEdited	QTMovie	The movie has been edited or changed in some way. Indicates that the movie should be saved.		
qtEventClassTemporal				
qtEventTimeWillChange	QTMovie	The current time position of the movie is about to change.	Yes	qtEventParamMovieTime: movie time (integer)
qtEventClassApplicationRequest				
qtEventEnterFullScreenRequest	QTMovie	The movie itself has requested to enter full-screen mode.	Yes	
qtEventExitFullScreenRequest	QTMovie	The movie itself has requested to exit full-screen mode.	Yes	
qtEventCloseWindowRequest	QTMovie	The movie has requested that the application close the window containing the movie.	Yes	
qtEventLinkToURLRequest	QTMovie	The movie has requested that the application load a URL.	Yes	qtEventParamURL: URL to be loaded (string)
qtEventShowStatusStringRequest	QTMovie	The movie has a status string to display, such as streaming status.	Yes	qtEventParamStatusString: status (string) qtEventParamStatusCode: status code (integer) 'flag': flags (integer)
qtEventShowMessageStringRequest	QTMovie	A sprite in a wired movie has sent a kActionDebugStr message.	Yes	qtEventParamMessageString: message (string)
qtEventGetNextURLRequest	QTMovie	The movie has requested that another URL be opened. Indicates that the current movie wishes to load another movie.	Yes	qtEventParamURL: URL to be loaded (string)
qtEventClassProgress				
qtEventExportProgress	QTExporter	The exporter progress has advanced.		qtEventParamAmount: 0–100 (floating point)

Table 5.3 QTEventObject Properties and Methods

Property/Method	Description
CanBeCanceled	True if it's possible to cancel the event
Context	A user-defined integer that can be assigned when registering for the event
EventClass	The class of the QuickTime event (e.g., qtEventClassStateChange)
EventID	The ID of the QuickTime event (e.g., qtEventRateWillChange)
GetParam	Given a parameter ID from QTEventObjectParametersEnum, returns the value of an event parameter
GetParams	Returns all parameters of the event in a CFObject
HasBeenCanceled	True if the event has already been canceled
ParamCount	The number of parameters

```
Private Sub AxQTControl1_QTEvent(ByVal sender As Object,
        ByVal e As AxQTOControlLib._IQTControlEvents_QTEventEvent)
        Handles AxQTControl1.QTEvent

  Select Case e.eventID

    Case QTEventIDsEnum.qtEventRateWillChange
      Dim rate = e.eventObject.GetParam(
          QTEventObjectParametersEnum.qtEventParamMovieRate)
      Debug.WriteLine("Rate Changing to:" + CStr(rate))

    Case QTEventIDsEnum.qtEventTimeWillChange
      Dim time = e.eventObject.GetParam(
          QTEventObjectParametersEnum.qtEventParamMovieTime)
      Debug.WriteLine("Time changing to:" + CStr(time))

    Case QTEventIDsEnum.qtEventAudioVolumeDidChange
      Dim vol = e.eventObject.GetParam(
          QTEventObjectParametersEnum.qtEventParamAudioVolume)
      Debug.WriteLine("Volume changed to:" + CStr(vol))

  End Select

End Sub
```

Now run Simple Player and load a movie, preferably one with a sound track. Play and stop the movie, click around in the movie controller to change the current time position and adjust the movie volume. You will get a stream of events producing an output something like this:

```
Rate Changing to:1
Rate Changing to:0
Rate Changing to:1
Rate Changing to:0
Time changing to:3197
Rate Changing to:0
Rate Changing to:0
Time changing to:6475
Rate Changing to:0
Rate Changing to:0
Volume changed to:0.875
Volume changed to:0.8515625
Volume changed to:0.8320313
Volume changed to:0.7890625
Volume changed to:0.7695313
Volume changed to:0.7460938
```

Sample: QuickTime Events Demo

Working with QuickTime events can be a bit bewildering to start with, especially if you are new to Visual Basic .NET or C#. QuickTime Events Demo is a simple but practical code sample designed to demonstrate the usefulness of QuickTime events in a real application. It is essentially a very basic movie composition application such as might be used in a newsroom to compile a 30-minute program from a series of shorter clips.

Looking at the application screenshot in Figure 5.2, the clips are loaded into the *Source* QuickTime Control on the left (AxQTControl1) and can be appended to the movie in the *Destination* control on the right (AxQTControl2) using the >> button in the center. The X button allows you to undo the most recent change. Each QuickTime Control has two buttons underneath on the left-hand side: the first is a Load button that brings up an Open Movie dialog, and the second is a combined Play/Stop button. The Destination movie has a New button that will create a new empty movie as a starting point, and a Save... button so that you can save your finished composition. Finally, at the bottom of the window below the Destination movie is a display of its current

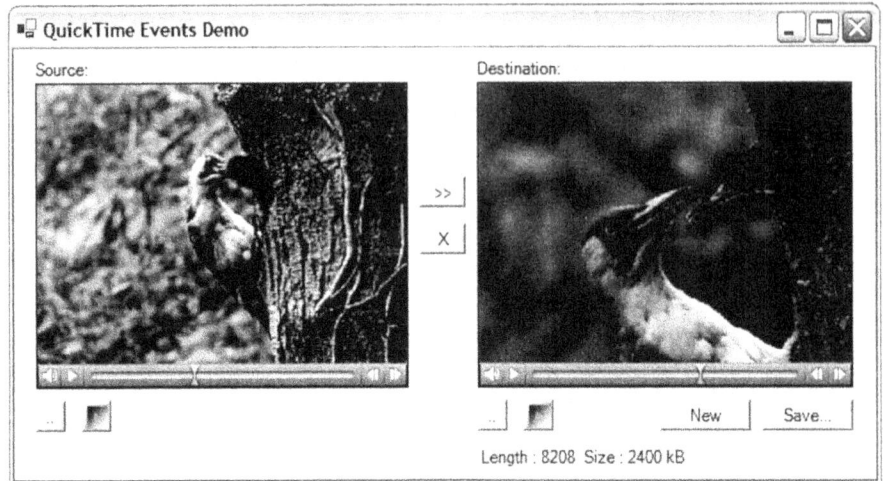

Figure 5.2 QuickTime Events Demo.

Length and Size. Simple enough in concept, but as we work through the implementation, we'll discover useful ways to apply QuickTime events.

First we'll set up the basic functionality. Good programming practice usually dictates that when you work with multiple instances of any object, common code should be shared. In this case we have two QuickTime Controls and two Load buttons and so we use a shared LoadMovie function, with the instance of the QuickTime Control passed as a parameter, along with an integer index:

```
Private Sub LoadMovie(ByVal qtCtrl As AxQTOControlLib.AxQTControl,
          ByVal idx As Long)

    Dim filter As String
    filter = "Movies|*.mov;*.mpg;*.avi;*.dv|"
    filter = filter + "Audio files|*.wav;*.aif;*.mp3;*.m4a;*.m4p|"
    filter = filter + "All files (*.*)|*.*"
    OpenFileDialog1.Filter = filter

    qtCtrl.Sizing =
          QTSizingModeEnum.qtMovieFitsControlMaintainAspectRatio

    If OpenFileDialog1.ShowDialog() = DialogResult.OK Then
          qtCtrl.URL = OpenFileDialog1.FileName()
    End If
```

```
  If qtCtrl.Movie Is Nothing Then Exit Sub

  MovieSetup(qtCtrl.Movie, idx)

End Sub
```

We'll come to MovieSetup later—for now just assume that it does exactly what it says.

The Click handlers for the Load buttons are trivial:

```
Private Sub btnLoad1_Click(...) Handles btnLoad1.Click

  LoadMovie(AxQTControl1, 1)

End Sub

Private Sub btnLoad2_Click(...) Handles btnLoad2.Click

  LoadMovie(AxQTControl2, 2)

End Sub
```

For the Play/Stop buttons, again we factor common code out into a Play-Stop routine:

```
Private Sub PlayStop(ByVal qtCtrl As AxQTOControlLib.AxQTControl)

  If qtCtrl.Movie Is Nothing Then Exit Sub

  If qtCtrl.Movie.Rate = 0 Then
    qtCtrl.Movie.Play()
  Else
    qtCtrl.Movie.Stop()
  End If

End Sub

Private Sub btnPS1_Click(...) Handles btnPS1.Click

  PlayStop(AxQTControl1)
```

```
End Sub

Private Sub btnPS2_Click(...) Handles btnPS2.Click

    PlayStop(AxQTControl2)

End Sub
```

Since we have a LoadMovie routine, it makes sense to have a similar New-Movie routine for our New button:

```
Private Sub NewMovie(ByVal qtCtrl As AxQTOControlLib.AxQTControl,
            ByVal idx As Long)

    qtCtrl.Sizing =
            QTSizingModeEnum.qtMovieFitsControlMaintainAspectRatio
    qtCtrl.CreateNewMovie()

    If qtCtrl.Movie Is Nothing Then Exit Sub

    MovieSetup(qtCtrl.Movie, idx)

End Sub

Private Sub btnNewMovie_Click(...) Handles btnNewMovie.Click

    NewMovie(AxQTControl2, 2)

End Sub
```

Continuing our basic functionality, we implement the Append (>>) and Undo (X) buttons:

```
Private Sub btnAppend_Click(...) Handles btnAppend.Click

    If AxQTControl1.Movie Is Nothing Then Exit Sub
    If AxQTControl2.Movie Is Nothing Then Exit Sub

    With AxQTControl1.Movie
        If .SelectionDuration = 0 Then .SelectAll()
        .Copy()
    End With
```

```
With AxQTControl2.Movie
  .Time = .Duration
  .Paste()
End With

End Sub

Private Sub btnUndo_Click(...) Handles btnUndo.Click

  If AxQTControl2.Movie Is Nothing Then Exit Sub

  AxQTControl2.Movie.Undo()

End Sub
```

In both cases, defensive programming dictates that we shouldn't attempt to do anything if there is no movie loaded. When we come to append, the user may already have made a selection in the Source movie (using the movie controller); if not, we select the entire movie. The selection is then copied to the clipboard. Appending the clip to the Destination movie involves first moving to the end of that movie before pasting the selection from the clipboard.

And finally of course, we mustn't forget the Save button, without which everything we've done so far would be a little pointless; again for consistency we have a SaveMovie routine:

```
Private Sub SaveMovie(ByVal qtCtrl As AxQTOControlLib.AxQTControl)

  If qtCtrl.Movie Is Nothing Then Exit Sub

  With qtCtrl.Movie
    .SetSelection(0, 0)
    .Time = 0
    If .CanUpdateMovieFile Then
      .Save()
    Else
      SaveFileDialog1.Title = "Save Movie As"
      SaveFileDialog1.FileName = "Untitled.mov"
      If SaveFileDialog1.ShowDialog() = DialogResult.OK Then
        .SaveSelfContained(SaveFileDialog1.FileName())
        btnSave.Enabled = False
      End If
```

```
      End If


      End With

   End Sub
```

SaveMovie has to be a little bit clever: it must do the right thing whether the Destination movie is a preexisting movie that we may have loaded, or a new movie. In the former case, the movie can just be saved to its current location, whereas for a new movie we must use a SaveFileDialog to prompt the user for a file name. SaveMovie checks the movie's CanUpdateMovieFile property so that it can decide which course of action to take: if this property is True, then the movie has been opened from a file and can be saved back into that file. Notice, too, that in the case of a new movie, we use SaveSelf-Contained rather than Save so that our newly created and saved movie is fully self-contained with all its own data resources, rather than just containing references to the bits of other movies that we've pasted into it.

If we build and run our sample application at this point, we should be able to load a movie into either QuickTime Control and be able to play and stop either movie independently using the Play/Stop buttons. It should be possible to create a new Destination movie, to append selections from the Source movie to it, and to save it.

So far so good, but what about QuickTime events you may ask with some justification? Well, now it's time to add a little polish.

First let's tackle those Play/Stop buttons: while the graphical button may look good, it really doesn't properly convey its dual function so long as it remains a static forward arrow (▶). Ideally, like any professional media player, it should change to a standard square Stop icon (■) while the movie is playing, and back to the arrow Play icon (▶) when the movie stops.

One perfectly valid way to do this would be to set up a timer on an interval of, say, 250 ms, which regularly polls the state of the movie—playing or stopped—and sets the button image accordingly. But there's something rather unsatisfying about such an approach—it smacks a little too much of brute force.

A much more elegant—and efficient—solution is to have the movie tell us when its play rate changes so that we can change the state of the button. To achieve this, we register for the QuickTime event qtEventRateWillChange to notify us any time the movie's play rate changes for whatever reason.

Second, a common requirement of good UI design is that a button or menu item should be enabled only when its function is available. This applies to our Save... button: by rights it should remain disabled unless the Destination movie is dirty (i.e., has been edited) and needs to be saved. Again, it turns out that we can use a QuickTime event to notify us whenever the movie has been changed: qtEventMovieWasEdited.

Registering for these QuickTime events just involves adding them to the movie's EventListeners collection. We will then be notified any time the play rate changes and any time the movie is changed for any reason. We do this in MovieSetup (remember this is called by both LoadMovie and NewMovie):

```
Private Sub MovieSetup(ByVal mov As QTMovie, ByVal idx As Long)

  If mov Is Nothing Then Exit Sub

  With mov
    .EventListeners.Add(QTEventClassesEnum.qtEventClassStateChange,
         QTEventIDsEnum.qtEventRateWillChange, 0, idx)
    .EventListeners.Add(QTEventClassesEnum.qtEventClassStateChange,
         QTEventIDsEnum.qtEventMovieWasEdited, 0, idx)
  End With

  btnSave.Enabled = False
  UpdateDestinationMovieStatus()

End Sub
```

One small detail is important here: notice that the idx parameter that is passed in to LoadMovie or NewMovie gets passed on as the Context (fourth parameter) when we register for the event. Glancing back at the Click event handlers for the Load buttons, you see that the value of idx will be either 1 or 2 depending on which QuickTime Control is being loaded.

Coming now to the event handler, the temptation is to add two QTEvent handlers—one for each control. And why ever not? Events from AxQT-Control1 will be handled by its own QTEvent handler, and those from the other QuickTime Control by a second dedicated QTEvent handler: no confusion, no risk, and anyway, who cares about the duplicate code? But there's that nagging feeling again—there must be a better way.

There is of course, and it involves sharing a single QTEvent handler. The .NET event model allows you to delegate the event handling from any number of objects to the same handler. In Visual Basic this simply involves tagging another item onto the Handles chain. Here's our skeleton shared QTEvent handler:

```
Private Sub OnQTEvent(ByVal sender As Object,
          ByVal e As AxQTOControlLib._IQTControlEvents_QTEventEvent)
          Handles AxQTControl1.QTEvent, AxQTControl2.QTEvent
End Sub
```

The syntax is self-explanatory: OnQTEvent *handles* AxQTControl1.QTEvent and AxQTControl2.QTEvent.

The complete QTEvent handler follows. Selecting e.eventID allows us to handle each event type appropriately:

```
Private Sub OnQTEvent(ByVal sender As Object,
          ByVal e As AxQTOControlLib._IQTControlEvents_QTEventEvent)
          Handles AxQTControl1.QTEvent, AxQTControl2.QTEvent

  Dim rate As Single
  Dim btn As Button = Nothing

  Select Case e.eventID

    Case QTEventIDsEnum.qtEventRateWillChange

      Select Case e.eventObject.Context
        Case 1
          btn = btnPS1
        Case 2
          btn = btnPS2
      End Select

      If btn Is Nothing Then Exit Sub

      rate = e.eventObject.GetParam(
          QTEventObjectParametersEnum.qtEventParamMovieRate)

      If rate = 0 Then
        btn.ImageIndex = 0   'Play
      Else
        btn.ImageIndex = 1   'Stop
      End If

    Case QTEventIDsEnum.qtEventMovieWasEdited
```

```
      If e.eventObject.Context = 2 Then
        btnSave.Enabled = True
        UpdateDestinationMovieStats()
      End If

   End Select

End Sub
```

Dealing first with qtEventRateWillChange, recall the Context value that we passed in when registering for this event: this can now be retrieved using e.eventObject.Context, used to determine which movie the event originated from, and therefore which Play/Stop button (left or right) we should operate on. Once we know which button we're working with, we extract the qtEvent-ParamMovieRate parameter that was passed with the qtEventRateWillChange event. The value of this, which indicates the current new play rate, can then be used to switch the ImageIndex of the button.

In handling qtEventMovieWasEdited, we're only interested in events from the Destination movie since that's the only movie that can be saved, so again we check the Context value before enabling the Save... button. The button is always disabled in MovieSetup. At this point, since the movie has changed, we also call UpdateDestinationMovieStats to refresh the statistics about the destination movie:

```
Private Sub UpdateDestinationMovieStats()

  Dim t As String
  If AxQTControl2.Movie Is Nothing Then
    LabelStatus.Text = ""
  Else
    t += "Length : " + CStr(AxQTControl2.Movie.Duration)
    t += "  "
    t += "Size : " + Format(AxQTControl2.Movie.Size / 1000, "0 kB")
    LabelStatus.Text = t
  End If

End Sub
```

Build and run the demo again now, and you should notice the icon on the Play/Stop buttons changing on cue. This should work correctly irrespective of how you start or stop the movie: clicking the Play/Stop button, double-clicking the movie, or using the movie controller. Click on the New button to create an empty movie and append a clip from the Source movie: the Save button should be enabled and the movie stats will be updated.

Deploying a couple of QuickTime events has allowed us to bring the user interface of this application up a step from crude functionality and closer to what would be expected in a professional application.

QuickTime Metadata

Whether it be a major sporting event, the latest blockbuster movie, or a song that we have just purchased, we are obsessed with information about whatever it is we are watching or listening to: who was playing, who starred, who was the director, the artist, and so on. In fact, such information *about* something can often be as important as the thing itself.

Take, for instance, the photograph shown in Figure 5.3 of an oversize chick staring out indignantly from its mud-bowl nest, looking for all the world like a fluffy toy with its ludicrously big feet and bill. As an image it's cute of course, but when we discover that this chick will one day become a full-grown black-browed albatross—a master of ocean flight—with a wingspan of almost 8 feet (2.5 meters), the picture takes on a whole lot more meaning. Our interest is further enhanced when we learn that this photo-

Title	Albatross Chick on Nest
Species	Black-browed albatross
Scientific name	*Diomedea melanophris*
Adult wingspan	2.5 meters (8 feet)
Place	Falkland Islands
Location	51° 22' S 60° 4' W
Date	2 February 2004

Figure 5.3 Image with associated metadata.

graph was taken on a small island in the South Atlantic—one of the Falkland Islands—at latitude 51° 22' S and longitude 60° 4' W, in the antipodean summer.

All of this information *about* a particular item of digital media is known in information technology circles as *metadata*.

When it comes to digital media, metadata is usually stored under a set of tags such as Title, Date, Description, and the like, as we can see in Figure 5.3. Some tags, such as Title, will be common to a wide variety of media types, while others, such as Album, may be specific to a particular type of media. Various efforts have been made to develop standards for metadata tags, but often the tags associated with a particular media collection are somewhat arbitrary.

With the burgeoning popularity of digital photography and personal music collections, many of us are amassing sizeable digital media collections running to thousands and even tens of thousands of files. Organizing these personal collections has become the new chore, with the laborious entering of metadata—such as captions for last summer's holiday snaps—replacing the once arduous task of writing on the back of each 4" x 6" print before stuffing it into an album. However, the end result, delivered to your relatives on a shiny CD-R, is (not surprisingly) just as boring!

So metadata is fast becoming a preoccupation of the digital classes, and any serious digital media technology had better be able to handle metadata convincingly. Fortunately, QuickTime is just such a technology and, in fact, has supported the concept of metadata long before the advent of the personal digital media collection.

Not only does QuickTime support its own metadata format, it makes a determined effort to unify access to the metadata standards of other digital media formats that it supports. So, for example, using the same API we can obtain the title of an MP3 song, the caption of a JPEG digital photograph, or the copyright information on a DV video clip. This layer of abstraction for metadata is one reason why QuickTime is so often the technology of choice for professional applications handling diverse media content.

Annotations

QuickTime can store and retrieve metadata items associated either with a movie itself or with any of the individual tracks in a movie. In the Quick-Time COM library metadata items are known as Annotations and may be

Table 5.4 Some of the Metadata Tags Available in QTAnnotationsEnum

Metadata Tag	Annotation ID	FourCharCode
Album	qtAnnotationAlbum	'albm'
Artist	qtAnnotationArtist	'arts'
Author	qtAnnotationAuthor	'auth'
Comments	qtAnnotationComments	'cmmt'
Composer	qtAnnotationComposer	'comp'
Copyright	qtAnnotationCopyright	'cprt'
Description	qtAnnotationDescription	'desc'
Director	qtAnnotationDirector	'dtor'
Title / Name	qtAnnotationFullName	'name'
Genre	qtAnnotationGenre	'genr'
Information	qtAnnotationInformation	'info'
Performers	qtAnnotationPerformers	'perf'
Producer	qtAnnotationProducer	'prod'
Software	qtAnnotationSoftware	'soft'
Writer	qtAnnotationWriter	'wrtr'

accessed individually through the Annotation property of the QTMovie and QTTrack objects. Whenever we use the Annotation property, we must supply an Annotation ID to indicate which particular annotation or metadata item we are referring to (Title, Description, Album, etc.) This Annotation ID is effectively the metadata tag and, not surprisingly, it is a FourCharCode (see "Meet the FourCharCode" in Chapter 4). For convenience, QTAnnotationsEnum contains a number of frequently used Annotation IDs, some of which are listed in Table 5.4.

Let's retrieve and display some basic metadata from a movie:

```
Dim s As String
If AxQTControl1.Movie Is Nothing Then Exit Sub
s = ""

With AxQTControl1.Movie
  s += " Name    : " + .Annotation(
        QTAnnotationsEnum.qtAnnotationFullName)
  s += vbCrLf
  s += "Album   : " + .Annotation(
        QTAnnotationsEnum.qtAnnotationAlbum)
```

```
    s += vbCrLf
    s += "Artist : " + .Annotation(
            QTAnnotationsEnum.qtAnnotationArtist)
End With

tbResults.Text = s
```

While the preceding code will often work fine, if we have the temerity to ask for an annotation that doesn't exist, the QTMovie object is very likely to deliver us a wrap across the knuckles in the form of an exception. Whether this actually does happen depends, of course, on the Error Handling mode of the QuickTime Control, but it's as well to be prepared. The safest way to do this is to use a very simple GetAnnotation function that just swallows any exceptions that might occur:

```
Function GetAnnotation(ByRef mov As QTMovie,
            ByVal annotationID As Long) As String

    Dim val As String = ""

    Try
      val = mov.Annotation(annotationID)
    Catch e As Exception
      'Ignore error
    End Try

    GetAnnotation = val

End Function
```

A more robust way of getting movie metadata then becomes

```
Dim s As String
If AxQTControl1.Movie Is Nothing Then Exit Sub
s = ""

With AxQTControl1
    s += "Name  : " + GetAnnotation(.Movie,
            QTAnnotationsEnum.qtAnnotationFullName)
    s += vbCrLf
    s += "Album : " + GetAnnotation(.Movie,
            QTAnnotationsEnum.qtAnnotationAlbum)
```

```
        s += vbCrLf
        s += "Artist: " + GetAnnotation(.Movie,
                    QTAnnotationsEnum.qtAnnotationArtist)
    End With


    tbResults.Text = s
```

Hint Experiment with the preceding code snippet on any iTunes MPEG-4 audio file (.m4a or .m4p) in your music collection.

Setting the value of annotations is equally straightforward:

```
With AxQTControl1.Movie
    .Annotation(QTAnnotationsEnum.qtAnnotationArtist) =
            "Ray Charles"
    .Annotation(QTAnnotationsEnum.qtAnnotationAlbum) =
            "The Great Tomato Blues Package"
    .Annotation(QTAnnotationsEnum.qtAnnotationFullName) =
            "Blues Is My Middle Name"
    .Annotation(QTAnnotationsEnum.qtAnnotationGenre) = "Blues"
End Width
```

Once an annotation has been added or changed in this way, the movie is marked as having been changed. If you want to permanently save the annotation changes you have made, you must remember to save the movie using its Save method. Before calling Save, it's usually good practice to check if the movie really does need to be saved:

```
If AxQTControl1.Movie.HasChanged Then AxQTControl1.Movie.Save()
```

I mentioned earlier that the QTTrack object also has an Annotation property and that it is equally possible to store/retrieve metadata to/from individual tracks in a movie. Access to metadata at the track level may not immediately appear to be a particularly useful feature, but there are cases when the ability to store data with the individual tracks that make up a movie can be valuable. Take, for instance, a news program that has been created by combining a number of shorter clips (as is very common in video editing) by putting each clip into a separate video track. QuickTime will of course combine the video tracks at playback time into what appears to be a single video track; however, the metadata for each clip (its title, source, etc.)

is retained and accessible in the track metadata. Here's an example that enumerates the name and source of each track in a movie:

```
Dim s As String
Dim i As Long
Dim trk As QTTrack
s = ""

With AxQTControl1.Movie
  For i = 1 To .Tracks.Count
    trk = .Tracks(i)
    s += "Track " + CStr(i) + vbCrLf
    s += "  Name  : " + trk.Annotation(
          QTAnnotationsEnum.qtAnnotationFullName)
    s += vbCrLf
    s += "  Source: " + trk.Annotation(
          QTAnnotationsEnum.qtAnnotationOriginalSource)
    s += vbCrLf
  Next i
End With
```

Custom Annotations

QuickTime provides a rich set of standard annotations in the form of QTAnnotationsEnum and, more often than not, these will serve our application needs perfectly. So, for example, if we want to store copyright information, we have qtAnnotationCopyright specifically for that purpose. However, there are sometimes situations where we would like to store proprietary data in the movies that our application deals with. Perhaps there are particular application settings that we use with each movie, or we have proprietary metadata in a particular format such as XML. In cases like these, it makes sense to use a custom annotation; this involves devising a new annotation ID, which shouldn't of course clash with any of the standard IDs, and using it with the Annotation property.

As an example, an aerospace manufacturer might wish to manage a collection of video clips of aircraft cabin interiors. While the name of the aircraft could easily be stored in the FullName annotation, the manufacturer's cabin specification needs to be stored separately; of course, one of the standard annotations could be appropriated for the purpose, but a custom annotation may be a more rigorous solution:

```
Dim qtu As New QTUtils
Dim cabinSpecificationID As Long

cabinSpecificationID = qtu.StringToFourCharCode("CABN")

With AxQTControl1.Movie
  .Annotation(QTAnnotationsEnum.qtAnnotationFullName) =
          "Airbus A340-300"
  .Annotation(cabinSpecificationID) = "Deluxe leather with fur trim"
End Width
```

Tip Notice that our custom annotation ID ("CABN") is in uppercase, the reason being that Apple reserves all lowercase FourCharCode IDs. If you want to ensure that your annotation ID will never clash with one of Apple's, make sure it's in uppercase.

Many content management systems now store metadata in an XML format, perhaps using a standard such as RDF (Resource Description Framework; see *www.w3.org/RDF* for more detail). Again, it makes sense to use a custom annotation to store the entire chunk of XML metadata with each movie. While annotations are more often than not short text strings, there is no reason why much larger chunks of data shouldn't be stored in an annotation.

Metadata in MPEG Files

As well as providing access to its own proprietary metadata storage as we've just seen, QuickTime also attempts to provide access to metadata stored in some common media file formats, including MPEG.

ID3 tags are special sections within an MP3 file in which information about the artist, album, title, and the like are stored. When QuickTime opens an MP3 file, the MP3 movie importer recognizes certain ID3 tags and maps them to movie annotations, as shown in Table 5.5. Unfortunately, only a limited selection of ID3 tags appears to be accessible through QuickTime.

iTunes stores songs in .m4a and .m4p files using the MPEG-4 AAC standard. Metadata in these files is stored not in ID3 tags but in AAC tags. Again, QuickTime takes care of this, providing access to many of these tags, as shown in Table 5.6.

Table 5.5 Annotation IDs for Some Common ID3 Tags

ID3 tag	Annotation ID / FourCharCode
Album	qtAnnotationAlbum
Artist	qtAnnotationArtist
Band/orchestra	qtAnnotationPerformers
Comment	qtAnnotationComment
Composer	qtAnnotationComposer
Copyright	qtAnnotationCopyright
Title/name	qtAnnotationFullName
Track number	'©trk'
Year/date of recording	'©day'

Table 5.6 Annotation IDs for Some Common AAC Tags

AAC tag	Annotation ID / FourCharCode
Album	qtAnnotationAlbum
Artist	qtAnnotationArtist
Comment	qtAnnotationComment
Composer	qtAnnotationAuthor
Name	qtAnnotationFullName
Grouping	'©grp'
Encoder software (iTunes version)	'©too'
Year/date of recording	'©day'
Apple ID (of purchaser from iTunes Music Store)	'apID'

Getting All the Annotations

As we've just seen, the Annotation property is invaluable in getting and setting individual annotations, but it's not a lot of use if we want to obtain a complete list of all the annotations in a movie or track. This is where the read-only Annotations (plural) property comes in handy: it returns a dictionary of *all* the annotations and their values keyed on the annotation (tag) IDs. This annotations dictionary comes packaged in a special data container object known as a CFObject. But before we can delve into its contents, we will have to learn a bit more about what a CFObject is.

CFObject and Its Uses

The CFObject is a data container object that is used throughout the Quick-Time Object Model, especially for complex data sets. It can contain data in a variety of formats from primitive types such as simple numbers or strings to more complex structures such as an array or dictionary, or even just raw bytes. Table 5.7 provides a summary.

If you have a CFObject, you can find out what type it is (or, more precisely, what type of data it contains) by examining its Type property. This will return one of the types listed in CFObjectTypesEnum, as shown in Table 5.7.

Table 5.7   The CFObject Data Types as Listed in CFObjectTypesEnum

CFObject Type	*Contains*
CFObjectTypeBoolean	True or False
CFObjectTypeNumber	Integer or floating-point number
CFObjectTypeString	String
CFObjectTypeArray	Array of CFObject
CFObjectTypeDictionary	Dictionary of key-value pairs. Key may be integer or string. Value may be any CFObject.
CFObjectTypeData	Raw data (i.e., bytes)
CFObjectTypeInvalid	Nothing

If the CFObject is a Boolean, Number, or String, you can get its value using the (default) Value property, which simply returns the value as a System.Object in .NET or Variant in VB6.

The CFObject is not just a read-only object. It is also possible to create a CFObject and put data into it. The following code snippet shows how to create a CFObject and use it with the primitive CFObject types:

```
Dim cf As New CFObject
Dim s As String

cf.Value = "Grasshopper"    'String
s += "Value : " + cf.Value + vbCrLf
s += "Type : " + CStr(cf.Type) + vbCrLf

cf.Value = 123              'Integer
s += "Value : " + CStr(cf.Value) + vbCrLf
s += "Type : " + CStr(cf.Type) + vbCrLf
```

```
cf.Value = 1234.5678         'Floating point
s += "Value : " + CStr(cf.Value) + vbCrLf
s += "Type : " + CStr(cf.Type) + vbCrLf

cf.Value = True              'Boolean
s += "Value : " + CStr(cf.Value) + vbCrLf
s += "Type : " + CStr(cf.Type) + vbCrLf

tbResults.Text = s
```

This produces the following output:

```
Value : Grasshopper
Type : 2
Value : 123
Type : 3
Value : 1234.5678
Type : 3
Value : True
Type : 1
```

You'll notice that we only used a single instance of CFObject and that its type changed based on the type of the value that was assigned to it.

In Depth

A CFObject is essentially a COM wrapper for a Core Foundation (CFType) object inside QuickTime. CFObject provides a convenient COM interface to the data while allowing the data itself to remain in its native internal format for efficiency.

Core Foundation is one of the core frameworks of Apple's OS X operating system. The various data types wrapped by CFObject are the fundamental data types used extensively within OS X and OS X applications. Developers working with OS X will be intimately familiar with these. Apple has ported elements of the OS X Core Foundation over to Windows in order to support the cross-platform QuickTime API.

Each CFObjectType in the QuickTime COM library corresponds to a CFType, as shown in Table 5.8. For convenience, CFObjects of a particular type are often referred to by their equivalent CFType name, so a CFObject of type CFObjectTypeDictionary is simply termed a CFDictionary.

Table 5.8 CFObjectType and Corresponding CFType

CFObjectType	*Equivalent CFType*
CFObjectTypeBoolean	CFBoolean
CFObjectTypeNumber	CFNumber
CFObjectTypeString	CFString
CFObjectTypeArray	CFArray
CFObjectTypeDictionary	CFDictionary
CFObjectTypeData	CFData
CFObjectTypeInvalid	—

CFObject Collection

In addition to holding primitive Boolean, Number, and String data values, a CFObject can also act as a *collection* of other CFObjects, either in the form of an array (CFObjectTypeArray) or a dictionary (CFObjectTypeDictionary). The items in an array or dictionary type CFObject are child items of the CFObject and may be accessed using its ChildItems property; this returns a collection (CFObjects). Like any collection object, CFObjects has a Count property that returns the number of items in the collection, and an Item property that returns an item (CFObject) from the collection. You can iterate over the items in a CFObjects collection just as you would with any other collection:

```
For i = 1 To cf.ChildItems.Count
  'Do something
Next
```

A CFObject containing an array is often referred to simply as a CFArray (after the Core Foundation type that it wraps) and a dictionary is a CFDictionary. We now look at this pair of collection objects in detail.

CFObject Array (CFArray)

To create a CFArray, we first create a new instance of a CFObject and set its type to CFObjectTypeArray. Then we can start adding other CFObjects to the array. Here's a code example that shows how to create and populate a CFArray and then how to list its contents:

```
Dim cfArray As New CFObject
Dim cf As New CFObject
Dim s As String
Dim i As Long

'Make the CFObject an array
cfArray.Type = CFObjectTypesEnum.CFObjectTypeArray

'Add items to the array
cf.Value = 1234.5678
cfArray.AddItem(cf)

cf.Value = "Dung Beetle"
cfArray.AddItem(cf)

cf.Value = True
cfArray.AddItem(cf)

'List items in the array
For i = 1 To cfArray.ChildItems.Count
  cf = cfArray.ChildItems(i)
  s += "Item " + CStr(i) + ":" + vbCrLf
  s += "  Type   : " + CStr(cf.Type) + vbCrLf
  s += "  Value : " + CStr(cf.Value) + vbCrLf
Next

tbResults.Text = s
```

This will produce the following output:

```
Item 1:
  Type   : 3
  Value : 1234.5678
Item 2:
  Type   : 2
  Value : Dung Beetle
Item 3:
  Type   : 1
  Value : True
```

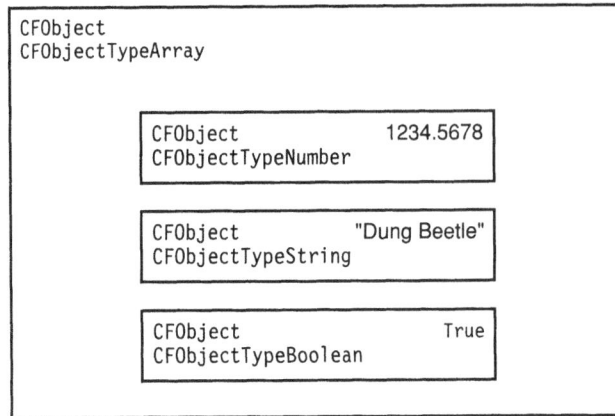

Figure 5.4 CFObject containing an array (CFArray).

The structure of the CFObjects collection that we've created is shown in Figure 5.4.

CFObject Dictionary (CFDictionary)

In a similar way, it is possible to create a dictionary of CFObjects containing key-value pairs, where the *key* is a string and the *value* is a CFObject. A *dictionary* is a collection in which any item can be retrieved with a key rather than just by index as with an array. This code example shows how to create a dictionary and then list all the items in it:

```
Dim cfDict As New CFObject
Dim cf As New CFObject
Dim s As String
Dim i As Long

'Make the CFObject a dictionary
cfDict.Type = CFObjectTypesEnum.CFObjectTypeDictionary

'Add items to the dictionary
cf.Value = "The Very Hungry Caterpillar"
cfDict.AddItem(cf, "Title")

cf.Value = "Eric Carle"
cfDict.AddItem(cf, "Author")
```

```
cf.Value = 1994
cfDict.AddItem(cf, "Year")

cf.Value = True
cfDict.AddItem(cf, "Classic")

'List items in the dictionary
For i = 1 To cfDict.ChildItems.Count
  cf = cfDict.ChildItems(i)
  s += "Item " + CStr(i) + ":" + vbCrLf
  s += "  Key    : " + cf.Key + vbCrLf
  s += "  Type   : " + CStr(cf.Type) + vbCrLf
  s += "  Value : " + CStr(cf.Value) + vbCrLf
Next

'Get item by key
s += vbCrLf
s += "Name : " + cfDict.ChildItems.ItemByKey("Title").Value + vbCrLf

tbResults.Text = s
```

Note that each time we use AddItem to add an item, we must pass the name of the key in the second parameter. The output from the preceding code is as follows:

```
Item 1:
  Key    : Title
  Type   : 2
  Value : The Very Hungry Caterpillar
Item 2:
  Key    : Author
  Type   : 2
  Value : Eric Carle
Item 3:
  Key    : Year
  Type   : 3
  Value : 1994
Item 4:
  Key    : Classic
  Type   : 1
  Value : True

Name : The Very Hungry Caterpillar
```

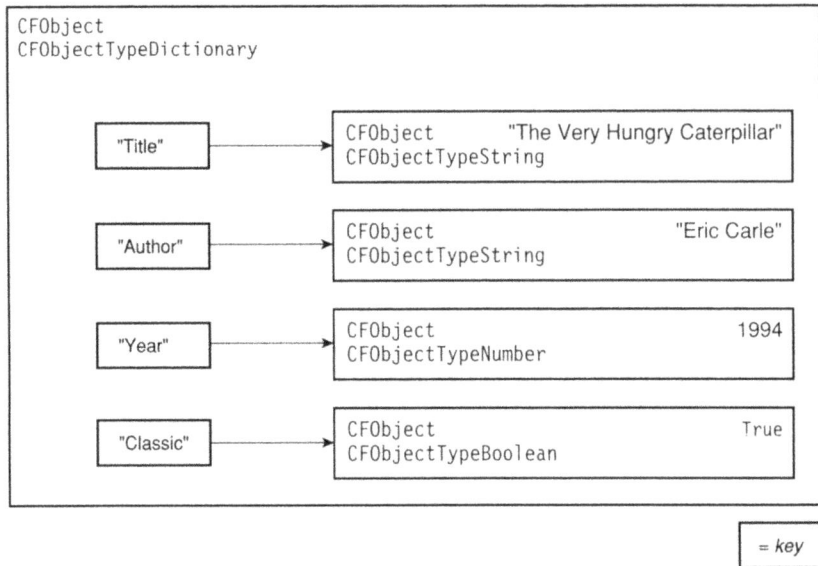

Figure 5.5 CFObject containing a dictionary (CFDictionary).

Figure 5.5 shows the structure of the dictionary we've created.

The Annotations CFDictionary

Browsing through the QuickTime Object Model, you will find the CFObject used in a number of cases to hold complex structured data. One example is the Annotations property of the QTMovie and QTTrack objects, which returns all of the annotations that exist in the movie or track packaged as a CFObject of type CFObjectTypeDictionary.

```
Dim cf As CFObject

If AxQTControl1.Movie Is Nothing Then Exit Sub

cf = AxQTControl1.Movie.Annotations
```

The CFObject that we get back contains a dictionary of key-value pairs, one for each annotation. The *key* for each annotation is the four-character ID of the annotation as a string (e.g., "albm" = qtAnnotationAlbum), while the *value* is another CFObject. In other words the Annotations dictionary contains a collection of child CFObjects keyed on annotation ID as illustrated in Figure 5.6.

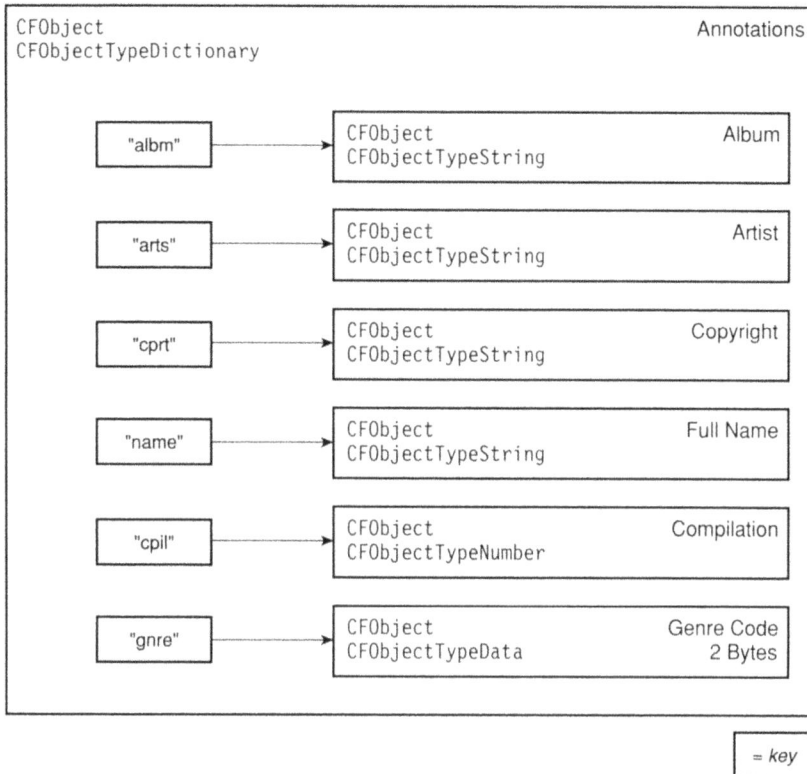

Figure 5.6 Annotations CFObject as a CFDictionary of key-value pairs.

It's easy to iterate over the items in the Annotations dictionary:

```
Dim cf As CFObject, cfAnn As CFObject
Dim s As String
Dim i As Long

If AxQTControl1.Movie Is Nothing Then Exit Sub

cf = AxQTControl1.Movie.Annotations

For i = 1 To cf.ChildItems.Count
  cfAnn = cf.ChildItems(i)
  If cfAnn.Type = CFObjectTypesEnum.CFObjectTypeString Then
    s += "Item " + CStr(i) + ":" + vbCrLf
    s += "  Key   : " + cfAnn.Key + vbCrLf
    s += "  Value : " + cfAnn.Value + vbCrLf
```

```
    End If
Next

tbResults.Text = s
```

Notice that not all the annotations in the dictionary shown in Figure 5.6 (typical of an iTunes song) share the same data type. In addition to the strings, the "cpil" annotation is a number while the "gnre" annotation is of type CFObjectTypeData and contains 2 bytes of data. This explains why, in the preceding example, we tested the Type of each item to make sure it was a string, since our simple code assumes that the value is a string.

We end up with a useful dump of all the string annotations within the movie:

```
Item 1:
  Key    : cprt
  Value  : ℗ 1996 Ricordi
Item 2:
  Key    : name
  Value  : Sotto vento
Item 3:
  Key    : arts
  Value  : Ludovico Einaudi
Item 4:
  Key    : ©day
  Value  : 1996-10-04T07:00:00Z
Item 5:
  Key    : albm
  Value  : Le Onde
```

Individual annotations may be retrieved from the dictionary by key using the ItemByKey property of the CFObjects collection:

```
s += "Name        : " + cf.ChildItems.ItemByKey("name").Value + vbCrLf
s += "Description : " + cf.ChildItems.ItemByKey("desc").Value + vbCrLf
s += "Comments    : " + cf.ChildItems.ItemByKey("cmmt").Value + vbCrLf
s += "Date        : " + cf.ChildItems.ItemByKey("©day").Value + vbCrLf
s += "Copyright   : " + cf.ChildItems.ItemByKey("cprt").Value + vbCrLf
```

Unfortunately, the `CFObjects` collection is rather unforgiving if we attempt to access an item in the dictionary that doesn't exist: it will generate an exception. This is quite likely to happen with the preceding code since a movie may well be missing one or more annotations. A more robust solution is to use a function with an exception handler to get each annotation item:

```
'Returns the value of a CFDictionary item or empty string if not found
Function GetDictionaryItem(ByVal dict As CFObject,
         ByVal key As String) As String

  Dim val As String = ""

  Try
    val = dict.ChildItems.ItemByKey(key).Value
  Catch e As Exception
    'Ignore error
  End Try

  GetDictionaryItem = val

End Function

s += "Name        : " + GetDictionaryItem(cf, "name") + vbCrLf
s += "Description : " + GetDictionaryItem(cf, "desc") + vbCrLf
s += "Comments    : " + GetDictionaryItem(cf, "cmmt") + vbCrLf
s += "Date        : " + GetDictionaryItem(cf, "©day") + vbCrLf
s += "Copyright   : " + GetDictionaryItem(cf, "cprt") + vbCrLf
```

What about those annotations with nonstring values? If the value is a number, then the value we get back is just a numeric `System.Object` (.NET) or `Variant` (VB6):

```
s += "Compilation : " + CStr(GetDictionaryItem(cf, "cpil")) + vbCrLf
```

yielding

```
Compilation : 1
```

However, if the value is of type `CFObjectTypeData`, then the value is returned as an array of bytes. How we interpret this will of course depend entirely on the structure of the data. In the case of "gnre" we might hazard a guess that the 2 bytes represent an integer:

```
Dim b() As Byte
b = cf.ChildItems.ItemByKey("gnre").Value
If IsArray(b) Then
  s += "Genre Code: " + CStr((b(0) * 256) + b(1))
End If
```

yielding

```
Genre : 21
```

Complex CFObject Data Structures

An item in a CFDictionary or CFArray need not contain merely a value such as a number or a string; it can also contain a more complex CFObject, perhaps another CFDictionary or CFArray. In turn, these CFObjects may hold further child objects to create an arbitrary *n*-deep hierarchical data structure.

As an example, let's examine the CFObject that we get back from the PotentialExporters property of a QTMovie or QTTrack. This property returns a list of all the exporters that can potentially be used with the track or movie. If we check the type of the CFObject that we get back from this property, we find that it has returned a CFDictionary. Examining one of the items of the CFDictionary, we discover that this in turn is yet another CFDictionary: so PotentialExporters gives us back a dictionary of dictionaries! The structure is shown in Figure 5.7. Each potential exporter in the dictionary has its own mini-dictionary containing three values keyed on ExporterKind, Type, and DefaultFileNameExtension.

Exploring such a structure would require a nested loop something like

```
Dim s As String
Dim cfExporters As CFObject
Dim cf As CFObject

If AxQTControl1.Movie Is Nothing Then Exit Sub

cfExporters = AxQTControl1.Movie.PotentialExporters
```

```
Dim i, j As Long
For i = 1 To cfExporters.ChildItems.Count
  cf = cfExporters.ChildItems(i)
  s += cf.Key + vbCrLf
  For j = 1 To cf.ChildItems.Count
    s += "   " + cf.ChildItems(j).Key
    s += " = " + cf.ChildItems(j).Value + vbCrLf
  Next
Next

tbResults.Text = s
```

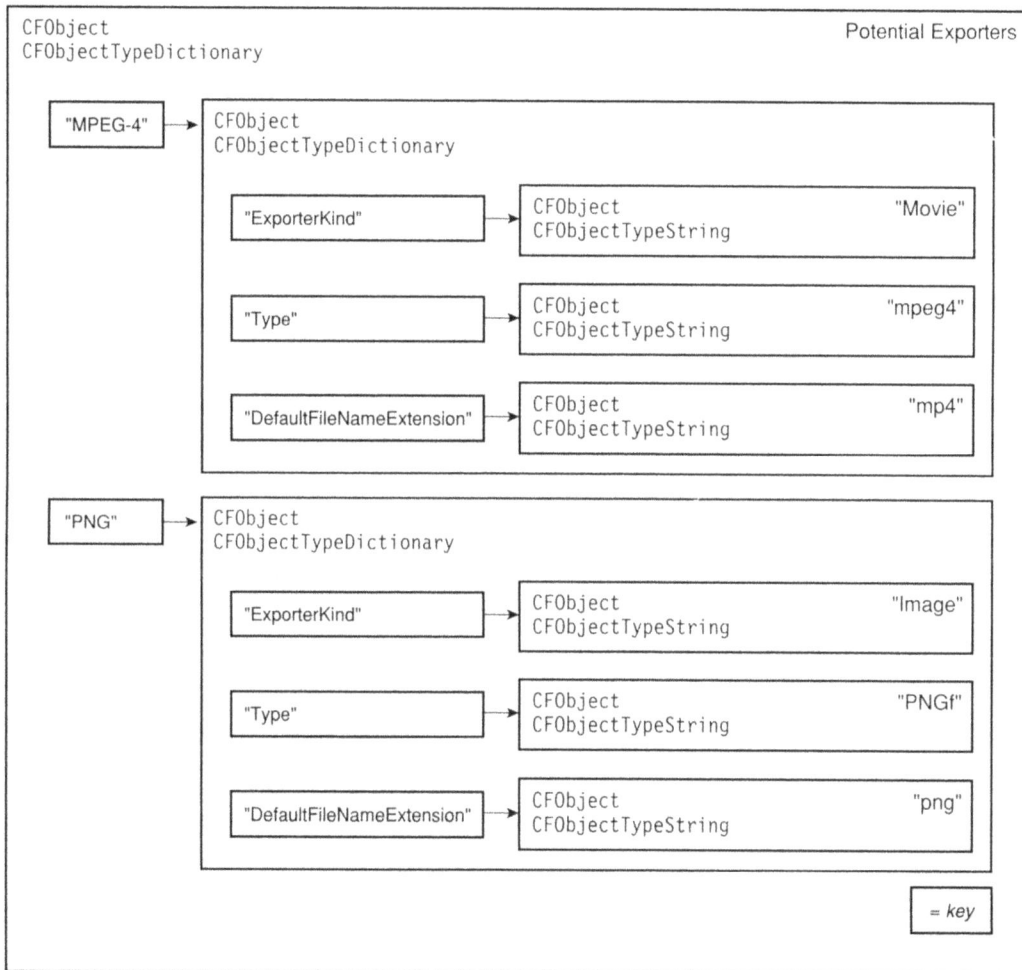

Figure 5.7 Potential Exporters CFDictionary (partial).

Inspecting a Complex CFObject

Studying the structure in Figure 5.7, you may immediately recognize the recursive nature of the "dolls-within-dolls" structure. Recursive structures beg recursive algorithms, so let's be ambitious and see if we can't come up with a recursive function that will allow us to explore *any* CFObject, irrespective of its structure or complexity. DumpCFObject is the surprisingly compact end result:

```
Sub DumpCFObject(ByVal item As CFObject, ByRef depth As Long,
          ByRef strOut As String)

  Dim i As Long
  Dim s As String = ""
  Dim key
  Dim Value As String
  Dim cfType As String

  Dim indent As New String(" ", depth * 3)

  Select Case item.Type
    Case CFObjectTypesEnum.CFObjectTypeDictionary : cfType =
          "<dictionary>"
    Case CFObjectTypesEnum.CFObjectTypeArray : cfType = "<array>"
    Case CFObjectTypesEnum.CFObjectTypeNumber : cfType = "<number>"
    Case CFObjectTypesEnum.CFObjectTypeString : cfType = "<string>"
    Case CFObjectTypesEnum.CFObjectTypeBoolean : cfType = "<boolean>"
    Case CFObjectTypesEnum.CFObjectTypeData : cfType = "<data>"
    Case Else : cfType = "<Unknown>"
  End Select

  Select Case item.Type

    Case CFObjectTypesEnum.CFObjectTypeDictionary,
          CFObjectTypesEnum.CFObjectTypeArray

      If IsDBNull(item.Key) Then
        s = cfType
      Else
        s = s + CStr(item.Key) + " = " + cfType
```

```
      End If
      strOut = strOut + indent + s + vbCrLf

      For i = 1 To item.ChildItems.Count
        DumpCFObject(item.ChildItems(i), depth + 1, strOut)
      Next i

    Case Else

      If IsDBNull(item.Value) Then
        Value = "<null>"
      Else
        If item.Type = CFObjectTypesEnum.CFObjectTypeData Then
          If (IsArray(item.Value)) Then
            Value = "[DATA : " +
              CStr(UBound(item.Value) -
              LBound(item.Value) + 1) + " bytes]"
          Else
            Value = "DATA"
          End If
        Else
          Value = CStr(item.Value)
        End If
      End If

      If IsDBNull(item.Key) Then
        s = s + Value + " " + cfType
      Else
        s = s + CStr(item.Key) + " = " + Value + " " + cfType
      End If

      If Len(s) <> 0 Then
        strOut = strOut + indent + s + vbCrLf
      End If

  End Select

End Sub
```

`DumpCFObject` takes a `CFObject`(item) together with two additional `ByRef` parameters:

depth : the depth of recursion (used to generate the appropriate indentation)

strOut : the string to which we append the output

To dump the contents of any `CFObject`, we simply call it as follows:

```
Dim s As String
Dim cfExporters As CFObject

If AxQTControl1.Movie Is Nothing Then Exit Sub

cfExporters = AxQTControl1.Movie.PotentialExporters

DumpCFObject(cfExporters, 0, s)

tbResults.Text = s
```

yielding something like the following extract:

```
<dictionary>
  MPEG-4 = <dictionary>
    ExporterKind = Movie <string>
    Type = mpg4 <string>
    DefaultFileNameExtension = mp4 <string>
  QuickTime Movie = <dictionary>
    ExporterKind = Movie <string>
    Type = MooV <string>
    DefaultFileNameExtension = mov <string>
  PNG = <dictionary>
    ExporterKind = Image <string>
    Type = PNGf <string>
    DefaultFileNameExtension = PNG <string>
```

So how exactly does `DumpCFObject` work? Well, it first inspects the type of the `CFObject` that it has been passed. This will be either a simple value such as a number or string, or it may be a collection: either an array or dictionary. If it's a simple value, all it has to do is print out the value and type. However, if the `CFObject` is a collection, life gets interesting: `DumpCFObject` then recursively calls itself for each of the child objects in the collection, incrementing depth as it does so. The end result, as we've seen, is a neatly formatted contents dump of any arbitrary CFObject.

Before we leave DumpCFObject, it's worth looking briefly at how it copes with a CFObject of type CFObjectTypeData. This type of CFObject is not a collection since it contains a value, and this value is an array of bytes, which could conceivably be of any length. Printing out each byte seems a little pointless, so DumpCFObject just extracts the length of the array:

```
If item.Type = CFObjectTypesEnum.CFObjectTypeData Then
  If (IsArray(item.Value)) Then
    Value = "[DATA : " + CStr(UBound(item.Value)
            - LBound(item.Value) + 1) + " bytes]"
```

For example, if you DumpCFObject the Annotations of an iTunes song, the Track Number annotation prints out something like

```
trkn = [DATA : 8 bytes] <data>
```

For the irredeemably curious, though, peeking inside the data is not difficult. The following addition prints out the data byte by byte in hex format, up to the first 16 bytes:

```
If item.Type = CFObjectTypesEnum.CFObjectTypeData Then
  If (IsArray(item.Value)) Then
    Value = "[" + CStr(UBound(item.Value) -
            LBound(item.Value) + 1) + " bytes]"
    Value += " = ["
    For i = LBound(item.Value) To UBound(item.Value)
      Value += Hex(item.Value(i)).PadLeft(2, "0") + "."
      If i > 16 Then
        Value += "..."
        Exit For
      End If
    Next i
    Value += "]"
  Else
    Value = "DATA"
  End If
Else
    Value = CStr(item.Value)
End If
```

Calling DumpCFObject on the Annotations dictionary of a song purchased from the iTunes Music Store yields something like the following—a fertile tramping ground for the reverse engineering enthusiast:

```
<dictionary>
  artw = [564801 bytes] =
            [89.50.4E.47.0D.0A.1A.0A.00.00.00.0D.49.48....] <data>
  trkn = [8 bytes] = [00.00.00.06.00.0D.00.00.] <data>
  cprt = © 1996 Ricordi <string>
  atID = -1690603264 <number>
  gnre = [2 bytes] = [00.0B.] <data>
  aART = Ludovico Einaudi <string>
  name = Tracce <string>
  meta = [567153 bytes] =
            [00.00.00.00.00.00.00.22.68.64.6C.72.00.00....] <data>
  arts = Ludovico Einaudi <string>
  rtng = 0 <number>
  apID = xxxx@yyyy.com <string>
  ©day = 1996-10-04T07:00:00Z <string>
  akID = 0 <number>
  disk = [6 bytes] = [00.00.00.01.00.01.] <data>
  albm = Le Onde <string>
  cnID = -1354367547 <number>
  geID = 218301808 <number>
  plID = -4.6754886448544E+18 <number>
```

DumpCFObject comes in handy anywhere that the property of a QuickTime object returns a CFObject. Here's another example.

Inspecting QuickTime Event Parameters

Earlier in this chapter we saw that in a QTEvent handler, we can retrieve specific event parameters through the GetParam method of QTEventObject, as long as you know the ID of the parameter that you want. The eagle-eyed may also have spotted a GetParams method; this returns a CFObject dictionary containing all the event parameters. If you ever want to explore the parameters of a QuickTime event, just pop the following into your QTEvent handler:

```
'Dump event params
Dim s As String
Dim qtu As New QTUtils
s = "Event ID: " + qtu.FourCharCodeToString(e.eventID) + vbCrLf
s += "["
DumpCFObject(e.eventObject.GetParams, 0, s)
s += "]" + vbCrLf
Debug.Write(s)
```

Here's what will appear in your output window for a selection of useful events:

```
Event ID: cvol
[<dictionary>
  volm = 0.703125 <number>
  ctxt = 0 <number>
]
Event ID: ctim
[<dictionary>
  time = 1640 <number>
  ctxt = 0 <number>
]
Event ID: size
[<dictionary>
  size = 0, 0, 480, 640 <string>
  ctxt = 0 <number>
]
Event ID: rate
[<dictionary>
  ctxt = 0 <number>
  rate = 1 <number>
]
```

Tip Event processing generally needs to be efficient if it is not to impact on your application's performance. Getting the parameters through the `GetParams` dictionary will inevitably be a lot less efficient than getting them directly by ID using `GetParam`.

Persistent CFObject

Given its ability to hold a data structure of arbitrary complexity, there is no reason why you shouldn't take advantage of the CFObject class to hold your own application data, as well as for interacting with QuickTime objects. When we discover how easy it is to serialize the data to and from an XML string so that, for example, we can save data to disk and load it again, the case for using CFObject is compelling.

The XML property of CFObject makes all this possible. This property returns an XML string representation of both the data and the structure contained in the CFObject. This is easiest to explain with a simple example. The following code populates a CFObject with some data, copies the XML property into a string, and then uses the string to load another CFObject:

```
Dim cfDict As New CFObject
Dim cf As New CFObject
Dim s As String
Dim xml As String
Dim i As Long

'Make the CFObject a dictionary
cfDict.Type = CFObjectTypesEnum.CFObjectTypeDictionary

'Add items to the dictionary
cf.Value = "The Very Hungry Caterpillar"
cfDict.AddItem(cf, "Title")

cf.Value = "Eric Carle"
cfDict.AddItem(cf, "Author")

cf.Value = 1994
cfDict.AddItem(cf, "Year")

cf.Value = True
cfDict.AddItem(cf, "Classic")

'Create another dictionary
Dim cfDict2 As New CFObject
cfDict2.Type = CFObjectTypesEnum.CFObjectTypeDictionary
```

```
cf.Value = "lettuce"
cfDict2.AddItem(cf, "Lunch")
cf.Value = "strawberry"
cfDict2.AddItem(cf, "Dessert")

'Add as child dictionary
cfDict.AddItem(cfDict2, "Food")

xml = cfDict.XML

s = ""
DumpCFObject(cfDict, 0, s)

s += vbCrLf
s += xml

'Create a new CFObject
Dim cfNew As New CFObject

'Load it from the xml
cfNew.XML = xml

s += vbCrLf

s += "Dessert : " +
  cfNew.ChildItems.ItemByKey("Food").ChildItems.ItemByKey(
          "Dessert").Value()

tbResults.Text = s
```

A DumpCFObject listing of the CFObject we've created looks like this:

```
<dictionary>
  Title = The Very Hungry Caterpillar <string>
  Classic = True <boolean>
  Food = <dictionary>
    Lunch = lettuce <string>
    Dessert = strawberry <string>
  Year = 1994 <number>
  Author = Eric Carle <string>
```

and the XML property returns the following:

```
<?xml version="1.0" encoding="UTF-8"?>
<!DOCTYPE plist PUBLIC "-//Apple Computer//DTD PLIST 1.0//EN"
            "http://www.apple.com/DTDs/PropertyList-1.0.dtd">
<plist version="1.0">
<dict>
  <key>Author</key>
  <string>Eric Carle</string>
  <key>Classic</key>
  <true/>
  <key>Food</key>
  <dict>
    <key>Dessert</key>
    <string>strawberry</string>
    <key>Lunch</key>
    <string>lettuce</string>
  </dict>
  <key>Title</key>
  <string>The Very Hungry Caterpillar</string>
  <key>Year</key>
  <integer>1994</integer>
</dict>
</plist>
```

If we then load a *new* CFObject (cfNew) with the preceding XML, we end up with exactly the same data that we had in our original object.

Querying it as follows

```
s += "Dessert : " +
    cfNew.ChildItems.ItemByKey("Food")
        .ChildItems.ItemByKey("Dessert").Value()
```

yields the expected result:

```
Dessert : strawberry
```

The XML format returned by the XML property of CFObject is in Apple's standard Property List or *PList* format. This is well-formed XML and can easily be imported and used by other XML parsers including System.XML.

Saving the contents of a CFObject to disk or, in software engineering parlance, making it *persistent*, is easily achieved using System.IO:

```
xml = cfDict.XML

'Save the XML to disk
Dim sw As StreamWriter = File.CreateText("d:\aaa\cfobject.plist")
sw.Write(xml)
sw.Close()
```

And loading a CFObject from the saved XML file is equally straightforward:

```
'Create a new CFObject
Dim cfNew As New CFObject

xml = ""

'Load CFObject from the XML on disk
Dim sr As StreamReader = New StreamReader("d:\aaa\cfobject.plist")
xml = sr.ReadToEnd
sr.Close()

cfNew.XML = xml
```

Saving Exporter Settings

One obvious use of this facility to save a CFObject is to save exporter settings. Whenever we bring up an Exporter Settings dialog, there may be quite a few options that we need to set before we can perform the export. If we ever want to use those settings again, it's a real pain if they all disappear the moment we dispose of the exporter. Now we have a ready means to save such settings:

```
Dim exp As QTOLibrary.QTExporter = qt.Exporters(1)

exp.TypeName = exporterType

'Load exporter settings if available
fPath = Application.StartupPath + "\Settings"
f = fPath + "\" + exporterType + ".plist"
```

```
If File.Exists(f) Then
  Dim sr As StreamReader = New StreamReader(f)
  Dim cf As New CFObject
  Dim xml = sr.ReadToEnd
  cf.XML = xml
  exp.Settings = cf
  sr.Close()
End If

exp.ShowSettingsDialog()

'Save exporter settings
If Not Directory.Exists(fPath) Then
  Dim di As DirectoryInfo = Directory.CreateDirectory(fPath)
End If
Dim sw As StreamWriter = File.CreateText(f)
sw.Write(exp.Settings.XML)
sw.Close()
```

The preceding code is wrapped around the exporter call to ShowSettings-Dialog. After the Exporter Settings dialog is closed, the current settings are saved in a file called *< exporter Type Name >.plist*. Before the settings dialog is opened, we look for a file with the same name and, if found, we load any previously saved settings.

With the simple addition of Open File and Save File dialogs, this could easily be extended so that the user would be able to load and save any number of specific export configurations. This is left as an exercise for the reader.

Error Handling

If your aim is to create a rugged, professional-grade application, then you ignore error handling at your peril. Developing with the QuickTime Control and QuickTime objects is no different: nasty and unexpected things happen, especially when someone is so inconsiderate as to allow your precious software to get into the grubby hands of real users. It pays to anticipate this.

Fortunately, the .NET framework has a powerful error handling facility in the form of its Exceptions mechanism. Any code that is liable to generate an error and throw an exception can be wrapped with a Try/Catch (C#: try/catch) block so that any exceptions are caught before they wreak havoc elsewhere. This exception handling is available in both Visual Basic and C#:

```
' VB.NET
Try

  'Try something risky in here

Catch ex As Exception

  'Catch and report exception errors in here

  MsgBox(ex.ToString)

End Try

// C#
try
{
// Try something risky in here
}
catch(Exception ex)
{
// Catch and report exception errors in here

  MessageBox.Show(ex.ToString());
}
```

The QuickTime COM control and objects can also generate COM exceptions when things go wrong. To make sure this happens, you should always explicitly configure the ErrorHandling property of the QuickTime Control as soon as possible after the control is loaded:

```
AxQTControl1.ErrorHandling =
         QTErrorHandlingOptionsEnum.qtErrorHandlingRaiseException
```

But COM exceptions are not the same as .NET exceptions. Fortunately, the COM Interop layer comes to the rescue once again and ensures that anytime a COM object returns an error or raises a COM exception, it gets translated into a .NET exception. A COM error code comes in the form of a 32-bit HRESULT. A few well-known HRESULT error codes are mapped to obvious named .NET exceptions such as OutOfMemoryException or NullReferenceException, but the vast majority are lumped together into a .NET exception known as a COMException, or more precisely as System.Runtime.InteropServices.COMException. Since COMException is ultimately derived from System.Exception, it behaves just like a regular .NET exception and can be caught in the catch-all exception handlers we have illustrated.

First, we'll look at how to handle a straightforward (and not uncommon) error. Here's an example of some code that's guaranteed to throw an exception as we attempt to access a movie object that doesn't exist:

```
AxQTControl1.URL = ""

Dim duration = AxQTControl1.Movie.Duration
```

And sure enough the resulting error message is predictably obtuse:

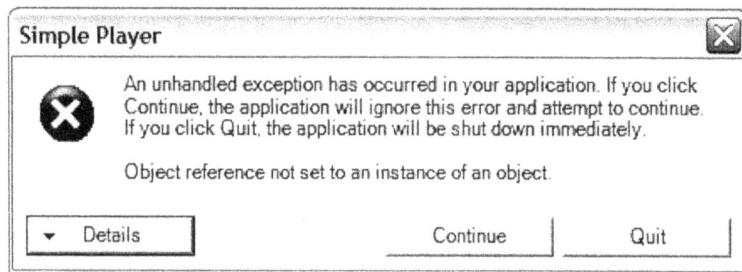

Adding the exception handler, as follows, this becomes somewhat more benign, although not a whole lot more meaningful. At least we have caught the exception and can choose to do something about it if we can.

```
Try

  AxQTControl1.URL = ""
  Dim duration = AxQTControl1.Movie.Duration

Catch ex As Exception

  MsgBox(ex.ToString)

End Try
```

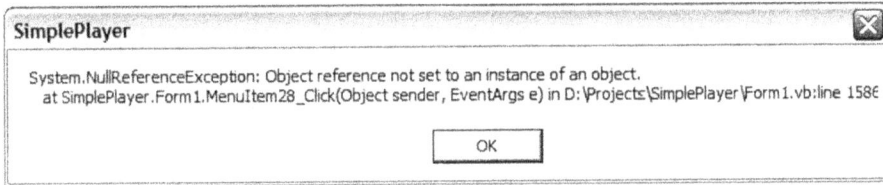

SimplePlayer

System.NullReferenceException: Object reference not set to an instance of an object.
at SimplePlayer.Form1.MenuItem28_Click(Object sender, EventArgs e) in D:\Projects\SimplePlayer\Form1.vb:line 158€

OK

We can now see that this particular error has generated a standard System.NullReferenceException rather than a COMException. That's simply because attempting to access objects that don't exist is a not-infrequent problem in .NET applications, the same as in any other application. We can of course improve on the error message:

```
Try

  AxQTControl1.URL = ""
  Dim duration = AxQTControl1.Movie.Duration

Catch ex As Exception

  Dim msg As String
  msg = "A calamitous event has occurred: I am so frightfully sorry!"
  msg += vbCrLf + vbCrLf
  msg += "Here are the details:" + vbCrLf
  msg += ex.Message()
  MsgBox(msg, MsgBoxStyle.Critical)

End Try
```

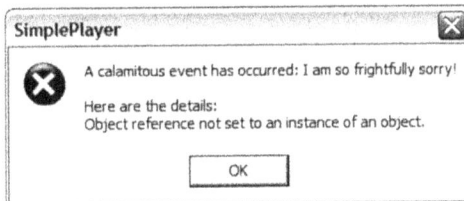

SimplePlayer

A calamitous event has occurred: I am so frightfully sorry!

Here are the details:
Object reference not set to an instance of an object.

OK

If we are concerned with this *particular* error and would like to present a polite message free from gobbledygook, we can always explicitly catch it:

```
Try

    AxQTControl1.URL = ""
    Dim duration = AxQTControl1.Movie.Duration

Catch ex As System.NullReferenceException

    MsgBox("The movie doesn't exist, dummy!", MsgBoxStyle.Exclamation)

Catch ex As Exception

    MsgBox(ex.ToString)

End Try
```

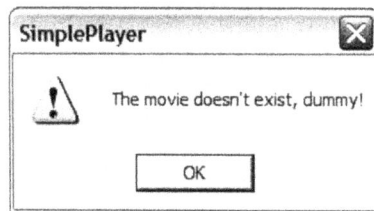

So far we've handled a straightforward .NET exception even though it has emanated from the QTMovie object. What follows is some code that will cause an error deep within QuickTime as we attempt to get an annotation that doesn't exist. The Annotation property of QTMovie will return an error that will, in turn, trigger a COM exception:

```
If AxQTControl1.Movie Is Nothing Then
    MsgBox("Please open a movie first and try again!",
            MsgBoxStyle.Exclamation)
    Exit Sub
End If
```

```
Try

    Dim mov As QTMovie = AxQTControl1.Movie
    Dim a = mov.Annotation(123456)        'Causes the exception

Catch ex As Exception

    Dim msg As String
    msg = "An error occurred!"
    msg += vbCrLf + vbCrLf
    msg += ex.Message()
    MsgBox(msg, MsgBoxStyle.Critical)

End Try
```

Even with the exception handler, the error message we get is far from illuminating:

The reason is that .NET knows nothing about the specific COM exception that occurred.

To get more details, we really need to trap the COMException explicitly:

```
If AxQTControl1.Movie Is Nothing Then
    MsgBox("Please open a movie first and try again!",
            MsgBoxStyle.Exclamation)
    Exit Sub
End If

Try
```

```
      Dim mov As QTMovie = AxQTControl1.Movie
      Dim a = mov.Annotation(123456) 'Causes the exception

Catch ex As COMException

  Dim msg As String
  Dim qtu As New QTUtils
  msg = "An error occurred!" + vbCrLf + vbCrLf
  msg += "Error code : " + Hex(ex.ErrorCode) + vbCrLf
  msg += "QT Error code : " +
          CStr(qtu.QTErrorFromErrorCode(ex.ErrorCode))
  MsgBox(msg, MsgBoxStyle.Critical)

Catch ex As Exception

  'Catch and report exceptions errors in here
  Dim msg As String
  msg = "An error occurred!"
  msg += vbCrLf + vbCrLf
  msg += ex.Message()
  MsgBox(msg, MsgBoxStyle.Critical)

End Try
```

Once we have a COMException, we can obtain the all-important HRESULT error code (in this case the hex value 0x8004F77F) from the exception's ErrorCode property. This is the error that originated in the QuickTime COM Control or in one of its child objects, and that triggered the COM exception in the first place. Looking this up in the documentation should help us track down the source of the problem.

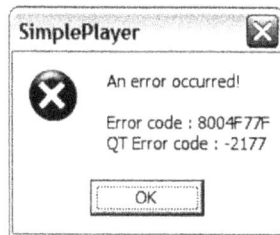

Embedded in the HRESULT may be an additional clue: if the HI word of the HRESULT equals 0x8004, then we can assume that the LO word is in fact a 16-bit QuickTime error code—in this case 0xF77F or -2177—which essentially means that the annotation we asked for could not be found. QuickTime error codes like this can often be looked up in .h header files provided with the QuickTime SDK. *MacErrors.h* is often a good place to start.

Exception handling can sometimes be necessary to handle even routine occurrences. One example is in the following code that implements the File | Export menu item in Simple Player:

```
Private Sub mnuExport_Click(...) Handles mnuExport.Click

  Dim qt As QTQuickTime = AxQTControl1.QuickTime

  If AxQTControl1.Movie Is Nothing Then Exit Sub

  qt = AxQTControl1.QuickTime

  If qt.Exporters.Count = 0 Then qt.Exporters.Add()

  Dim exp As QTExporter = qt.Exporters(1)
  exp.SetDataSource(AxQTControl1.Movie)
  exp.ShowExportDialog()

End Sub
```

If you happen to hit the Cancel button in the Export Dialog, the exporter will throw a COM exception with an HRESULT error code of 0x8004FF80. Clearly this should not be considered an error, and so we can tactfully ignore this particular error code in our COMException handler:

```
Private Sub mnuExport_Click(...) Handles mnuExport.Click

  Dim qt As QTQuickTime = AxQTControl1.QuickTime

  If AxQTControl1.Movie Is Nothing Then Exit Sub
```

```
Try

    qt = AxQTControl1.QuickTime

    If qt.Exporters.Count = 0 Then qt.Exporters.Add()

    Dim exp As QTExporter = qt.Exporters(1)
    exp.SetDataSource(AxQTControl1.Movie)
    exp.ShowExportDialog()

Catch ex As COMException

    If ex.ErrorCode = &H8004FF80 Then
        'Canceled - ignore
    Else
        Dim msg As String
        msg = "An error occurred!" + vbCrLf + vbCrLf
        msg += "Error code : " + Hex(ex.ErrorCode) + vbCrLf
        MsgBox(msg, MsgBoxStyle.Critical)
    End If

Catch ex As Exception

    MsgBox(ex.ToString)

End Try

End Sub
```

As a general rule, make sure to add exception handling code to any routines or functions in your code that involve input/output (I/O), such as opening movies or saving and exporting movies. Remember also that exceptions thrown in lower-level routines percolate up the calling chain and are caught in the exception handling code of higher-level functions. However, if you depend entirely on this, you will often miss out on the specific context in which an exception occurred in a low-level function.

⬤ Summary

If you've completed this chapter and spent some time perusing the code samples available online at *www.skylark.ie/qt4.net/Samples*, you should feel considerably more confident about tackling real-world QuickTime applications. The judicious use of QuickTime events will ensure that your application performs well in an event-driven environment. Well-thought-out error handling will contribute to a robust application, while comprehensive error reporting will help in tracking down any problems that do arise, whether the source is in your application or in QuickTime itself. Familiarity with the CFObject data container ensures that you will be in a position to use some of the more powerful features of the QuickTime COM objects, with the added bonus of a useful general-purpose container class to add to your bag of tricks.

If you're working with QuickTime content in a production environment or developing software tools for production, the ability to access QuickTime's metadata capabilities can be a major bonus.

6

Create and Edit

Creating and Editing
QuickTime Content

Introduction

Not many years ago, the process of video production and editing was mainly the preserve of an exclusive priesthood of professionals working with expensive equipment, and even more expensive software, usually in the hallowed studios of television and movie production companies. How things have changed! It seems that almost anyone with a handheld DV camera and a home computer is now an aspiring video editor, capable of transforming those hours of insipid poolside footage (you know the kind: little Jack on the waterslide; little Jill on the waterslide; Jack going down the waterslide head-first, upside-down, backwards; Jack being ejected by the pool attendant...) into gripping hour-long episodes peppered with special video effects and captions. Millions of grandparents will happily attest to the soporific effects of their output.

While dramatically lowered hardware size and cost have undoubtedly contributed to this democratization of video production, advances in video-editing software have been no less significant. In recent years Apple has led the way, both with its professional-grade, yet affordable *Final Cut Pro* and, at a more basic level, with *iMovie*, the home video-editing package. It shouldn't come as a surprise to learn that both of these applications draw heavily upon QuickTime.

While few of us will aspire to creating video production applications as sophisticated as these, the underlying video creation and editing capabilities of QuickTime do provide a powerful platform for developing both commercial and in-house content production applications. In this chapter we examine the editing and content creation features of QuickTime that are exposed through the QuickTime COM Control and object library.

The Joy of Cut, Copy, and Paste

When it comes to basic movie creation and editing, such as the compilation of multiple short clips, or shots, into a single movie, the Pro version of QuickTime Player can be perfectly adequate. It has the undeniable advantages of simplicity and low cost. Much can be achieved simply by opening movies in multiple QuickTime Player windows, copying and pasting between them, and finally saving or exporting the result.

Implementing the Edit Menu

Since much of this capability derives from the Edit menu in QuickTime Player, let's begin by looking at what it takes to add a similar Edit menu to the Simple Player application that we kicked off with in Chapter 2. The starting point, of course, is to add and populate the Edit menu in Visual Studio. As you insert the menu items, don't forget to add the requisite standard keyboard shortcut to each menu item. You should end up with a menu like that shown in Figure 6.1.

Now we can add the code behind the menu items. It turns out that most of the edit functions can be implemented as single-line calls to the appropri-

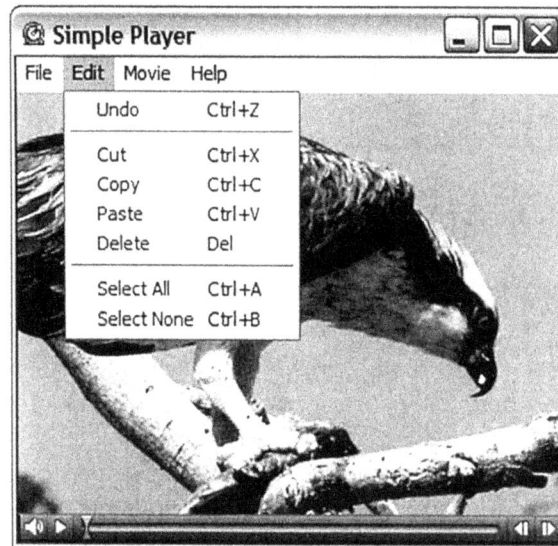

Figure 6.1   Simple Player showing basic Edit menu.

ate methods of the QTMovie object, and so it seems logical to handle all the Edit menu items together in one single event handler:

```
Private Sub OnEditMenu_Click(ByVal sender As System.Object,
        ByVal e As System.EventArgs)
    Handles mnuUndo.Click, mnuCut.Click,
        mnuCopy.Click, mnuPaste.Click,
        mnuDelete.Click, mnuSelectAll.Click,
        mnuSelectNone.Click

  If AxQTControl1.Movie Is Nothing Then Exit Sub

  With AxQTControl1.Movie

    If sender Is mnuUndo Then
      .Undo()
    ElseIf sender Is mnuCut Then
      .Cut()
    ElseIf sender Is mnuCopy Then
      .Copy()
    ElseIf sender Is mnuPaste Then
      .Paste()
    ElseIf sender Is mnuDelete Then
      .DeleteSelection()
    ElseIf sender Is mnuSelectAll Then
      .SelectAll()
    ElseIf sender Is mnuSelectNone Then
      .SelectionDuration = 0
    End If

  End With

End Sub
```

The sender object that we are passed as a parameter to the event handler comes into play here: we compare it with each of the menu items in turn until we find the MenuItem object that it matches. Note that the apparently more suitable Select Case statement can't be used here since it only copes with *value* equivalence (=) and not *object* equivalence (Is).

Saving the Movie

Now that we have an Edit menu, we can open a movie, shuffle sections around by cutting from one part of the movie and pasting into another, delete bits out of it, and generally monkey around with the movie. Once we are happy with the result, we will want to save the movie to disk. Any self-respecting editor application will have both Save and Save As... menu items in the File menu. Implementing the Save menu item is trivial:

```
Private Sub mnuSave_Click(...) Handles mnuSave.Click

  If AxQTControl1.Movie Is Nothing Then Exit Sub

  AxQTControl1.Movie.Save()

End Sub
```

Implementing Save As... to save the movie to a different file is pretty straightforward as well:

```
Private Sub mnuSaveAs_Click(...) Handles mnuSaveAs.Click

  If AxQTControl1.Movie Is Nothing Then Exit Sub

  SaveFileDialog1.Title = "Save Movie As"
  SaveFileDialog1.FileName = "Untitled.mov"
  If SaveFileDialog1.ShowDialog() = DialogResult.OK Then
    AxQTControl1.Movie.SaveSelfContained(SaveFileDialog1.FileName())
  End If

End Sub
```

The Windows Forms SaveFileDialog component is used to prompt for a file name and location.

Note that in this case we use the movie's SaveSelfContained method rather than Save. If you are already familiar with QuickTime Player, you will know that when you save an existing movie that you have edited, the edits are saved in the movie file, but the data within the movie file remains unchanged. This is for efficiency, especially when editing large files. Save-SelfContained saves all of the movie data into a specified new file. We explore the distinction in more detail later in this chapter in "Saving a New Movie."

Creating a New Movie

Editing and saving existing movies is all fine and well, but many of us have a yearning to create something new and original. The starting point for this is an empty movie, which we obtain by calling the CreateNewMovie method of the QuickTime Control. This method sports a single optional parameter movieIsActive: in general, we *do* want our new movie to be active so that we can play it, and since movieIsActive defaults to True if we leave it out, we can often safely ignore this parameter. Enhancing the File menu in Simple Player, as shown in Figure 6.2, we can add a *New Movie* menu item.

The New Movie implementation couldn't be much simpler:

```
Private Sub mnuNewMovie_Click(...) Handles mnuNewMovie.Click

    AxQTControl1.CreateNewMovie()

End Sub
```

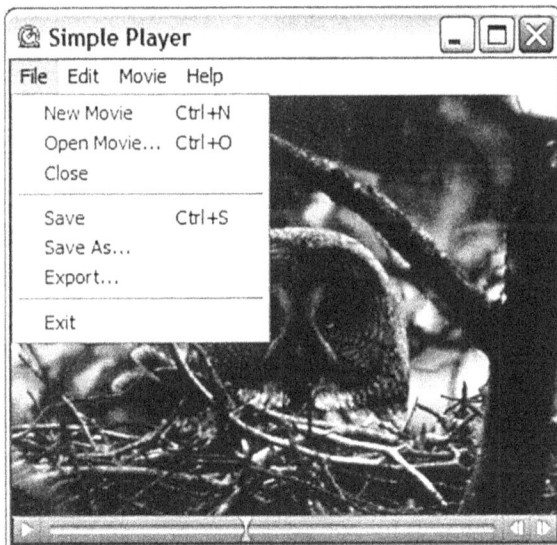

Figure 6.2 Simple Player showing File menu.

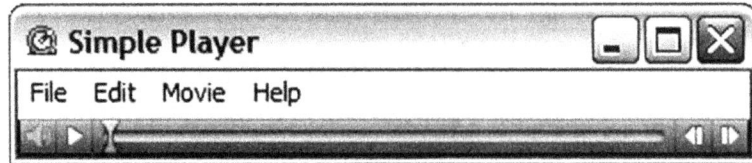

Figure 6.3 Simple Player with a new empty movie.

Choose File | New Movie, and Simple Player hosts an empty movie (Figure 6.3), just inviting you to populate it with some exciting content.

The simplest way to add anything—images, video clips, sounds—to this movie is by pasting them from the clipboard. While this may sound a bit crude, it is quite an effective means of assembling a movie, especially when you remember that virtually any application is capable of putting something on the clipboard and can therefore serve as a content source. For example, if you copy an image from a graphics application such as Photoshop and select Edit | Paste in Simple Player, the image will be added to the movie as a single frame at the current time position. If the dimensions of the image are larger than the current movie size, the movie will be enlarged to accommodate this. By pasting in a sequence of images one by one, you can create an entire movie, albeit rather laboriously.

By employing QuickTime Player, or another instance of Simple Player as our content source, we can copy entire movies or movie selections onto the clipboard and paste them into the movie that we are assembling. Longer movies can easily be created from a series of shorter movies in this way. Admittedly, this technique is a rather tedious manual route to a finished movie. Nonetheless, if we can *automate* both the source player (opening files and copying to the clipboard) and the destination player (pasting in from the clipboard), we possess an eminently practical tool for assembling digital content.

Movie Builder

In order to illustrate how the movie creation and editing features of the QuickTime Control and object library can be deployed in a real-world environment, we will develop a sample application called Movie Builder. The basic concept is quite simple: we open a source folder containing a collection of movies, and these individual movies are then automatically assembled into a single composite movie. Later in this section, we will extend Movie

Builder with a few interesting bells and whistles. The Movie Builder sample can be found on the website

www.skylark.ie/qt4.net/Samples/MovieBuilder

Assembling a Movie

The Movie Builder user interface is shown in Figure 6.4. At the top there is a Source frame containing a CheckedListBox control (CheckedListBox1) on the left, with a QuickTime COM Control (AxQTControl1) beside it. The idea is that, on choosing File | Select Source Folder…, all the files (movies, images, audio files, etc.) in the source folder are listed in CheckedListBox1. Clicking

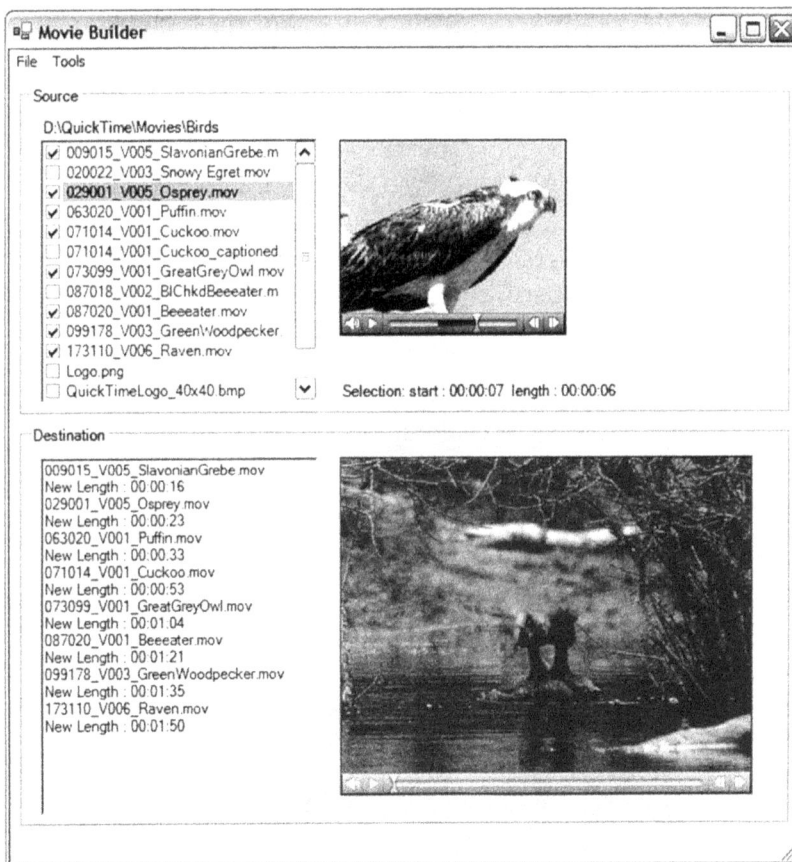

Figure 6.4 Movie Builder.

on any file name will open and display that file as a movie in the QuickTime Control opposite. In the Destination frame below, we have another Quick-Time COM Control (AxQTControl2) in which the new movie will be assembled, as well as a TextBox (tbLog) in which we can log activity.

Once the list of source files is populated, we can uncheck any files that we don't want to assemble into our composite movie and then choose Tools | Build Movie. This will create a new empty movie in the destination Quick-Time Control, and then, opening each source movie in turn, it will append them one by one to the destination movie. At that point we can choose File | Save As... or File | Export... to save or export the movie that has just been assembled.

First let's look at the code for opening a folder and populating the list of files. Using a FolderBrowserDialog component, we prompt for the path to the source folder, which we then stash in member variable m_SourcePath. CheckedListBox1 is then populated with the names of all the files in that folder:

```
Private Sub mnuSelectSource_Click(...) Handles mnuSelectSource.Click

  Dim srcFile As String

  If m_SourcePath <> "" Then
    FolderBrowserDialog1.SelectedPath = m_SourcePath
  End If
  If FolderBrowserDialog1.ShowDialog() = DialogResult.OK Then

    m_SourcePath = FolderBrowserDialog1.SelectedPath
    lblSource.Text = m_SourcePath

    CheckedListBox1.Items.Clear()

    Dim srcFiles As String() = Directory.GetFiles(m_SourcePath, "*.*")
    If srcFiles.Length = 0 Then Exit Sub

    For Each srcFile In srcFiles
      Dim fi = New FileInfo(srcFile)
      CheckedListBox1.Items.Add(fi.Name, True)
    Next

  End If

End Sub
```

Adding some code to handle the `SelectedIndexChanged` event of Checked-ListBox1 allows us to load and display a file in AxQTControl1 any time an item is selected.

```
Private Sub CheckedListBox1_SelectedIndexChanged(...)
          Handles CheckedListBox1.SelectedIndexChanged

  Dim msg As String = ""
  Dim fName As String = CheckedListBox1.SelectedItem.ToString()

  Try

    Dim f = m_SourcePath + "\" + fName

    Cursor.Current = Cursors.WaitCursor
    AxQTControl1.URL = f
    Cursor.Current = Cursors.Default

  Catch ex As COMException

    msg = "Error loading file: " + fName
    msg += " (" + Hex(ex.ErrorCode) + ")"

  End Try

  StatusBar1.Text = msg

End Sub
```

Note the exception handler: there is a distinct possibility of something going wrong should we attempt to load a corrupt file, or a file type that cannot be imported by QuickTime.

An interesting and useful refinement would be the ability to define the *in* and *out* points for each source clip so that, rather than appending the entire clip to the destination movie, only that portion of the clip between its *in* and *out* points gets added. The movie selection is ideally suited to this purpose, as Figure 6.5 illustrates, since it is possible to set the selection using the movie controller bar (just hold down the Shift key while clicking and dragging in the controller). An added bonus is that the current selection is saved whenever the movie is saved so that the *in* and *out* points can be permanently saved for any clip.

Figure 6.5 Movie showing *in* and *out* points as start and end of the movie selection.

Even more useful for our editor users would be a real-time display of the position and length of the selection. This is easily accomplished by registering for the qtEventMovieSelectionDidChange event from the movie so that we are notified any time the selection changes.

With these additions, our SelectedIndexChanged handler starts to become a little more complex. To ensure that any changes to the movie selection are saved before another movie is opened, we check the m_bSelectionChanged flag and save the movie if necessary:

```
'Save changes to current movie
If Not AxQTControl1.Movie Is Nothing Then
  With AxQTControl1.Movie
    If m_bSelectionChanged And .CanUpdateMovieFile Then
      AxQTControl1.Movie.Save()
    End If
  End With
End If
```

Unnecessary movie saves are avoided by using the Boolean flag m_bSelectionChanged, which gets set any time the movie selection is changed in our qtEventMovieSelectionDidChange handler:

```
Private Sub AxQTControl1_QTEvent(...) Handles AxQTControl1.QTEvent

    Select Case e.eventID
```

```
      Case QTEventIDsEnum.qtEventMovieSelectionDidChange
        m_bSelectionChanged = True
        lblSelection.Text = GetMovieSelectionInfo(AxQTControl1.Movie)

    End Select

End Sub
```

lblSelection is a text label underneath the source movie that displays the current selection information. It is updated when the movie is opened, and any time the selection is changed. GetMovieSelectionInfo returns a string with the selection details for a movie:

```
Private Function GetMovieSelectionInfo(ByVal mov As QTMovie) As String

  Dim s = ""
  GetMovieSelectionInfo = ""

  If mov Is Nothing Then Exit Function
  s += "Selection: "
  With mov
    If .SelectionDuration = 0 Then
      s += "none"
    Else
      s += "start : "
      s += CStr(GetTimeCode(mov, .SelectionStart))
      s += "  length : "
      s += CStr(GetTimeCode(mov, .SelectionDuration))
    End If
  End With
  GetMovieSelectionInfo = s

End Function
```

Condemning our long-suffering editor to work in units of movie time would be to impose an unnatural burden, and so we use the function GetTimeCode to translate movie time into a format that is more familiar to video editors. The timecode format is as follows:

< hours > : < minutes > : < seconds > . < movie time units > = hh:mm:ss.tt

Hours, minutes, and seconds should be self-explanatory: the fourth field represents a fraction of a second and is denominated in units of movie time, as defined by the movie's time scale. So, if a movie has a typical time scale of 600, the last field would be in the range 0–599. For example, the timecode 01:35:46.120 is equivalent to 1 hour, 35 minutes, 46 seconds, and 120/600ths of a second, for a movie whose time scale is 600. In passing, it's worth noting that if the movie's frame rate is the same as its time scale, the last field may also be interpreted as frames—hh:mm:ss.ff.

```
'Converts movie time to timecode (HH:MM:SS.ttt) format
Private Function GetTimeCode(ByVal mov As QTMovie, ByVal t As Long)

  Dim ss As Long, mm As Long, hh As Long, tt As Long

  Dim dSecs As Double = t / mov.TimeScale
  Dim totalSecs As Long = Math.Floor(dSecs)

  ss = totalSecs Mod 60
  mm = totalSecs \ 60
  hh = mm \ 60
  mm = mm Mod 60
  hh = hh Mod 24

  tt = t - (totalSecs * mov.TimeScale)

  GetTimeCode = Format(hh, "00:") + Format(mm, "00:") +
          Format(ss, "00") + "." + Format(tt, "000")

End Function
```

The complete enhanced SelectedIndexChanged handler follows:

```
Private Sub CheckedListBox1_SelectedIndexChanged(...)
          Handles CheckedListBox1.SelectedIndexChanged

  Dim msg As String = ""
  Dim fName As String = CheckedListBox1.SelectedItem.ToString()

  Try
```

```
    'Save changes to current movie
    If Not AxQTControl1.Movie Is Nothing Then
      With AxQTControl1.Movie
        If m_bSelectionChanged And .CanUpdateMovieFile Then
          AxQTControl1.Movie.Save()
        End If
      End With
    End If


    'Load next movie
    Dim f = m_SourcePath + "\" + fName

    Cursor.Current = Cursors.WaitCursor
    AxQTControl1.URL = f

    m_bSelectionChanged = False

    lblSelection.Text = GetMovieSelectionInfo(AxQTControl1.Movie)

    With AxQTControl1.Movie
      .EventListeners.Add(QTEventClassesEnum.qtEventClassStateChange,
          QTEventIDsEnum.qtEventMovieSelectionDidChange)

    End With

  Catch ex As COMException

    msg = "Error loading file: " + fName
    msg += " (" + Hex(ex.ErrorCode) + ")"

  Finally

    Cursor.Current = Cursors.Default

  End Try

  StatusBar1.Text = msg

End Sub
```

Returning once more to our core objective, let's look at the code required to assemble the new movie from our collection of clips. The first thing to do is to create a new empty destination movie in AxQTControl2 using CreateNew-Movie. Then we need to iterate over the checked file names in CheckedListBox1 using its convenient CheckedItems collection. Each source movie is loaded in turn into AxQTControl1; the selection can be copied to the clipboard and then pasted into the destination movie (AxQTControl2) using just a few lines of code:

```
If AxQTControl1.Movie.SelectionDuration = 0 Then
  AxQTControl1.Movie.SelectAll()
End If


AxQTControl1.Movie.Copy()
AxQTControl2.Movie.Paste()
```

While this does indeed serve the purpose perfectly adequately, copy and paste via the clipboard is really a bit of a blunt instrument, and it can be slow. Fortunately, there is a better way: the InsertSegment method of QTMovie directly copies a movie segment from another QTMovie object, avoiding the need for the clipboard stopover entirely. This useful method has the following parameters, the last three of which are optional:

srcMovie	: The source QTMovie object from which the segment is to be copied.
srcStartTime	: The start time (in movie units) of the selection to be copied from the source movie. Defaults to the current selection start time if not supplied.
srcDuration	: The duration (in movie units) of the selection to be copied from the source movie. Defaults to the current selection duration if not supplied.
insertionTime	: The time position (in movie units) at which the new segment should be inserted. Defaults to the current time if not supplied.

Rather than relying too much on the defaults for optional parameters (never a great idea), we will specify them fully as follows:

```
If AxQTControl1.Movie.SelectionDuration = 0 Then
  AxQTControl1.Movie.SelectAll()
End If
```

```
AxQTControl2.Movie.InsertSegment(AxQTControl1.Movie,
        AxQTControl1.Movie.SelectionStart,
        AxQTControl1.Movie.SelectionDuration,
        AxQTControl2.Movie.Duration)
```

This appends the current selection from AxQTControl1.Movie to the end of the movie in AxQTControl2 and is significantly more efficient than the equivalent copy and paste option.

The complete build movie routine is as follows:

```
Private Sub mnuBuildMovie_Click(...) Handles mnuBuildMovie.Click
  Dim i As Integer
  Dim fName As String
  Try
    tbLog.Text = ""
    AxQTControl2.CreateNewMovie(True)

    If AxQTControl2.Movie Is Nothing Then Exit Sub

    If CheckedListBox1.CheckedItems.Count = 0 Then Exit Sub

    For i = 0 To CheckedListBox1.CheckedItems.Count - 1

      fName = CheckedListBox1.CheckedItems(i).ToString

      AxQTControl1.URL = m_SourcePath + "\" + fName

      If Not AxQTControl1.Movie Is Nothing Then

        If AxQTControl1.Movie.SelectionDuration = 0 Then
          AxQTControl1.Movie.SelectAll()
        End If

        With AxQTControl2.Movie
          .InsertSegment(AxQTControl1.Movie,
            AxQTControl1.Movie.SelectionStart,
            AxQTControl1.Movie.SelectionDuration,
            .Duration)
```

```
                    tbLog.Text += fName + vbCrLf
                    tbLog.Text += "New Length : "
                    tbLog.Text += CStr(GetTimeCode(AxQTControl2.Movie,
                       .Duration)) + vbCrLf
                End With

                Application.DoEvents()

            End If
        Next i

        AxQTControl2.Movie.Rewind()
        AxQTControl2.Movie.SelectionDuration = 0

    Catch ex As COMException

        tbLog.Text = "Error : " + Hex(ex.ErrorCode)

    End Try

End Sub
```

Once the movie has been built, it can either be saved as a self-contained movie or exported to any desired format. The Save As... implementation is identical to that shown earlier in this chapter for Simple Player, except that the movie being saved is AxQTControl2.Movie. The Export... facility is equally straightforward.

```
Private Sub mnuExport_Click(...) Handles mnuExport.Click

    If AxQTControl2.Movie Is Nothing Then Exit Sub

    Try
        Dim qt As QTQuickTime = AxQTControl1.QuickTime
        If qt.Exporters.Count = 0 Then qt.Exporters.Add()
        Dim exp As QTExporter = qt.Exporters(1)
        exp.SetDataSource(AxQTControl2.Movie)
        exp.ShowExportDialog()
    Catch ex As COMException
```

```
If ex.ErrorCode = &H8004FF80 Then
  'Canceled - ignore
Else
  Dim msg As String
  msg = "An error occurred!" + vbCrLf + vbCrLf
  msg += "Error code : " + Hex(ex.ErrorCode) + vbCrLf
  MsgBox(msg, MsgBoxStyle.Critical)
End If

End Try

End Sub
```

Adding an Overlay

Branding has become a fixation with a lot of TV channels nowadays—so much so that they insist on having their logos conspicuously and intrusively superimposed on all transmitted output. Imagine that our fledgling Movie Builder application is destined for one of these identity-obsessed corporations and that we've been asked to provide a facility to automatically overlay the logo on each newly created movie.

Conceptually this is not particularly difficult in QuickTime: all that's required is to have the logo graphic in a separate video track that is in parallel with, and the same length as, the content video track (Figure 6.6). So long as the logo track is above the content track in the z-order, and is positioned correctly relative to the video track, QuickTime will ensure that the logo is superimposed on the entire movie clip.

Well, so much for the theory, but how do we achieve this in practice? We need some means of creating another video track. This comes in the guise of

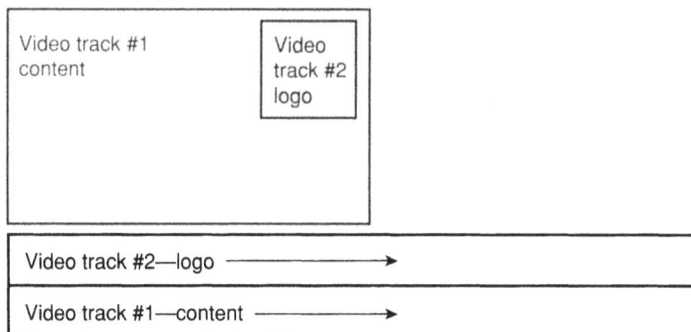

Figure 6.6 Logo video track superimposed on content video track showing spatial arrangement (above) and temporal arrangement (below).

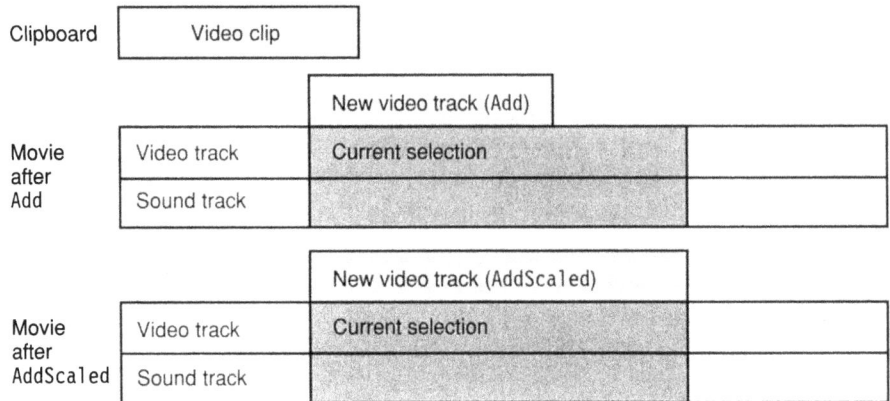

Clipboard	Video clip		

Figure 6.7 Comparison of `Add` and `AddScaled` methods.

the `Add` and `AddScaled` methods of `QTMovie`, both of which add the contents of the clipboard to the movie in a new track parallel with the current movie selection. In the case of `Add`, the new track starts at the beginning of the current selection, or the current movie time if there is no selection; the length of the new track is the length of whatever was on the clipboard. With `AddScaled`, the length of the new track is scaled to the length of the current movie selection or, if there is no selection, to the length of the entire movie. Figure 6.7 illustrates the difference. In both cases the X-Y dimensions of the new track will match those of whatever is on the clipboard.

So, in order to superimpose a logo on the movie, we can copy a logo graphic of the correct size to the clipboard (perhaps using `AxQTControl1`), select the entire destination movie, and then call `AddScaled`:

```
AxQTControl2.Movie.SelectAll()
AxQTControl2.Movie.AddScaled()
```

The logo will end up deposited in the top-left corner of our movie, and this may not be where we would ideally like to see it. However, since the logo is in a new track of its own, we can use the spatial properties of the track to position it wherever we want—perhaps in the top-right corner of the movie.

```
WithAxQTControl2.Movie
  Dim trkLogo As QTTrack = .Tracks(.Tracks.Count)
  If Not trkLogo Is Nothing Then
    trkLogo.left = .right - trkLogo.Width - 10
```

```
            trkLogo.top = 10
        End If
    End With
```

Note that since the logo track has just been added to the movie, it is always going to be the last track in the Tracks collection of the movie at this point.

While we're at it, we can impart a more professional look to the logo by blending it with the movie. When QuickTime renders a visual track, it uses the track's transfer mode to determine how the track is rendered onto the movie. The default transfer mode for a video track is a dither copy (qtTransferModeDitherCopy) that simply copies the track onto the underlying movie. By changing the TransferMode property of the logo track to one of the blend modes (see QTTransferModesEnum), the logo will be blended with the underlying movie. We even have some control over the degree of transparency with the OperationColor property, which takes a triplet of RGB values (in the range 0–65535) in the form of a comma-delimited string. The ultimate effect will of course depend on the combination of colors in the logo and the background movie itself. Finally, to ensure that QuickTime carries out this rendering operation to best effect, we set the track's HighQualityMode to True.

```
trkLogo.TransferMode =
            QTTransferModesEnum.qtTransferModeStraightAlphaBlend
trkLogo.OperationColor = "32768, 32768, 32768"        '50%
trkLogo.HighQualityMode = True
```

The end result is a logo neatly ensconced in the top corner of our movie as shown in Figure 6.8.

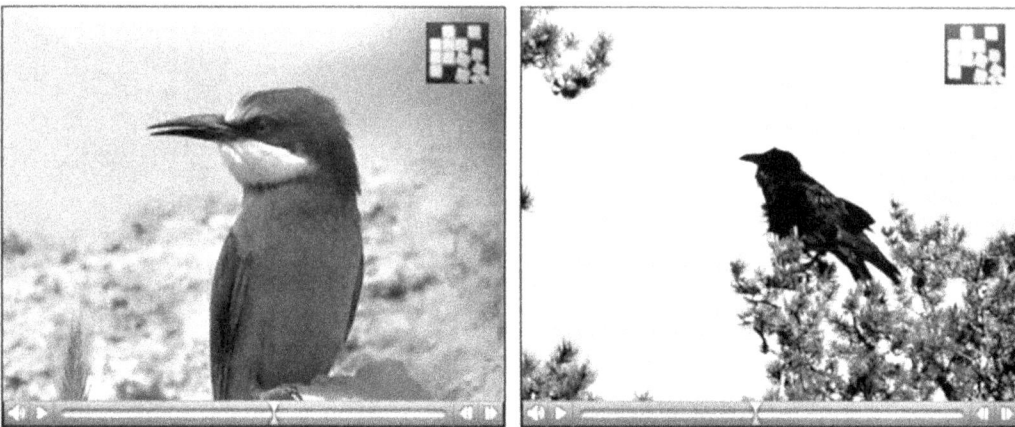

Figure 6.8 Movie with logo overlay.

The complete code listing for our logo overlay feature is shown below, demonstrating how OpenFileDialog1 is initially used in conjunction with AxQTControl1 to get the required logo graphic onto the clipboard in the first place:

```
Private Sub mnuInsertLogo_Click(...) Handles mnuInsertLogo.Click

  Try
    Dim filter As String = ""
    filter += "Images|*.bmp;*.gif;*.png;*.jpg;*.tif|"
    filter += "All files (*.*)|*.*"
    OpenFileDialog1.Filter = filter

    If OpenFileDialog1.ShowDialog() <> DialogResult.OK Then Exit Sub
    AxQTControl1.URL = OpenFileDialog1.FileName()

    AxQTControl1.Movie.Copy()

    With AxQTControl2.Movie
      .SelectAll()
      .AddScaled()
      Dim trkLogo As QTTrack = .Tracks(.Tracks.Count)
      If Not trkLogo Is Nothing Then
        trkLogo.left = .right - trkLogo.Width - 10
        trkLogo.top = 10
        trkLogo.TransferMode =
            QTTransferModesEnum.qtTransferModeStraightAlphaBlend
        trkLogo.OperationColor = "32768, 32768, 32768"
        trkLogo.HighQualityMode = True
      End If
      .Time = 0
      .SelectionDuration = 0
    End With

  Catch ex As COMException

    tbLog.Text = "Error : " + Hex(ex.ErrorCode)

  End Try

End Sub
```

Subtitling the Movie

Not content with automating the process of stamping a logo into the corner of each of the movies, our demanding client is now wondering aloud about whether it might just be possible to automatically add text subtitles as well! Tempting though it is to disabuse him of such a notion, coming as it does so late on a Friday afternoon, we have to grudgingly admit that, at least conceptually anyhow, this most certainly *is* possible.

Live text (as opposed to text that is burned into the video itself) in a QuickTime movie resides in a special type of track known as a *text track*. A text track contains a series of text samples, each with a start time. Just like any other visual track, the text track can run in parallel with other tracks and may be superimposed on top of them. But how do we go about adding a text track to the movie?

If you launch QuickTime Player and point it at a plain text file, this should give you a clue. Player will indeed open the file, creating a text track and adding a sample for each line in the file. Play the resulting movie, and each text sample will appear one after another frame by frame as the movie plays: this is the QuickTime text importer in action. It does in fact provide rather more sophisticated control over the creation of text tracks from text files. The key to this is the use of a special *text descriptor* that describes the text format and the individual text samples.

The following is an example of a simple text descriptor file:

```
{QTtext} {timeScale:30} {width:150} {height:40}
{timeStamps:absolute} {language:1} {textEncoding:0}
{font:Verdana} {size:12} {bold} {justify:center} {dropShadow:off}
{textColor: 65535, 65535, 65535} {backColor: 0, 0, 0}
[00:00:00.00]
Mary had a little lamb,
[00:00:03.00]
Her father shot it dead.
[00:00:05.00]
Now it goes to school with her
[00:00:09.00]
Between two chunks of bread.
[00:00:12.00]
```

The text descriptor always begins with {QTtext}, which is usually followed by some formatting details such as text font, size, and color. After that comes a series of text samples, each with a starting timecode in square brackets. The timecode in the very last line of the text descriptor is the time at which the text track should end, which often corresponds to the end of the movie. Full documentation for the QuickTime text descriptor format is available at

http://developer.apple.com/documentation/QuickTime/REF/
refDataExchange.6.htm

Opening the preceding text file in QuickTime Player, we get a movie with four frames, each displaying one text sample and lasting whatever length has been specified (Figure 6.9).

To add our subtitles track in Movie Builder, we need to do the following:

1. Get the subtitle for each constituent movie: this could, for example, come from the Full Name annotation (qtAnnotationFullName) of the movie.

2. Generate a text descriptor for the subtitles text track. This will contain a text sample for each of the individual movie clips that we used to build our composite movie, and each sample will begin at precisely the same time as each of the clips begins.

3. Save the subtitles text descriptor to a temporary file.

4. Open the subtitles text descriptor file in a QuickTime Control (AxQTControl1). If all goes well, the QuickTime text importer will ensure that we end up with a movie containing a single text track and of exactly the same length as our composite movie in AxQTControl2.

5. Copy the entire subtitles movie from AxQTControl1 to the clipboard. Add the contents of the clipboard to the composite movie in AxQTControl2. This will add a new subtitles text track in parallel with the movie, and at the top of the movie z-order so that it is superimposed on top of any other video track(s).

6. Position and format the subtitles text track.

[00:00:00.00]	[00:00:03.00]	[00:00:05.00]	[00:00:09.00] [00:00:12.00]
Mary had a little lamb,	Her father shot it dead.	Now it goes to school with her	Between two chunks of bread.

Figure 6.9 Movie containing text track imported from text descriptor.

Let's look at the code required to generate the text descriptor. The first thing to do is to write out the header formatting information for the track and text, carefully inserting the TimeScale and Width of the movie that we eventually want this track to overlay:

```
Dim td As String

If AxQTControl2.Movie Is Nothing Then Exit Sub

td = ""
td += "{QTtext} "
td += "{timeScale:" + CStr(AxQTControl2.Movie.TimeScale) + "} "
td += "{width:" + CStr(AxQTControl2.Movie.Width) + "} "
td += "{height:22}" + vbCrLf
td += "{timeStamps:absolute} {language:1} {textEncoding:0}" + vbCrLf
td += "{font:Verdana} {size:12} {bold} {justify:center}
         {dropShadow:off}" + vbCrLf
td += "{textColor: 65535, 65535, 65535} {backColor: 0, 0, 0}" +
         vbCrLf
```

The next step is to iterate over the constituent movie clips just as we did earlier to build the movie, except that this time we write out a timecode (currentTime, the cumulative time position in the movie) and the text (qt-AnnotationFullName) for each subtitle, followed, at the very end, by a final timecode corresponding to the end of the movie.

```
Dim currentTime As Long = 0

If CheckedListBox1.CheckedItems.Count = 0 Then Exit Sub

For i = 0 To CheckedListBox1.CheckedItems.Count - 1
  fName = CheckedListBox1.CheckedItems(i).ToString
  AxQTControl1.URL = m_SourcePath + "\" + fName

  If Not AxQTControl1.Movie Is Nothing Then

    td += "[" + CStr(GetTimeCode(AxQTControl1.Movie,
         currentTime)) + "]" + vbCrLf
```

```
            With AxQTControl1.Movie
              Try
                td += .Annotation(QTAnnotationsEnum.qtAnnotationFullName)
              Catch ex As Exception
                td += ""
              End Try
            End With
            td += s + vbCrLf

            If AxQTControl1.Movie.SelectionDuration = 0 Then
              currentTime += AxQTControl1.Movie.Duration
            Else
              currentTime += AxQTControl1.Movie.SelectionDuration
            End If

            Application.DoEvents()
          End If

      Next i

      td += "[" + CStr(GetTimeCode(AxQTControl1.Movie, currentTime)) + "]"
                + vbCrLf

      tbLog.Text = td
```

Dumping all this out to our log text field tbLog, the complete text descriptor should appear something like

```
{QTtext} {timeScale:600} {width:320} {height:22}
{timeStamps:absolute} {language:1} {textEncoding:0}
{font:Verdana} {size:12} {bold} {justify:center} {dropShadow:off}
{textColor: 65535, 65535, 65535} {backColor: 0, 0, 0}
[00:00:00.000]
Puffin
[00:00:09.408]
Blue-cheeked Bee-eater
[00:00:20.192]
Green Woodpecker
[00:00:34.000]
Raven
[00:00:48.360]
```

Saving this to a temporary file is really a piece of cake with the aid of System.IO.StreamWriter:

```
f = Application.StartupPath + "\subtitles.txt"
Dim sw As StreamWriter = File.CreateText(f)
sw.Write(td)
sw.Close()
```

Now that we have the subtitles text descriptor committed to a file, we can just open it with the QuickTime Control (AxQTControl1), invoking the magic of QuickTime's text importer in the process:

```
AxQTControl1.URL = f
```

At this point, if all has gone to plan, we should have two movies of the same length, as shown in Figure 6.10. The movie in AxQTControl2 is the new composite movie that we built earlier, and that in AxQTControl1 contains the subtitles text track. Combining the latter into the former, via the clipboard, is the next step.

Copying the entire text track movie, we Add it into the destination movie at Time = 0, creating a new text track in parallel with the existing movie. Note that AddScaled is *not* what we want here since both movies should be the same length in the first place, and even if they weren't, scaling the text track to fit the movie would defeat the purpose of our carefully generated timecodes.

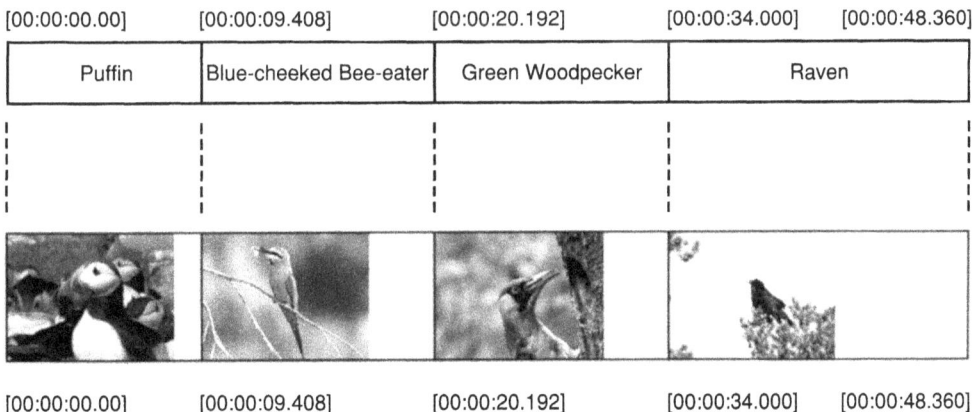

Figure 6.10 Movie containing text track in AxQTControl1 (top) ready to Add to composite movie in AXQTControl2 (bottom).

```
If Not AxQTControl1.Movie Is Nothing Then

  AxQTControl1.Movie.SelectAll()
  AxQTControl1.Movie.Copy()

  With AxQTControl2.Movie
    .SelectionDuration = 0
    .Time = 0
    .Add()
  End With

End If
```

Lastly, the positioning and formatting of the subtitles text track is similar to that for the logo track, except that we want the text track across the bottom of our movie. Giving it a 50 percent blend, along with the black background, produces a translucent effect that helps the subtitles to stand out, as can be seen in Figure 6.11.

```
With AxQTControl2.Movie

  Dim trkSubtitle As QTTrack = .Tracks(.Tracks.Count)
  If Not trkSubtitle Is Nothing Then
    trkSubtitle.top = .Height - trkSubtitle.Height
```

Figure 6.11 The final result: a movie with logo and subtitles.

```
    trkSubtitle.TransferMode =
            QTTransferModesEnum.qtTransferModeBlend
    trkSubtitle.OperationColor = "32768, 32768, 32768"
    trkSubtitle.HighQualityMode = True
  End If
  .Time = 0
  .SelectionDuration = 0
End With
```

Summary of the Edit Capabilities of QTMovie

Techniques similar to those we've just used in Movie Builder can, with a little ingenuity, be used to develop powerful tools for use in a production environment workflow. At the core of all of this are the various edit methods of QTMovie, which are summarized in Table 6.1.

Creating a Movie from Images

At their most basic, movies are comprised of individual frames. When creating QuickTime content, it is not unusual to have, as a starting point, a folder containing dozens—perhaps hundreds—of individual images that will end up as frames in the movie. Combining these together into a single movie can easily be accomplished using the same technique that we've used in Movie Builder, namely, opening an image in one QuickTime Control and inserting it into another. In fact, if you simply select a folder of images in Movie Builder, creating a movie from them will work perfectly well. You will end up with a movie containing a frame for each image with a default frame rate of 15 fps (frames per second). This movie can, of course, then be exported in any format you like.

But, yet again, there is an easier—and more efficient—way that involves handing more of the drudgery over to QuickTime. This is the CreateNew-MovieFromImages method of the QuickTime Control, which happily does exactly what it says on the label and creates for us a new movie from a folder full of images. The only proviso is that the images should be sequentially numbered so that QuickTime knows what order you want your movie's frames in. So, for example, the first image might be *Frame0001.png*, the second *Frame0002.png*, and so on. The source of the image sequence is immaterial: it might have been exported from an animation or a 3D rendering package, or it could be the product of time-lapse photography of a growing bacterial culture—anything that can produce a sequence of image files.

Table 6.1 The Edit Methods of `QTMovie`

Method	Parameters	Description
Add		Adds the contents of the clipboard in a new track in parallel with the current movie selection.
AddScaled		Adds the contents of the clipboard in a new track in parallel with, and scaled to the length of, the current movie selection.
Copy		Copies the current movie selection to the clipboard.
CopyFrame	Time (Long) [optional]	Copies a single frame from the movie to the clipboard, optionally at a specified movie time.
Cut		Cuts the current movie selection to the clipboard.
DeleteSelection	StartTime (Long) [optional] Duration (Long) [optional]	Deletes the current selection, or a specified segment, from the movie.
InsertEmptySegment	StartTime (Long) Duration (Long)	Inserts an empty segment into the movie.
InsertSegment	srcMovie (QTMovie) srcStartTime (Long) [optional] srcDuration (Long) [optional] insertionTime (Long) [optional]	Inserts all or part of another movie into the current movie, optionally at a specified movie time.
Paste		Pastes the contents of the clipboard into the movie at the current movie time.
ReplaceSelection		Replaces the current movie selection with the contents of the clipboard.
ScaleSegment	newSegmentDuration (Long) oldSegmentStart (Long) [optional] oldSegmentDuration (Long) [optional]	Scales the current movie selection, or a specified segment of the movie, to a new duration.
TrimToSelection		Trims the movie leaving only the current selection.
Undo		Undoes the last movie edit.

CreateNewMovieFromImages takes the following parameters:

bstrFirstFilePath	:	The full path, including file name, of the first image in the sequence
rate	:	Play rate of the new movie (Single) in either fps or spf (seconds per frame)
rateIsFramesPerSecond	:	True : rate is in frames per second False : rate is in seconds per frame

The code below pops up a File Open dialog prompting for the name of the first image in the sequence. Once a file name has been chosen, Create-NewMovieFromImages is invoked to generate a movie that is 12.5 fps.

```
Private Sub mnuMovieFromImages_Click(...)
        Handles mnuMovieFromImages.Click

  Try
    Dim filter As String = ""
    filter += "Images|*.bmp;*.gif;*.png;*.jpg;*.tif|"
    filter += "All files (*.*)|*.*"
    OpenFileDialog1.Filter = filter

    If OpenFileDialog1.ShowDialog() <> DialogResult.OK Then Exit Sub

    AxQTControl2.CreateNewMovieFromImages
            (OpenFileDialog1.FileName(), 12.5, True)

  Catch ex As COMException

    tbLog.Text = "Error : " + Hex(ex.ErrorCode)

  End Try

End Sub
```

● SMIL the Movie

So far in this chapter, the assumption has been that a movie can only be constructed from source material in a piecemeal fashion, adding a movie clip here, or a text track there until we have built up the complete movie that we want. Indeed, this is the way in which many of us tackle DIY jobs: we start out with a grand idea and dive in with more enthusiasm than ability, cobbling bits together and tacking things on. The sensible alternative, of course, would be to devote our energies to sketching out proper plans, before handing the whole lot over to a professional builder and heading to the mountains for a few days.

Well, the good news, at this point in our story, is that QuickTime *is* that construction professional: everything that we so laboriously achieved with our carefully crafted code in Movie Builder—well, QuickTime can just about do it all for us. All we need do is draw up the plans and hand them over.

The secret here is SMIL (pronounced, "smile") or *Synchronized Multimedia Integration Language*, an XML-based description language for integrating diverse media elements into a single synchronized presentation. SMIL is a W3C recommendation and, as such, enjoys widespread industry support. QuickTime supports a useful subset of the SMIL standard and offers a few extensions of its own. If we can describe the composite movie we want in SMIL, then QuickTime can import our SMIL description and present us with the finished movie, so the theory goes.

New to SMIL?

If you're new to SMIL, there are several good tutorials out there on the Web, and I would recommend skimming through at least one of them before continuing.

W3 School

www.w3schools.com/smil/default.asp

QuickTime and SMIL

*http://developer.apple.com/documentation/QuickTime/IQ_InteractiveMovies/
quicktimeandsmil/chapter_10_section_1.html*

Synchronized Multimedia on The Web

www.webtechniques.com/archives/1998/09/bouthillier/

The easiest way to explain the power of SMIL, in this context, is to assemble a SMIL document that describes, as closely as possible, the composite movie that we were able to create with Movie Builder. You will recall that this consisted of a series of movies concatenated together into a single movie, with the addition of logo and subtitle overlays.

A SMIL document has two main sections: the `<head>` section that describes the layout and the `<body>` section that defines the content that gets presented in the layout. The `<layout>` section defines one or more regions, and each media element in the body section is then associated with a particular region. A very simple SMIL document that presents a single movie looks like this:

```
<?xml version="1.0"?>
<smil xmlns:qt="http://www.apple.com/quicktime/resources/
            smilextensions"
    qt:time-slider="true">
  <head>
    <layout>
      <root-layout width="320" height="240"
            background-color="white" />
      <region id="r1" left="0" top="0" width="320" height="240" />
    </layout>
  </head>
  <body>
    <par>
      <!-- Video Track -->
      <video src="../Birds/099178_V003_GreenWoodpecker.mov"
            region="r1" />
    </par>
  </body>
</smil>
```

The <video> element is associated with region *r1* and has a src attribute containing the URL to the movie itself. This URL can be absolute, or, as in this instance, it can be relative to the location of the SMIL document.

To define a sequence of movies one after the other in SMIL, we use a <seq> element in the body section. When this sequence plays, each movie starts as soon as the previous movie has finished:

```
<body>
  <seq>
    <video src="../Birds/063020_V001_Puffin.mov" region="r1" />
    <video src="../Birds/087018_V002_BlChkdBeeeater.mov"
            region="r1" />
    <video src="../Birds/099178_V003_GreenWoodpecker.mov"
            region="r1" />
    <video src="../Birds/173110_V006_Raven.mov" region="r1" />
  </seq>
</body>
```

Adding the logo is a little more of a challenge. We need to add an image element in parallel with the preceding sequence, and we need to make sure that it remains visible for the entire length of the sequence. Since the logo is in a different spatial location from the main video that plays in region *r1*, we need to define a new region *r2* located in the top-right corner of the movie, as well as the correct size for our logo.

```
<layout>
  <root-layout width="320" height="240" background-color="white" />
  <region id="r1" left="0" top="0" width="320" height="240" />
  <region id="r2" left="270" top="10" width="40" height="38" />
</layout>
```

Adding in the logo then involves adding a <par> or parallel <img> element, whose src is our chosen logo graphic and which is located in region *r2*:

```
<body>
  <par>
    <seq id="s1">
      <video src="../Birds/063020_V001_Puffin.mov" region="r1" />
      <video src="../Birds/087018_V002_BlChkdBeeeater.mov"
            region="r1" />
      <video src="../Birds/099178_V003_GreenWoodpecker.mov"
            region="r1" />
      <video src="../Birds/173110_V006_Raven.mov" region="r1" />
    </seq>
    <img region="r2" src="../Birds/Logo.png"
            qt:composite-mode="blend;50%" end="id(s1)(end)" />
  </par>
</body>
```

To ensure that our logo doesn't fizzle out before the end of our movie sequence, we set its end attribute so that it ends at the same time as the sequence whose id is *s1*:

```
end="id(s1)(end)"
```

And, using one of the QuickTime SMIL extensions, we can even specify the graphics transfer mode for our logo, confusingly called qt:composite-mode:

```
qt:composite-mode="blend;50%"
```

Finally, all that remains is to overlay the subtitles. For these we will require a third region, this time across the bottom of the movie:

```
<layout>
  <root-layout width="320" height="240" background-color="white" />
  <region id="r1" left="0" top="0" width="320" height="240" />
  <region id="r2" left="270" top="10" width="40" height="38" />
  <region id="r3" left="0" top="220" width="320" height="20" />
</layout>
```

The subtitle itself can be described in a SMIL <text> element whose src attribute contains, not a URL this time, but a QuickTime text descriptor:

```
<text src="data:text/plain,{QTtext}{font:Arial}{size:12}{bold}
        {width:320}{height:20} Puffin"

    region="r3" end="id(v1)(end)" qt:composite-mode="blend;50%" />
```

The text descriptor is prefixed with a data specifier and MIME type ("data:text/plain") to distinguish it as in-line data rather than a URL, and it can specify a series of timecoded text samples just as we used earlier for creating a text track.

To add the subtitles, we need another parallel track. We have a choice here. We could use a single <text> element in parallel with the entire movie sequence, containing a series of text samples carefully timed to appear at the point that each movie begins. Or, we could be a little lazier (or more robust, depending on your point of view) and simply add a <text> element in parallel with each of the movies in our sequence. Opting for the latter, we tie a <text> element to each video element inside a dedicated <par> element:

```
<par>
  <video region="r1" id="v1" src="../Birds/063020_V001_Puffin.mov" />
  <text region="r3" end="id(v1)(end)" qt:composite-mode="blend;50%"
        src="data:text/plain,{QTtext}{font:Arial}{size:12}{bold}
        {width:320}{height:20} Puffin" />
</par>
```

Notice again how we must force the text to hang out to the bitter end by slaving its end attribute to the end of the associated video track.

The complete SMIL description for our composite movie follows:

```
<?xml version="1.0"?>
<smil xmlns:qt="http://www.apple.com/quicktime/resources/
          smilextensions" qt:time-slider="true">
  <head>
    <layout>
      <root-layout width="320" height="240" background-color="white" />
      <region id="r1" left="0" top="0" width="320" height="240" />
      <region id="r2" left="270" top="10" width="40" height="38" />
      <region id="r3" left="0" top="220" width="320" height="20" />
    </layout>
  </head>
  <body>
    <par>
    <seq id="s1">
      <par>
        <video region="r1" id="v1" src="../Birds/
            063020_V001_Puffin.mov" />
        <text region="r3" end="id(v1)(end)"
            qt:composite-mode="blend;50%"
            src="data:text/plain,{QTtext}{font:Arial}{size:12}{bold}
            {width:320}{height:20} Puffin" />
      </par>
      <par>
        <video region="r1" id="v2" src="../Birds/
            087018_V002_BlChkdBeeeater.mov" />
        <text region="r3" end="id(v2)(end)"
            qt:composite-mode="blend;50%"
            src="data:text/plain,{QTtext}{font:Arial}{size:12}{bold}
            {width:320}{height:20} Blue-cheeked Bee-eater" />
      </par>
      <par>
        <video region="r1" id="v3" src="../Birds/
            099178_V003_GreenWoodpecker.mov" />
        <text region="r3" end="id(v3)(end)"
            qt:composite-mode="blend;50%"
            src="data:text/plain,{QTtext}{font:Arial}{size:12}{bold}
            {width:320}{height:20} Green Woodpecker" />
      </par>
      <par>
```

```
        <video region="r1" id="v4" src="../Birds/
            173110_V006_Raven.mov" />
        <text region="r3" end="id(v4)(end)"
            qt:composite-mode="blend;50%"
            src="data:text/plain,{QTtext}{font:Arial}{size:12}{bold}
            {width:320}{height:20} Raven" />
          </par>
        </seq>
        <img region="r2" qt:composite-mode="blend;50%" src="../Birds/
            Logo.png"
            end="id(s1)(end)"   />
      </par>
    </body>
</smil>
```

A credible alternative implementation for Movie Builder, then, would be to generate a SMIL description similar to the preceding, and then open it in a QuickTime Control. In practice, playback performance of SMIL sequences is not always what it should be in QuickTime, but once you export the sequence as a new movie, you will end up with a movie that is virtually indistinguishable from the one created the hard way.

SMIL is a serious tool in the portfolio of anyone working in QuickTime production. Since SMIL descriptions are well-formed XML, any software or tools that can generate or manipulate XML can readily be used, including the XML tools built into .NET in the form of System.Xml.

Unfortunately, the QuickTime SMIL implementation has remained rather static since its inception with QuickTime 5, so many of the features of the newer SMIL versions are not supported. This makes for interoperability problems with other SMIL players. Thus, despite its promise, SMIL has never really developed as a universal media integration standard, which is a pity.

Creating a Movie Using GDI

It's not difficult to think of cases where the frames for a movie come, not from a collection of image files somewhere on the hard disk, but directly from an application that generates them—perhaps using the graphical libraries supported by the .NET Framework, such as GDI +. This is likely to be the case, for example, with computer-generated graphics, or movie scenes rendered using powerful dedicated software, or perhaps even with the more prosaic output from a scientific experiment.

As with examples earlier in this chapter, the staging ground between graphic and movie is the clipboard. Each time our application generates a new graphic, it must put it on the clipboard and then paste it into the movie under construction. This technique works very well, the only downside being the evident inefficiency of copying to and from the clipboard.

Let's look at a very simple example, this time in C# for a change. We will create a movie by drawing its frames one by one, adding a random colored ball in each frame (Figure 6.12). A rather trivial example, admittedly, but given what *could* be done with GDI+, you will appreciate the potential. This sample can be found on the website

www/skylark.ie/qt4.net/Samples/GDICreateMovie

We start off with a single form with a QuickTime Control on it (axQTControl1) and a button. The first thing we must do is create a Bitmap into which we will draw each frame. We keep this in a member variable (m_bmpFrame) to avoid having to re-create it every time we draw a frame, and we initialize it in the form's Load event handler:

Figure 6.12 Computer-generated movie.

```
// C#
private Bitmap m_bmpFrame = null;

private void OnLoad(object sender, System.EventArgs e)
{
  m_bmpFrame = new Bitmap(300,300);
}
```

Clicking the button on the form gets the ball rolling, so to speak. In the initialization process, we create a new and empty movie in axQTControl1, and clear m_bmpFrame to white. Generating the movie then involves calling AddNewMovieFrame repeatedly until we have as many frames as we want.

```
// C#
private void OnCreateMovieClick(object sender, System.EventArgs e)
{
  axQTControl1.CreateNewMovie(true);

  int frameCount = 100;

  Graphics g = Graphics.FromImage(m_bmpFrame);
  g.FillRectangle(new SolidBrush(Color.White),
          new Rectangle(0,0,320,240));
  g.Dispose();

  for(int i = 0; i < frameCount; i++)
  {
    AddNewMovieFrame(axQTControl1.Movie);
  }

  axQTControl1.Movie.SetSelection(0, 0);
  axQTControl1.Movie.Time = 0;

}
```

Adding a new frame to the movie consists of drawing the new frame onto our Bitmap, setting the Bitmap onto the clipboard, and finally calling the movie's Paste method to actually append the frame to the movie:

```csharp
// C#
private void AddNewMovieFrame(QTOLibrary.QTMovie mov)
{
  DrawRandomBallFrame(m_bmpFrame);

  DataObject dataobj = new DataObject();
  dataobj.SetData(DataFormats.Bitmap, m_bmpFrame);
  Clipboard.SetDataObject(dataobj);

  if (mov != null)
    mov.Paste();
}
```

DrawRandomBallFrame is the function that draws an individual frame, taking the Bitmap as a parameter. Picking a random color and size, it plops a single ball somewhere on the Bitmap.

```csharp
// C#
private void DrawRandomBallFrame(Bitmap bmp)
{
  Graphics g = Graphics.FromImage(bmp);
  g.SmoothingMode = SmoothingMode.AntiAlias;

  Random rand = new Random();

  SolidBrush b = new SolidBrush(Color.FromArgb(rand.Next(255),
          rand.Next(255),rand.Next(255)));

  int rad = rand.Next(100);
  g.FillEllipse(b, rand.Next(bmp.Width), rand.Next(bmp.Height),
          rad, rad);

  g.Dispose();
}
```

Needless to say, the preceding draw function could do something considerably more sophisticated, not to mention useful, and that's really the whole point of this exercise: if your application can generate potential movie frames using GDI+, and get them onto the clipboard, you are well on the way to being able to generate content in any of the myriad formats that QuickTime supports.

Saving a New Movie

Once we have created a movie in the QuickTime Control, by whatever means, it is instructive to review our options for saving the new movie to a file. Essentially we have three choices:

- **Save the Movie.** Calling the movie's Save method and passing a file name will indeed create a new movie file. If we open this file in Quick-Time Player for a quick check, it will appear and play exactly as we would expect, with everything in place. A glance at the size of the file on disk, though, might cause some disquiet: it is likely to be unusually small—perhaps only several tens of kilobytes—and nowhere near what we might expect it to be, given all the movie clips or images we were under the impression we stuffed into it.

  Here's the explanation: when the contents of our new movie originated in other files, what actually gets added to the movie is a sequence of references to the data in its original source files, rather than a copy of the data itself. So when we Save the movie, only the data references get saved. You can easily see this if you create a movie from a sequence of movies in Movie Builder, Save it, and then open it in QuickTime Player. Choose Window | Show Movie Properties and select the Resources tab: you will see a list of all the original movie files from which your movie was constructed. Close the movie, move or rename any of these original files, and then attempt to reopen it. You will be confronted with an error message stating that one or more of your movie's resource files cannot be located.

  If we know that our original source files are going to stay where they are, movies containing just references can be a very efficient means of pulling together content from various sources without the overhead of actually having to copy large chunks of data. But, more often than not, this is decidedly not the way in which we want to save our new movie, which brings us to the other two options.

- **Save the Movie as Self-Contained**. If we want to be certain that all the data resources required by our new movie are indeed stored in the movie itself, then we should call SaveSelfContained rather than Save. This will copy all of the data from the various original sources into the new file so that the movie has no dependencies, but it doesn't do anything with that data, leaving it in its original format without any recompression. While nowhere near as quick as Save, SaveSelfContained can still be quite efficient since all it really has to do is to bulk-copy data from all the source files into the new movie file. The resulting movie, however, couldn't be considered in particularly good shape when it comes to efficient playback, since its data is not optimized in any way.

- **Export the Movie.** As we've seen in previous chapters, exporting the movie involves handing the movie over to a QTExporter object, which will recompress the movie data in the desired format, optimizing it for efficient playback and space utilization. While often time-consuming, especially with the most efficient codecs, this really is the only option for the final stage in your production workflow.

Summary

Hopefully, this chapter has opened up a window on all the possibilities for using the QuickTime Control in a production environment. You should now be familiar with the movie creation methods of the QuickTime Control, together with the various editing methods of the QTMovie object, that make all this possible. Using these capabilities effectively in the .NET and COM environments requires a range of techniques that we have explored conceptually and then implemented in working code samples. The use of SMIL introduces another dimension to the whole business of assembling and synchronizing content and has a very useful role to play in certain aspects of content production. If your workflow is likely to require the regular creation of QuickTime content on Windows, you stand to gain a lot by familiarizing yourself with what can be achieved using the QuickTime Control in combination with a few scripts.

7

Browsing the Media

Design and Build a
Complete QuickTime Application

For the Birds

If you were a nineteenth-century ornithologist and wanted to identify an unfamiliar bird, you generally had to be a pretty good shot—the standard of binoculars and telescopes was then just so poor. In fact, pick any leading Victorian ornithologist and you'll find that he (yes, invariably *he*) was quite handy with the rifle. Nowadays, as with big-game hunters, the rifle-toting birdwatcher is thankfully a fading memory, only to be replaced by an army of recreational birders wielding nothing more harmful than the latest bins, 'scopes, digital cameras, DV cameras, motorized lenses, PDAs, and digital sound gear, not to mention the obligatory designer birding jacket and pants. Well, at least the wee birds don't get hurt anymore, although sometimes I wonder what they make of it all.

When this lot come home, they no longer worry about how to keep the cat away from their catch before they get down to the taxidermist. Instead, they are faced with a whole new set of concerns: how to identify, label, and organize the hundreds of digital images, movie clips, sound clips, and field notes that comprise the 'catch.' The digital photography of birds has become so popular that an entire new subculture known as *digiscoping* has evolved around the activity of taking pictures with a digital camera stuck on the end of a telescope!

In fact, come to think of it, birds have to be the perfect subject for the new digital media collector: they form photogenic subjects for stills, unlike coins, for example; their flight and other movements make for stunning video sequences, unlike stamps; and, unlike trains, their evocative songs and calls just have to be captured on disk. And they generally don't bite.

In this chapter we are going to work through the development of a basic media browser application for a digital media collection such as this, using Visual Basic .NET and QuickTime. Rather than just hacking the sample together, we deliberately pay close attention to the design process. If you're relatively new to object-oriented programming, you should learn a little about the essential design process involved and how your own real-world projects will benefit from the application of sound design methodology. In the process, of course, we learn more about how the QuickTime Control can best be deployed in the object-oriented environment.

Design Decisions

Before launching straight into the fun bit—coding—most seasoned developers have learned to give in to their pangs of conscience and spend a little time beforehand considering functionality and design. Whatever software design paradigm you happen to subscribe to, it's hard to beat having some notion of what you plan to do before you start, even if the design process turns out to be highly iterative. Since we are using .NET, this inevitably means some object-oriented thinking. One of the most convincing benefits of the object-oriented programming (OOP) approach is the close synergy between the functionality and the software implementation of that functionality. Once you have worked out the various things your application needs to do, the objects that you need to implement these functions tend to fall quite naturally out of the process. And if they don't, you should probably worry about whether you really understand the problem in the first place.

The Objects

So, putting on our object-oriented thinking caps, what functionality will we require of our media browser and what objects will we need to implement it? First of all, assuming our collection of media files is organized in some kind of logical folder structure, we will need a folder or directory navigator so that we can find our way around the collection: a *DirectoryNavigator* object. Think the left-hand panel of Windows Explorer.

Now that we have a DirectoryNavigator to locate a folder of interest, we will want something like the right-hand panel of Windows Explorer in which to view the media files in that folder; let's call this our *MediaDisplayPanel* object. Of course, we could just list the names of all the media files in this panel, but that wouldn't exactly be mind-blowing. No, this is where Quick-Time comes in: we'll have QuickTime open each of the media files in the folder, if it can, and display the contents of that file, together with a few tidbits of useful information about the file. Recalling the sheer variety of media file types that QuickTime can open, you can begin to visualize the outcome.

If you're thinking slightly ahead of me at this point, you will already have realized that the MediaDisplayPanel will have to contain a collection of QuickTime Controls as child objects—one for each media file in the folder. The good news is that you're right; and the bad news? Well, you've fallen into the all-too-frequent trap of jumping to *implementation* decisions too early. For now, forget you know that such a thing as a QuickTime Control exists, and let's stick with high-level design. What we *can* say at this point is that the MediaDisplayPanel object should contain a *MediaViewer* object for each file in the folder, without making any assumptions just yet about how that MediaViewer object might be implemented.

What additional functionality might we wish for? How about a property inspector for the media files—one of those almost ubiquitous floating property palettes that can usually be found a right-click or two away in any serious application. Our *MediaInspector* object should display as much as possible of the metadata about a selected media file.

Finally, if our collection of objects is to coalesce as an application, we need some kind of overall container object: let's call this *MediaBrowser*. In addition to hosting the various objects we've just discussed, this container object must also provide some of the essentials of any application such as a menu bar and workspace.

Visualizing the Design

A propelling pencil is arguably one of the more essential tools in the object-oriented designer's toolbox. In conjunction with the back of a business card, beer mat, airplane sick bag, or, if all else fails, a clean sheet of white paper, you have a sophisticated visual design tool at your disposal. Use it! Visualizing the objects in our simple application so far, we can sketch a diagram like that shown in Figure 7.1.

The various objects that we've identified so far comprise the core functionality of our Media Browser, but they clearly can't stand on their own. It is the relationships and connections *between* the objects that really make our application tick. In common with most GUI applications, our Media Browser is predominantly event-driven.

This is where the visual sketch comes into its own: we can now begin to identify and add in the various events that will drive our application, as shown in Figure 7.2 and detailed in companion Table 7.1.

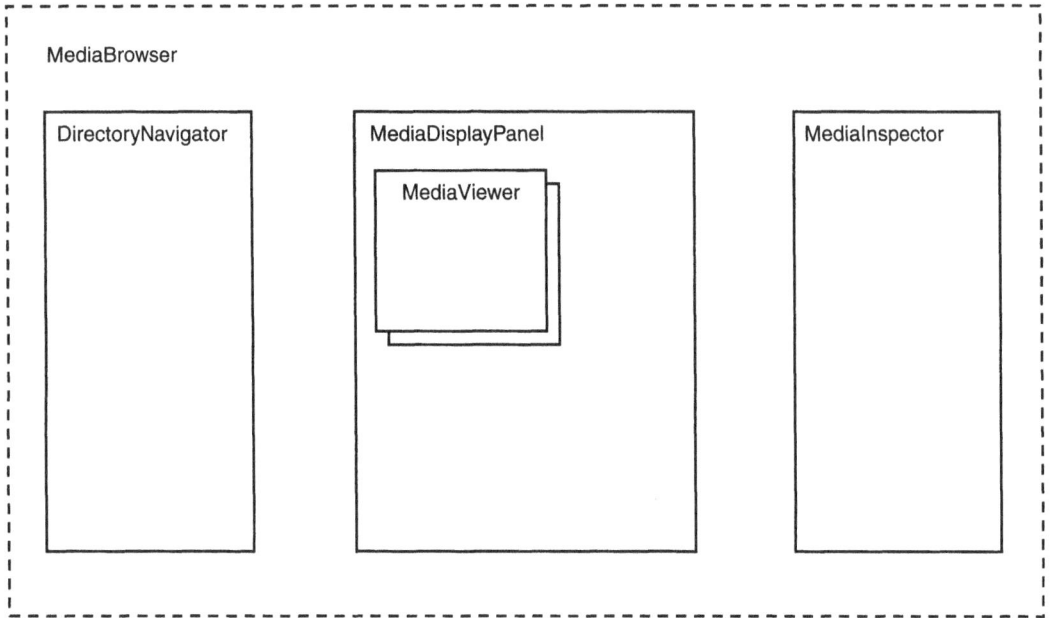

Figure 7.1 Visualizing the objects.

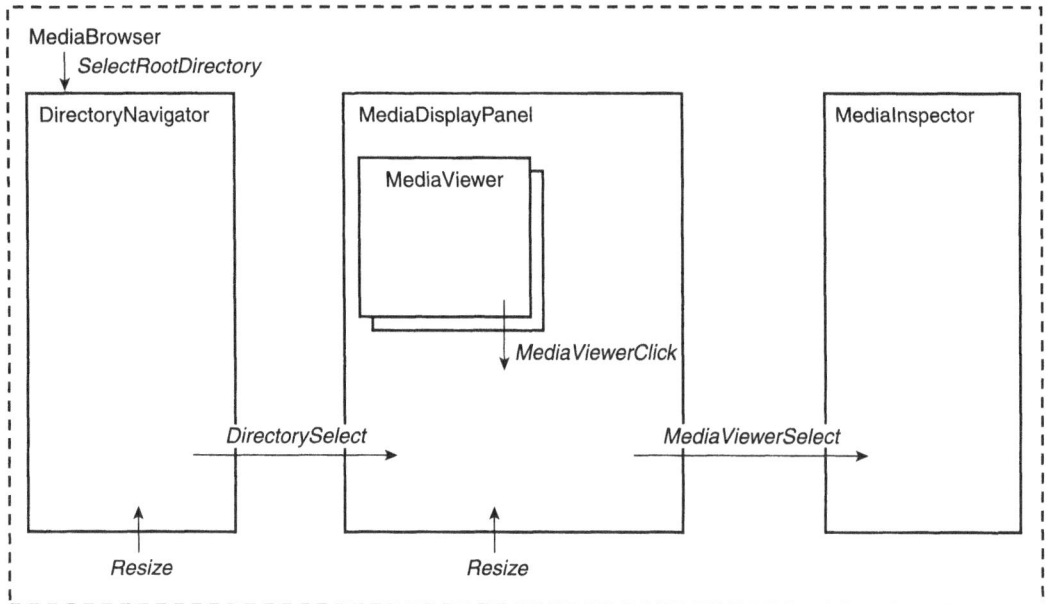

Figure 7.2 Visualizing the objects and the events that connect them.

Table 7.1 Principal Events in the Media Browser Application

Event	Source	Destination	Description
SelectRootDirectory	MediaBrowser via main menu	DirectoryNavigator	Assuming we have a main menu that allows the user to choose a root directory, this event is sent to the DirectoryNavigator and triggers it to load a new directory structure.
DirectorySelect	DirectoryNavigator	MediaDisplayPanel	Once a user selects a directory to browse, this event tells the MediaDisplayPanel to load a new set of files.
MediaViewerClick	MediaViewer	MediaDisplayPanel	When a MediaViewer is clicked, this event tells the MediaDisplayPanel to mark the MediaViewer as the currently selected viewer.
MediaViewerSelect	MediaDisplayPanel	MediaInspector	When a MediaViewer is selected, this event tells the MediaInspector to load a fresh set of data from the newly selected viewer.
Resize	MediaBrowser	DirectoryNavigator MediaDisplayPanel	When the application is resized, this event tells the DirectoryNavigator and MediaDisplayPanel to resize themselves. The MediaDisplayPanel should then reorganize its collection of MediaViewers.

In summary, we've now identified the core functional objects in our application and the key connections between those objects. Note that we very deliberately haven't yet talked much about user interface (UI), nor have we discussed any implementation details of the objects themselves. The object-based application that we have designed could in fact, at this stage, be implemented in any of a whole variety of different OOP languages and frameworks: C++, Java, Visual Basic, C#, Qt, REALbasic, to mention but a few.

Implementation

Having gotten the tedious bit out of the way, and brandishing our object-oriented design on the torn-off flap of a cornflake box, we can move on to worrying about more practical matters—like how to actually implement the design we've come up with.

Picking the Components

A core feature of the .NET Framework is *Windows Forms*—a rather unimaginative name for what turns out to be quite a comprehensive and useful collection of reusable standard UI objects. We begin our implementation design by looking carefully at each of our objects in turn and, where possible, selecting UI objects from Windows Forms upon which to base each object.

- `DirectoryNavigator`. Since any directory structure is essentially a tree structure, we must look for some kind of tree-view control that will allow us to display and navigate the structure. A tree-view is a very common UI requirement and it's not surprising to find the necessary class in Windows Forms known simply as `System.Windows.Forms.TreeView`. Unfortunately, the `TreeView` class out of the box is not smart enough to build itself from a directory structure, so some additional coding will be required.

- `MediaDisplayPanel`. Nothing particularly fancy required here: just a class capable of containing a collection of `MediaViewers` and managing them within a piece of screen real estate. Windows Forms has just such an unassuming class known as `System.Windows.Forms.Panel`. Not quite as dumb as it sounds, `Panel` inherits from `ScrollableControl` the ability to intelligently manage a scrolling display area, which turns out to be useful.

- `MediaViewer`. Clearly, this has to be based on the QuickTime Control. Incidentally, it's worth pointing out that the object-oriented design that we have come up with would equally allow the `MediaViewer` object to be implemented using a Windows Media Player control, a Flash control, or any other kind of media control, without fundamentally affecting the overall application design.

- `MediaBrowser`. Sticking to the conventional here, we will use a standard resizeable form with a `MainMenu` along the top and `StatusBar` along the bottom. The client area within the form will be divided between the `DirectoryNavigator` on the left and the `MediaDisplayPanel` on the right. A nice touch might be to add a `Splitter` object between the `DirectoryNavigator` and the `MediaDisplayPanel` so that their relative widths can be changed.

```
┌ ─ ─ ─ ─ ─ ─ ─ ─ ─ ─ ─ ─ ─ ─ ─ ─ ─ ─ ─ ─ ─ ─ ─ ─ ─ ─ ─ ─ ─ ─ ┐
│ MediaBrowser                                                  │
│ Form                                                          │
│  ┌──────────────────┐   ┌──────────────────┐  ┌────────────┐  │
│  │ DirectoryNavigator│  │ MediaDisplayPanel │  │MediaInspector│ │
│  │ TreeView         │   │ Panel            │  │ ??         │  │
│  │                  │   │  ┌─────────────────┐│  │            │  │
│  │                  │   │  │ MediaViewer     ││  │            │  │
│  │                  │   │  │ QTControl       ││  │            │  │
│  │                  │   │  │ (QuickTime Control)││  │            │  │
│  │                  │   │  │                 ││  │            │  │
│  │                  │   │  └─────────────────┘│  │            │  │
│  └──────────────────┘   └──────────────────┘  └────────────┘  │
└ ─ ─ ─ ─ ─ ─ ─ ─ ─ ─ ─ ─ ─ ─ ─ ─ ─ ─ ─ ─ ─ ─ ─ ─ ─ ─ ─ ─ ─ ─ ┘
```

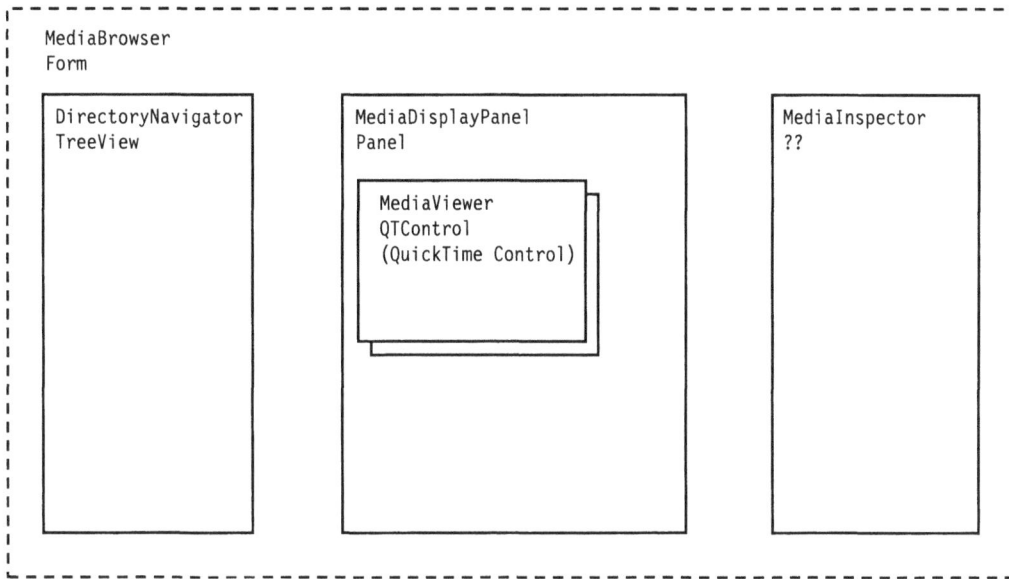

Figure 7.3 Media Browser application objects and their base classes.

- MediaInspector. We live in the real world, so let's just assume for now that we've only a vague idea what we might wish for here and postpone implementation decisions until later.

Now we can revisit our object diagram and fill in the names of the Windows Forms classes that we plan to use in the implementation of each object, as shown in Figure 7.3.

Having gone through this exercise, it should be apparent how much of the boilerplate functionality of our simple application the .NET Framework conveniently provides. Instead of wasting time reinventing basic UI elements, we can get on with wiring the .NET objects together and writing our own application code.

Building the Bare Bones

Even in a supposedly *Rapid* Application Development (RAD) environment such as Visual Basic .NET, assembling the bare bones of an application from scratch is always tedious. If you're like me, you invariably spend a while rooting through previous projects or samples looking for a starting point—anything to avoid File | New | Project.

To get started with this project, download the *MediaBrowserVB/BareBones* project from

www.skylark.ie/qt4.net/Samples

Just open MediaBrowserVB.sln in the *BareBones* folder. Start it (F5), and you'll be pleased to discover that I've saved you the trouble. In fact, I've even gone a little farther and created skeleton classes for the DirectoryNavi‐gator and MediaDisplayPanel and arranged for them to neatly fill the application form with a splitter bar in between.

So what have we got here? MainForm, as you might imagine, is our main application form, and it acts as a container for the DirectoryNavigator and MediaDisplayPanel (Figure 7.4).

As usual in Visual Basic .NET, we're faced with the conundrum of whether to place UI elements on the form in design mode or add them ourselves using handcrafted code in the New handler. In this case I've opted to give the form a menu bar in design mode and I've dropped a FolderBrowserDialog component on the form for later use. All the other setup code is in the InitializeMe rou-

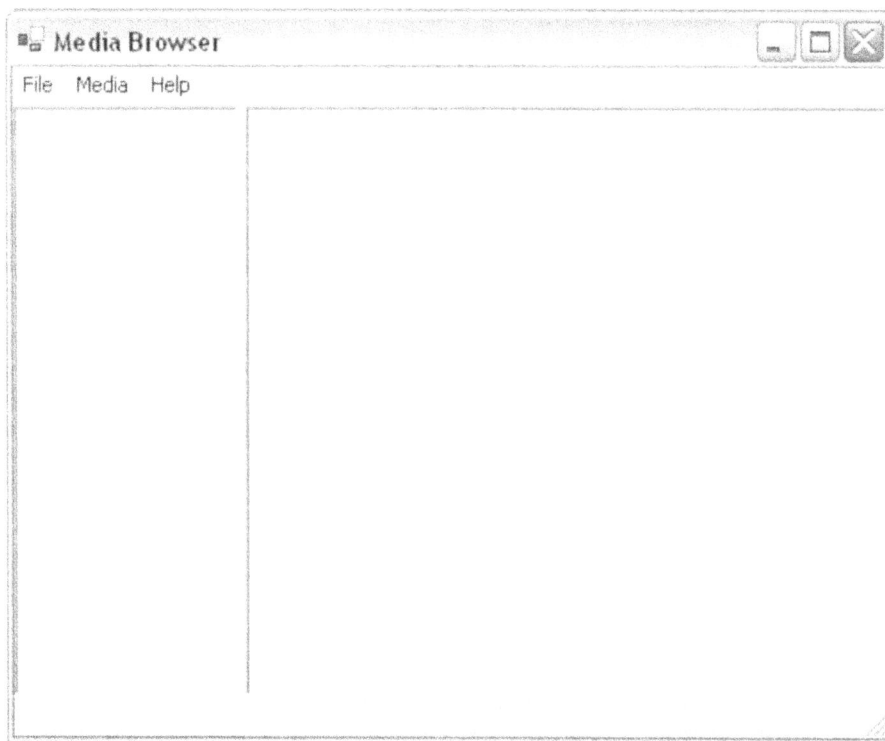

Figure 7.4 Bare-bones Media Browser.

tine that gets called at the end of New, after InitializeComponent has executed the autogenerated code from design mode. In InitializeMe you can see how we create and initialize the two principal child objects that will fill our form:

```
'Create a DirectoryNavigator
m_directoryNavigator = New DirectoryNavigator
m_directoryNavigator.Parent = Me
m_directoryNavigator.Dock = DockStyle.Left

'Create RHS display Panel
m_mediaDisplayPanel = New MediaDisplayPanel
m_mediaDisplayPanel.Parent = Me
m_mediaDisplayPanel.Dock = DockStyle.Fill 'Fills remainder of window
m_mediaDisplayPanel.BackColor = System.Drawing.Color.White
m_mediaDisplayPanel.BorderStyle = BorderStyle.Fixed3D
m_mediaDisplayPanel.AutoScroll = True
m_mediaDisplayPanel.SetAutoScrollMargin(15, 15)
```

Notice how the Dock property of both child objects is used to park the DirectoryNavigator on the Left and to allow the MediaDisplayPanel to Fill the rest of the available space. Setting AutoScroll = True for the MediaDisplayPanel immediately gives us all the benefits of a managed scrolling region, which we will come to appreciate later. The addition of a Splitter object between the two panels and a StatusBar at the bottom completes the initial layout of our form.

Before firing up our bare-bones application for the first time, let's take a quick look at the start-up code. While it might seem sensible to just have MainForm as the start-up object for our project, I've elected instead to use a Main subroutine in a separate module—MediaBrowser—as the entry point for our application. This has several advantages:

- We have a chance to carry out some initial checks *before* we attempt to load the main form. For example, we could check for the presence of QuickTime.

- Wrapping the loading of our MainForm with a Try...Catch construct allows us to gracefully handle any unexpected application errors that might occur anywhere in our application, since an exception will bubble up from wherever it was raised until it is eventually trapped here if not caught beforehand.

- It is often useful to load application configuration information as early as possible, since some of the application settings may well determine what happens during the subsequent start-up phase.

Every nontrivial application should have a configuration file of some sort, where settings and preferences can be stored and in this case, it's *Media-Browser.ini*:

```
[Settings]
RootPath=E:\Book\Data\Species
FileExtensions=jpg,bmp,gif,tif,png

[MediaDisplayPanel]
MarginWidth=15
ViewerWidth=128
ViewerHeight=96
ViewerSpacing=10
```

Sub Main() creates an instance of the IniFile class for reading and writing INI files and initializes it with the name of the INI file. Since the reference to our IniFile object, g_IniSettings, is declared Public within a module, it is available globally to other objects in the application—debatably one of the few legitimate uses for a global variable in an object-oriented application.

The MainForm menu events are wired up to Exit the application, to Open a new root folder, and to show the About dialog. The handy AboutForm class was borrowed from one of the .NET samples: it conveniently populates itself with information from its parent form and from the application assembly.

Press F5 and we have a great starting point for building the real meat of our application. Try dragging the splitter bar or resizing the main form and you'll recognize how much functionality we've essentially gotten "for free" from the .NET Framework and for very little effort.

Before moving on, I suggest you move to the *MediaBrowserVB/WorkIn-Progress* version of this project available from

www.skylark.ie/qt4.net/Samples

Directory Browsing

Our DirectoryNavigator class subclasses the Windows Forms TreeView control. Unfortunately, that really hasn't gotten us very far. In order to graphically represent our folder structure, we will finally have to give in and resort to some serious coding to turn our TreeView into a DirectoryNavigator.

A TreeView object is made up of a hierarchical set of TreeNode objects, where each TreeNode represents a named branch of the tree and may in turn have its own child nodes—ideally suited to graphically representing a directory structure. So populating our TreeView requires a straightforward walk through the directory tree structure within our root directory:

1. Add a TreeNode for the current directory.

2. Add a child TreeNode for each subdirectory to the node we just created.

3. Open each subdirectory, go back to step 1, and keep repeating this process until we end up at the leaves of the tree; that is, until we run out of subdirectories.

Many of you will instantly note the scope for recursion, but before looking at how we might implement this algorithm, let's start by configuring our DirectoryNavigator class. Each TreeNode can be assigned a label and a pair of images in its constructor. The images are set using indexes into an ImageList, which we set up in the New() routine of the DirectoryNavigator with one image to represent a closed folder and another for the open folder:

```
Me.ImageList = New ImageList
With Me.ImageList.Images
   .Add(New Bitmap("..\Images\FolderClosed.bmp"))
   .Add(New Bitmap("..\Images\FolderOpen.bmp"))
End With
```

Referring back to our design sketches, we can see that the DirectoryNavigator must respond to a SelectRootDirectory event by loading a new directory structure, and so we give it a Load method that takes an optional rootPath parameter.

```
Public Sub Load(Optional ByVal rootPath As String = "")

   BeginUpdate()     'Prevent repainting flicker while we add nodes

   Nodes.Clear()

   'Build root nodes of tree
   If rootPath <> "" Then
     Dim tnRootPath As New TreeNode(rootPath, 0, 1)
     Nodes.Add(tnRootPath)
     AddDirectories(tnRootPath)
```

```
      'Expand root node
      tnRootPath.Expand()
    Else
      'No root path so make disk drives the root nodes
      Dim diskDrives As String() = Directory.GetLogicalDrives()

      Dim drv As String
      For Each drv In diskDrives
        Dim tnDrive As New TreeNode(drv, 0, 1)
        Nodes.Add(tnDrive)
        AddDirectories(tnDrive)
      Next

    End If

    EndUpdate()

End Sub
```

If the rootPath parameter is present, then we create a new TreeNode object, give it the name rootPath, and add our new node to the Nodes collection of the TreeView. If no rootPath was passed in, we gather up a list of all the disk drives and add a new node for each to the Nodes collection.

But the real magic here is in AddDirectories, which simply takes a node representing a directory, obtains a list of all its subdirectories, and adds child nodes for each one:

```
Sub AddDirectories(ByVal tn As TreeNode)

  Dim di As DirectoryInfo
  Dim dirs() As DirectoryInfo

  tn.Nodes.Clear()

  di = New DirectoryInfo(tn.FullPath)

  Try
    'Get array of all subdirectories
    dirs = di.GetDirectories()
```

```
Catch exp As Exception
  Exit Sub
End Try


For Each di In dirs

  'Create a child node for every subdirectory, passing in
  'the directory name and the images its node will use
  Dim tnDir As New TreeNode(di.Name, 0, 1)

  ' Add the new child node to the parent node
  tn.Nodes.Add(tnDir)

  AddDirectories(tnDir)

Next
End Sub
```

Note use of `tn.FullPath`: the `FullPath` property of a `TreeNode` returns a delimited string of the labels of all the nodes in the complete path from its root node. Since we label our nodes with the name of the corresponding directory, and since the default delimiter or `PathSeparator` is a backslash (\), `FullPath` effectively returns just that—a full path to the directory represented by the node.

Intriguingly, `AddDirectories` calls itself for each of the new nodes it has added. This is known as a recursive call and makes for a very elegant solution: a single call to `AddDirectories` in the `Load` routine populates our entire `DirectoryNavigator`! Sadly, while it's certainly elegant, it's not really a lot of use in practice. Imagine calling

```
Load("c:\")
```

You might have time for a quick coffee while `AddDirectories` churns recursively through every folder on your drive adding thousands of nodes as it goes! So, sadly, the neat recursive bit gets commented out.

Thinking about it, however, it's obvious that we only really need to add nodes to our tree *on demand* whenever the user chooses to open a folder by expanding its node. And sure enough, `TreeView` has an `OnBeforeExpand` event that is just the ticket. We override this to call `AddDirectories` on demand for each child node of the node that the user has chosen to expand:

```
Protected Overrides Sub OnBeforeExpand(
        ByVal tvcea As TreeViewCancelEventArgs)

  MyBase.OnBeforeExpand(tvcea)

  BeginUpdate()    'Prevent repainting flicker while we add nodes

  Dim tn As TreeNode

  'Add child nodes for each child node in the expanded
  For Each tn In tvcea.Node.Nodes
    AddDirectories(tn)
  Next tn

  EndUpdate()

End Sub
```

Media Display

Now that we can use our `DirectoryNavigator` to select a folder of media files, let's move on to the `MediaDisplayPanel` that is going to provide us with a view of those files.

During the design discussion, I mentioned that the `MediaDisplayPanel` would manage a collection of `MediaViewer` objects: one for each media file in the selected folder. So, clearly, it will need methods to

- Load the `MediaViewer` objects from a directory in response to a `Directory-Select` event from the `DirectoryNavigator`.
- Lay out the `MediaViewer` objects within the available space on the `Media-DisplayPanel`.

Let's look at the `Load` subroutine. Having unloaded any existing `Media-Viewer` instances and switched the cursor to an hourglass—this could take a while—we get a list of all the files in the directory that was passed as a parameter to `Load`:

```
Public Sub Load(ByVal dir As String)

  'Save directory path
  m_directoryPath = dir

  'Clear any existing media viewers
  Unload()

  Cursor.Current = Cursors.WaitCursor 'This might take some time


  Dim di As New DirectoryInfo(m_directoryPath)
  Dim myFiles() As FileInfo

  'Get an array of all files in the directory
  Try
    myFiles = di.GetFiles("*.*")
  Catch
    MessageBox.Show("Unable to get list of files from folder:" & _
            vbCrLf & vbCrLf & m_directoryPath, "Error")
    Cursor.Current = Cursors.Default
    Return
  End Try

  ...

End Sub
```

The error trap here is useful in case for some reason our directory has gone away, for example, the DVD-ROM was ejected or a network share disappeared.

Now, while QuickTime is pretty adept at working out whether it can or cannot open a particular file, we may prefer a little more control over this. For example, confronted with a text file, QuickTime will quite happily make a movie out of it containing a text track with one frame per line in the file. However, reading text files with the aid of a movie controller isn't exactly pleasurable, so maybe we'd like a means of limiting the kinds of files that our Media Browser can open to certain types, such as MP3 files or Flash movies. For this purpose I've added a FileExtensions setting in *Media-Browser.ini* that contains a list of all the file extensions we would like to be able to browse. For example

```
FileExtensions=jpg,bmp,avi,pic,mov,dv,gif,tif,png,wav,aif,mpg,
              mp3,mp4,swf,m4a,m4p
```

This comma-delimited list of extensions is loaded from the INI file in the Form1_Load routine of MainForm, split into an array of strings, and passed to the MediaDisplayPanel by calling its SetExtensions method:

```
Private Sub Form1_Load(ByVal sender As System.Object, _
            ByVal e As System.EventArgs) Handles MyBase.Load

  Dim exts() As String

  exts = LCase(g_IniSettings.GetSetting("Settings",
          "FileExtensions", "jpg,mov")).Split(CType(",", Char))

  'Set qualifying file extensions
  m_mediaDisplayPanel.SetExtensions(exts)


  ...


End Sub
```

SetExtensions takes the array of strings and converts it into a StringCollection held in the m_extensionsCollection member variable:

```
Public Sub SetExtensions(ByVal exts() As String)
  m_extensionsCollection = New StringCollection
  m_extensionsCollection.AddRange(exts)
End Sub
```

Back in our Load routine, as we can see in the following listing, all we have to do is loop through the list of files we have obtained from the folder, filtering out any that don't have extensions in our list and creating new MediaViewer objects one by one to load the files that we *do* want to view.

```
Dim di As New DirectoryInfo(m_directoryPath)
Dim myFiles() As FileInfo

'Get an array of all files in the directory
```

```vbnet
Try
  myFiles = di.GetFiles("*.*")
Catch
  MessageBox.Show("Unable to get list of files from folder:" +
          vbCrLf + vbCrLf + m_directoryPath, "Error")
  Cursor.Current = Cursors.Default
  Return
End Try


'Load the media viewers one at a time
Dim fi As FileInfo
Dim ext As String
Dim mv As MediaViewer
For Each fi In myFiles

  ext = LCase(Mid(fi.Extension, 2))  'Strip period: ".JPG" -> "jpg"

  'Check if file extension in extensions collection
  If m_extensionsCollection.Contains(ext) Then

    'Create new media viewer
    Try
      mv = New MediaViewer

      'Configure media viewer
      mv.Parent = Me
      mv.Visible = False  'Keep hidden until after we position later
      mv.BorderStyle = BorderStyle.FixedSingle
      mv.Size = m_sizeViewer

      mv.Load(fi.FullName)

      'Add media viewer to controls collection of MediaDisplayPanel
      Controls.Add(mv)

    Catch e As Exception

      Dim errMsg As String = "Unable to load media viewer: "
      errMsg += "[" + fi.FullName + "]"
      errMsg += vbCrLf + e.Message
```

```
        Debug.WriteLine(errMsg)

        'Dispose of media viewer - we won't be needing it
        mv.Dispose()
        mv = Nothing

      End Try

    End If

  Next fi
```

Once each `MediaViewer` is created and loaded, we add it to the `Controls` collection of the `MediaDisplayPanel`. If an exception occurs while attempting to load a `MediaViewer`—the file might be corrupt—we log the error and dispose of the `MediaViewer`.

Media Viewer

Up to this point we haven't said a whole lot about the `MediaViewer` class that we have been so merrily creating instances of. What precisely is a `Media-Viewer`, and what is the code in the preceding Load routine actually doing?

Well, our `MediaViewer` class actually subclasses the QuickTime Control—it inherits all of its properties and methods:

```
Public Class MediaViewer
    Inherits AxQTOControlLib.AxQTControl
```

Why not just use the QuickTime Control as is instead of going to all this trouble? The answer is that, in line with good OOP practice, we want to wrap a layer of abstraction around the implementation details of the `Media-Viewer`. The `MediaDisplayPanel` should not need to be overly concerned with the precise semantics of the QuickTime Control. Rather, it should be able to deal with a more abstract `MediaViewer` class with a well-defined interface specific to its own needs.

This approach has several advantages:

■ Should a new or updated QuickTime Control come on the scene, any changes we may find necessary are likely to be confined to the private code of our `MediaViewer` class.

- If we opted to replace the QuickTime Control with some other media control, it is conceivable that we could create a drop-in replacement for our MediaViewer control.

Encapsulation vs. Inheritance

While subclassing allows us to inherit all the functionality and interfaces of the QuickTime Control, and to extend it, it does not provide any real degree of information-hiding or encapsulation. Encapsulation means literally putting something "inside a shell" and is one of the pillars of object-oriented design. If our MediaViewer were to *encapsulate* the QuickTime Control, instead of inheriting the QuickTime Control class, it would create its own private instance of the control through a private member variable.

```
'Subclass/Inheritance
Public Class MediaViewer
  Inherits AxQTOControlLib.AxQTControl
End Class

'Encapsulation
Public Class MediaViewer
  Private m_qtControl as AxQTOControlLib.AxQTControl

    Sub New()
      m_qtControl = New AxQTOControlLib.AxQTControl
    End Sub
End Class
```

None of the control's interface would be exposed, and all access would be through the public MediaViewer interface. Any class using MediaViewer would be dealing with a black box. While this degree of abstraction has some clear advantages, it does add an additional layer of complexity, since additional code has to be added to MediaViewer to access the encapsulated control.

Since, at this stage, we are more concerned with how our MediaDisplay-Panel class loads and positions MediaViewer objects than with the Media-Viewer itself, let's take advantage of the layer of abstraction we've allowed ourselves. Instead of having the MediaViewer subclass the QuickTime Control, let's forget about QuickTime for now and make our life a little simpler by having MediaViewer subclass a PictureBox, the Windows Forms class for displaying images:

```
Public Class MediaViewer
  Inherits PictureBox
```

Once we have everything working the way we want it with a Picture-Box-based MediaViewer, we'll see how easy it is to switch the base class of the MediaViewer back to the QuickTime Control class. Here's our starter Media-Viewer class:

```
Public Class MediaViewer
  Inherits PictureBox

  Private m_loadedFileName As String

  Public ReadOnly Property LoadedFileName() As String
    Get
      Return m_loadedFileName
    End Get
End Property

  Public Sub Load(ByVal fileName As String)

    m_loadedFileName = fileName

    If fileName = "" Then
      Image = Nothing
    Else
      Image = Image.FromFile(fileName)
      SizeMode = PictureBoxSizeMode.StretchImage
    End If

  End Sub

  'Unload viewer
  Public Sub Unload()

    m_loadedFileName = ""
    Image = Nothing

  End Sub

End Class
```

Notice that we have given the MediaViewer both Load and Unload methods together with a LoadedFileName property. These simple additions allow us to disguise the fact that we are working with a PictureBox. Later, when we switch MediaViewer to inherit the QuickTime Control class, we'll retain this interface so as not to disrupt the client (MediaDisplayPanel), even though the *implementation* of the methods will of course change.

Keeping the Viewers in Order

Having loaded a MediaViewer for each media file of interest in the selected directory, we turn our attention to the problem of how to lay out our collection of MediaViewer objects. Given that the media files, or at least those with a visual representation such as movies or images, are likely to come in a variety of different sizes and aspect ratios, it probably makes sense to use a fixed-size MediaViewer and to scale the media display accordingly. For our simple PictureBox-based MediaViewer, the following line does the trick by ensuring that the image loaded into the PictureBox is stretched to fit the control.

```
SizeMode = PictureBoxSizeMode.StretchImage
```

Later, when we introduce the QuickTime Control, we'll get more fussy about exactly how we control the scaling.

After each MediaViewer is created in the MediaDisplayPanel.Load routine, it is first hidden and then sized and given a single-pixel border:

```
mv.Parent = Me
mv.Visible = False  'Keep hidden until after we position later
mv.Size = m_sizeViewer
mv.BorderStyle = BorderStyle.FixedSingle
```

The member variable m_sizeViewer holds the required viewer size and is set through the MediaDisplayPanel.ViewerSize property. This is one of several layout settings that are read from the INI file in MainForm.Form1_Load.

The MediaDisplayPanel.PositionMediaViewers routine has the rather unenviable task of having to impose some spatial order on our collection of MediaViewer objects, such as arranging them neatly in a grid. We decreed earlier that they should all be the same size, so this makes the task a little easier. Here are the parameters we have to work with:

- MediaDisplayPanel width and height
- MediaViewer width and height (m_sizeViewer)

- Margin width, or distance between edge of panel and viewers (m_margin-Width)
- Viewer spacing, or distance between adjacent viewers (m_viewerSpacing)
- Number of MediaViewers

Pencil and paper come to the rescue here once again. Correctly visualizing this sort of problem is usually half the battle won, as can be seen in Figure 7.5.

Start with the assumption that that if we have too many viewers to display in the available space, we would rather they scrolled vertically—a bit like a long web page. Fortunately, the scrolling is taken care of for us since, as you will recall, MediaDisplayPanel inherits from Panel, which in turn inherits from ScrollableControl. But that still leaves us with the task of positioning the controls in a grid. To achieve this we first need to work out the maximum

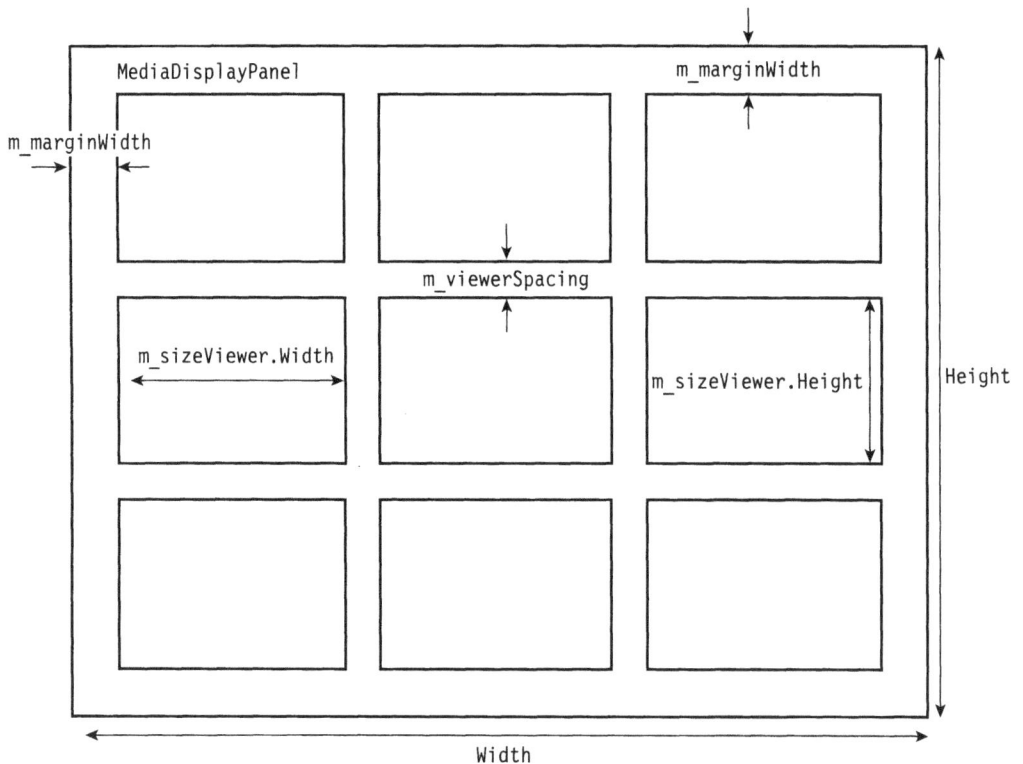

Figure 7.5 Parameters involved in positioning MediaViewers on the MediaDisplayPanel.

number of viewers that will fit across a single row in the available width, taking into account the desired margin and spacing:

```
'How many columns can we fit in available width?
nMaxCols = CInt(Math.Floor((Width - (m_marginWidth * 2)) /
         (m_sizeViewer.Width + m_viewerSpacing)))
```

Math.Floor ensures that we obtain the largest whole number of viewers that will fit; were we to use CInt on its own, it would be as likely to round up as down, leading us to believe that 4 viewers might fit where there is really only room for 3.8.

Now that we've figured out the number of columns, we can loop through our viewers collection and line them all up in a grid. Since our MediaDisplayPanel has no other child objects in it, we can safely assume that its Controls collection is synonymous with the collection of viewers.

```
'Position all the media viewers in a grid within the available space
Sub PositionMediaViewers()

  Dim nMaxCols As Integer, nCenterHOffset As Integer

  If Controls.Count = 0 Then Exit Sub

  'How many columns can we fit in available width?
  nMaxCols = CInt(Math.Floor((Width - (m_marginWidth * 2)) /
           (m_sizeViewer.Width + m_viewerSpacing)))

  'Position the media viewers
  Dim ctl As Control
  Dim locn As New Point
  Dim nCol As Integer, nRow As Integer

  nCol = 0 : nRow = 0
  For Each ctl In Controls

    If (nCol >= nMaxCols) Then
      nRow += 1 'New row
      nCol = 0
    End If
```

```
    locn.X = m_marginWidth +
            (nCol * (m_sizeViewer.Width + m_viewerSpacing))
    locn.Y = m_marginWidth +
            (nRow * (m_sizeViewer.Height + m_viewerSpacing))

    ctl.Location = locn
    ctl.Visible = True    'Show viewer

    nCol = nCol + 1

  Next ctl

End Sub
```

The logic here should be self-explanatory, but notice how we make each viewer visible *after* we position it using its Location property. By hiding the viewers on creation and only making them visible once we have positioned them, we ensure an orderly screen update. Of course, we could be a little smarter and precompute nMaxCols *before* loading our viewers, working out the position of each viewer as we create it and allowing it to pop into place immediately—an exercise for the reader!

Resizing MainForm or even dragging the splitter bar has the effect of resizing our MediaDisplayPanel. We want to be informed when this happens so that we can call our PositionMediaViewers routine to do its thing. The best way to do this is to override the MediaDisplayPanel's Resize event handler, making sure to call the base handler:

```
'Overrides Resize event handler to reposition viewers
Protected Overrides Sub OnResize(ByVal e As EventArgs)

  PositionMediaViewers()

  MyBase.OnResize(e)

End Sub
```

Wiring Up the Connections

You will recall from our earlier design discussion that this application is very much *event-driven*. Now is the time to take the various objects that we've created and connect them to each other so that they begin to work together.

Where better to start than with File | Open Folder… on our main menu, which allows the user to pick a root folder from which the DirectoryNavigator is populated. Selecting this menu item raises the menu's Click event, thus our code to respond to it must go inside the mnuOpen_Click event handler of MainForm. When you present your user with a file/folder open dialog, it's only courteous to ensure that the starting point for browsing is the current working file or folder. And so first we retrieve the RootPath setting from our INI file and use it to preconfigure the FolderBrowserDialog component, which you will recall we placed on MainForm in design mode:

```
'Start with current root folder
Dim currentRootFolder As String =
            g_IniSettings.GetSetting("Settings", "RootPath", "")

If currentRootFolder <> "" Then
            folderBrowserDialog1.SelectedPath = currentRootFolder
```

ShowDialog presents the user with a standard Windows folder browser from which a new root folder can be selected. Once chosen, the new folder path is saved straight back out to the INI file before we call Load on our DirectoryNavigator object:

```
'Browse for new root folder
If folderBrowserDialog1.ShowDialog() = DialogResult.OK Then

  'Save new root folder
  g_IniSettings.SetSetting("Settings", "RootPath",
            folderBrowserDialog1.SelectedPath())

  'Load directory tree from root folder
  m_directoryNavigator.Load(folderBrowserDialog1.SelectedPath())

End If
```

And so with just a few lines of event handling code, we've succeeded in connecting our File | Open Folder… menu to our DirectoryNavigator object.

The next significant event occurs whenever the user selects a directory in the DirectoryNavigator. Glancing back at our design sketches, we can see that this event has to be wired to our MediaDisplayPanel object. The only problem is that our DirectoryNavigator object is blissfully unaware of the existence of the MediaDisplayPanel and vice versa! And, in a sense, this is exactly as it should be in a proper object-oriented system: neither of these objects *needs* the other to accomplish its *own* particular function so why introduce unnecessary dependencies?

The real responsibility for connecting these two objects falls upon Main-Form, their shared parent object. Since our DirectoryNavigator inherits from the TreeView control, it will emit an AfterSelect event whenever a directory is selected. All we have to do is add a handler for this event to MainForm after we create the DirectoryNavigator instance:

```
'Create a DirectoryNavigator instance
m_directoryNavigator = New DirectoryNavigator
m_directoryNavigator.Parent = Me
m_directoryNavigator.Dock = DockStyle.Left

'Add an AfterSelect event handler
AddHandler m_directoryNavigator.AfterSelect,
        AddressOf DirectoryNavigatorOnAfterSelect
```

Our event handler routine then does nothing more than extract the full path to the selected directory from the selected node and call the Load method of our MediaDisplayPanel:

```
'Handles the AfterSelect event for the DirectoryNavigator
Private Sub DirectoryNavigatorOnAfterSelect(ByVal obj As Object,
        ByVal tvea As TreeViewEventArgs)

  'Load media display panel from directory
  m_mediaDisplayPanel.Load(tvea.Node.FullPath)

End Sub
```

This indirect linkage between the between DirectoryNavigator and Media-DisplayPanel is illustrated in Figure 7.6.

And with that, we should have a fully functional Image Browser based on a PictureBox, as shown in Figure 7.7. Check it out by navigating to any folder that contains JPEG, GIF, or BMP images. Now is a good chance to do some testing and to add in any functional tweaks we might wish for before we ditch the PictureBox in favor of a much more serious piece of kit.

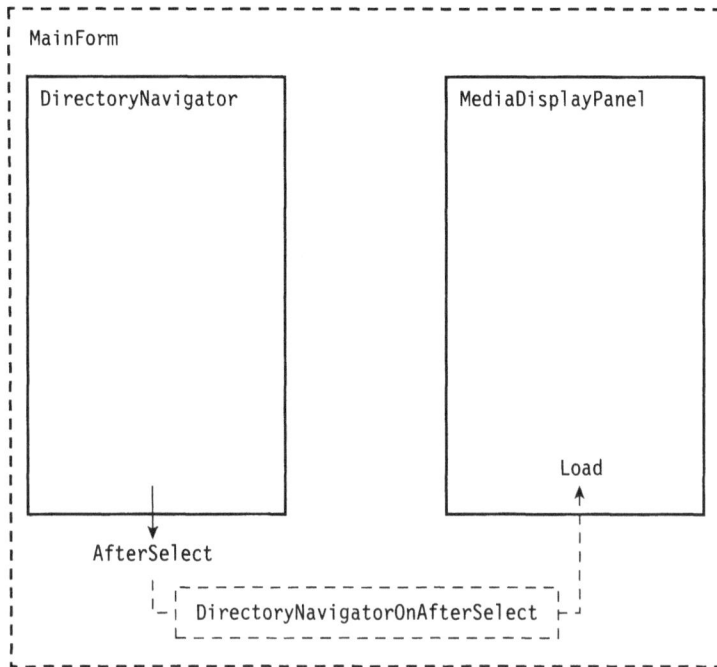

Figure 7.6 Indirect link between `DirectoryNavigator` and `MediaDisplayPanel`.

Adding the QuickTime Control

Having elected earlier to wrap our media control with a `MediaViewer` class, switching from a `PictureBox`-based implementation to a QuickTime Control–based viewer should be a matter of changing

```
Public Class MediaViewer
   Inherits PictureBox
```

to

```
Public Class MediaViewer
   Inherits AxQTOControlLib.AxQTControl
```

not forgetting, of course, to add the necessary reference to the QuickTime Control to our project—as we learned in Chapter 2—and making some alterations to the `MediaViewer.Load` routine.

Figure 7.7 Image Browser based on `PictureBox` control.

In practice, it is a little more complicated than this, but not very much more. Here's our new `MediaViewer` class:

```
Public Class MediaViewer
    Inherits AxQTOControlLib.AxQTControl

    Private m_loadedFileName As String
    Private m_loadErrorCode As Integer

    Public ReadOnly Property LoadedFileName() As String
        Get
            Return m_loadedFileName
        End Get
    End Property
```

```
Public ReadOnly Property LoadErrorCode() As Integer
  Get
    Return m_loadErrorCode
  End Get
End Property

'Load viewer from a file
Public Sub Load(ByVal fName As String)

  Me.ErrorHandling =
          QTErrorHandlingOptionsEnum.qtErrorHandlingRaiseException
  Me.Sizing =
          QTSizingModeEnum.qtMovieFitsControlMaintainAspectRatio

  Me.MovieControllerVisible = True

  Try
    Me.URL = fName
    m_loadedFileName = fName
    m_loadErrorCode = 0

    If Microsoft.VisualBasic.Left(Me.Movie.MIMEType, 5) =
            "image" Then
      Me.MovieControllerVisible = False
    End If

  Catch e As COMException
    m_loadErrorCode = e.ErrorCode
    Throw e
  End Try

End Sub

'Unload viewer
Public Sub Unload()

  m_loadedFileName = ""
  Me.URL = ""

End Sub
End Class
```

Our Load routine has been toughened up by adding an exception handler to catch any COMException that the QuickTime Control might throw while attempting to load a file. Rather than reporting an error here, the exception handling code just saves the error code in a member variable m_loadError-Code, and then proceeds to throw the exception once again so that it can be recaught in the routine that is attempting to load the control. The LoadError-Code property of MediaViewer can then be checked to find out what went wrong.

Setting the Sizing mode to MediaFitsControlMaintainAspectRatio ensures that the image, video, or whatever is scaled to fit within the bounds of the control, but in such a way as to preserve the original aspect ratio of the media. This means that there may be some white-space at top/bottom or left/right of the media where its aspect ratio differs from that of the control.

If a movie is loaded, we make sure it has a visible movie controller:

```
Me.MovieControllerVisible = True
```

But if an image happens to be loaded, it's a bit pointless having a movie controller, so we'd like to turn it off. This is easier said than done: since the QuickTime Control opens an image as a single-frame movie, how can we possibly tell that it's an image? This is where the MIMEType property of QTMovie comes in handy. The MIME content type of an image (or, more specifically, of any file that is opened using a QuickTime Graphics Importer) can always be relied upon to be "image" so we can add the following after we've opened the file:

```
If Microsoft.VisualBasic.Left(Me.Movie.MIMEType, 5) = "image" Then
  Me.MovieControllerVisible = False
End If
```

With these few changes we should now be able to point our Directory-Navigator at a folder of movies, images, or sound files, or even a mixture of any of the many types of media files that QuickTime can open, and watch them pop into our browser. Of course, don't forget to edit the FileExtensions setting in your *MediaBrowser.ini* file to include a few more file types:

```
FileExtensions=jpg,bmp,avi,mov,dv,gif,tif,png,wav,aif,mpg,
         mp3,mp4,m4a,m4p,swf
```

Media Inspector

It's all very well being able to view and even play the media files we're browsing, but that doesn't help a whole lot if we've no idea what we're looking at or listening to! As we learned in Chapter 5, many movies, images, and sound files contain valuable information about themselves locked up in their embedded metadata. The QTMovie class conveniently exposes this embedded data through its Annotation and Annotations properties, providing us with a unified means of obtaining metadata from many of the diverse file types that QuickTime can handle. A fuller explanation and examples can be found in Chapter 5. In addition to the metadata, QuickTime also allows us to extract lots of interesting and even not-so-interesting tidbits of information about a particular media file, such as its color depth, the codec used to compress the data, the length of a track, and the like.

If you open your movies one at a time in QuickTime Player and choose Window | Show Movie Info and Window | Show Movie Properties, you can of course find a lot of this information, but it's tedious and they make you work for it. What we would like for our Media Browser is a concise view of as much of this metadata as possible, preferably in a floating palette. Ideally, all we should have to do is click on a media file of interest in our browser and the palette will instantly display all the data we want. Welcome to the Media Inspector! (See Figure 7.8.)

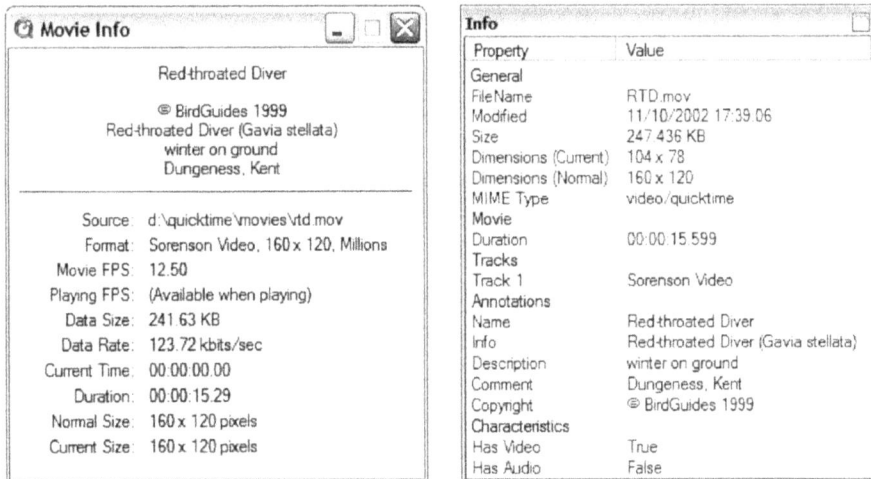

Figure 7.8   QuickTime Player Movie Info vs. Media Inspector for the same movie.

Stepping back for a moment, let's consider what functionality we require of our MediaInspector object and how best we can implement it. The first thing that's really kind of obvious, but still worth stating, is that it can only "inspect" one media file at a time, so clearly our MediaInspector must have a means of being told which MediaViewer to inspect.

Paying homage once more to OOP fundamentals, we should encapsulate as much functionality as possible *within* our MediaInspector so that its clients need not concern themselves too much with what goes on inside it. Ideally, all our application should have to do is create an instance of the MediaInspector, size and position it, and then hand it a MediaViewer to inspect. Property inspectors in various contemporary applications tend to vary in sophistication from elaborate tree-based structures with collapsible sections to humbler lists of name-value pairs. In our case we'll opt for the simpler name-value property list, although we will split this up into sections of related properties.

Moving on to implementation, if the MediaInspector is to be a floating palette separate from our main application form, then we need to start with a stand-alone Form (MediaInspector) whose FormBorderStyle is SizableTool-Window and that will *not* show up in the task bar separately from our main application form. It's just as convenient to set these properties of the form in design mode.

The name-value property pairs can conveniently be presented in a two-column ListView component that fills the client area of our MediaInspector form, for which we declare the member variable m_lvInfo. Here's an outline of our new two-column property inspector class:

```
Public Class MediaInspector
  Inherits System.Windows.Forms.Form

  Private m_lvInfo As ListView
  Private m_viewer As MediaViewer

  Public Sub New()
    MyBase.New()

    'This call is required by the Windows Form Designer
    InitializeComponent()
```

```
'Add any initialization after the InitializeComponent() call

'Create Info List View to fill window
m_lvInfo = New ListView
m_lvInfo.Parent = Me
m_lvInfo.Dock = DockStyle.Fill
m_lvInfo.BorderStyle = BorderStyle.None

m_lvInfo.Items.Clear()
m_lvInfo.View = View.Details
m_lvInfo.GridLines = True
m_lvInfo.HeaderStyle = ColumnHeaderStyle.Nonclickable

'Add two columns
m_lvInfo.Columns.Add("Property", -2, HorizontalAlignment.Left)
m_lvInfo.Columns.Add("Value", -2, HorizontalAlignment.Left)

'Set Initial Size
Me.Size = New Size(350, 400)

    End Sub
End Class
```

Notice that I have slipped in member variable m_viewer. This is destined to hold a reference to the MediaViewer that is currently under inspection. Before we look at this in detail, though, let's finish off the housekeeping by adding a resize handler to the inspector form:

```
'Handles the Resize event
Private Sub MediaInspector_Resize(ByVal sender As Object, _
            ByVal e As System.EventArgs) Handles MyBase.Resize

  If IsNothing(m_lvInfo) Then Exit Sub

  'Resize the list view intelligently
  m_lvInfo.Size = Me.ClientSize

  If m_lvInfo.Columns.Count >= 2 Then
    If m_lvInfo.Width < 300 Then
      m_lvInfo.Columns(0).Width = CInt(m_lvInfo.Width / 2)
      m_lvInfo.Columns(1).Width = CInt(m_lvInfo.Width / 2)
```

```
    Else
      m_lvInfo.Columns(0).Width = 150
      m_lvInfo.Columns(1).Width = m_lvInfo.Width - 150
    End If
  End If

End Sub
```

All this does is to ensure that, above a certain width, our Property column does not get any wider at the expense of the Value column where space is at a premium.

Tip   Note this small but important check at the beginning of our Resize handler:

```
If IsNothing(m_lvInfo) Then Exit Sub
```

Without this check, it's conceivable that our Resize handler could be called before the ListView object is created, for example, when the form is first set to its default size, in which case referencing m_lvInfo would throw a rather scary NullReferenceException. Try commenting out this check and you'll see what I mean!

The moral of course is to never assume that object variables invariably reference an actual object. Ruthless natural selection soon weeds out C and C++ programmers who don't religiously check for null pointers, but because Visual Basic does such a masterful job of masking the concept of pointers from the casual developer, it's easy to become careless with object references.

Now all that's left is to write the code that actually populates the ListView in our MediaInspector. The starting point for this is to assign a particular MediaViewer to be inspected through the public SetViewer method of Media-Inspector.

```
Public Sub SetViewer(ByRef mv As MediaViewer)

  If IsNothing(mv) Then Exit Sub

  m_viewer = mv

  'Clear all existing info
  m_lvInfo.Items.Clear()
```

```
'Populate Inspector
...

End Sub
```

Once we have a `MediaViewer` to inspect, we can then proceed to populate the `ListView` with as much information as we care to extract from the Media-Viewer. First, we create a "General" section with some useful data that would be common to most media files:

```
'Add the General section
AddSection("General")

Dim fi As FileInfo = New FileInfo(mv.FileName)
AddProperty("FileName", fi.Name)
AddProperty("Modified", fi.LastWriteTime.ToString())
AddProperty("Size",
            Format(m_viewer.Movie.Size / 1000, "0.000") + " KB")
w = m_viewer.Movie.Width
h = m_viewer.Movie.Height
AddProperty("Dimensions (Current)", CStr(w) + " x " + CStr(h))
Dim rNatural As QTRECT = m_viewer.Movie.NaturalRect
w = rNatural.right - rNatural.left
h = rNatural.bottom - rNatural.top
AddProperty("Dimensions (Normal)", CStr(w) + " x " + CStr(h))
AddProperty("MIME Type", m_viewer.Movie.MIMEType)
```

`AddSection` and `AddProperty` are private helper routines that I have added to our `MediaInspector` class to make life easier. `AddSection` simply adds a row to the `ListView` in a different color and gives it a heading, while `AddProperty` adds a row and sets the contents of the Property and Value columns.

```
'Adds a section heading to the ListView
Private Sub AddSection(ByVal heading As String)

  Dim item As New ListViewItem(heading, 0)
  item.BackColor = System.Drawing.Color.Wheat
  m_lvInfo.Items.Add(item)

End Sub
```

```
'Adds a property and its value to the ListView
Private Sub AddProperty(ByVal prop As String, ByVal value As String)

  Dim item As New ListViewItem(prop, 0)
  item.SubItems.Add(value)
  m_lvInfo.Items.Add(item)

End Sub
```

Different types of media files have particular properties of interest, so it's useful to be able to differentiate between the fundamental types of media files that QuickTime can open, such as video, image, and audio files. The MIMEType property comes in handy here again. If the file opened is an image, then we create a new "Image" section in our property list and add several pertinent properties of the image; whereas, if it's an audio file, we add an "Audio" section. The "Movie" section is really a catchall for everything else.

```
Dim bIsImage As Boolean
Dim bIsAudio As Boolean

bIsImage = Microsoft.VisualBasic.Left(m_viewer.Movie.MIMEType, 5)
          = "image"
bIsAudio = Microsoft.VisualBasic.Left(m_viewer.Movie.MIMEType, 5)
          = "audio"

If bIsImage Then

  AddSection("Image")
  AddProperty("Format", m_viewer.Movie.Tracks(1).Format)
  AddProperty("Color Depth", CStr(m_viewer.Movie.Tracks(1).Depth))

ElseIf bIsAudio Then

  AddSection("Audio")
  AddProperty("Duration", CStr(m_viewer.Movie.Duration))
  AddProperty("Format", m_viewer.Movie.Tracks(1).
          AudioFormatSummaryString)
  AddProperty("Channels", CStr(m_viewer.Movie.Tracks(1).
          AudioChannelCount))
  AddProperty("Channel Layout", m_viewer.Movie.Tracks(1).
          AudioChannelLayoutString)
```

```
Else

    AddSection("Movie")
    AddProperty("Duration", CStr(m_viewer.Movie.Duration))

    'Iterate over tracks
    For i = 1 To m_viewer.Movie.Tracks.Count
      If i = 1 Then AddSection("Tracks")
      AddProperty("Track " + CStr(i), m_viewer.Movie.Tracks(i).Format)
    Next i

End If
```

Last, we turn to Annotations. As we have already discovered in Chapter 5, QuickTime does a reasonably competent job of unifying access to metadata irrespective of its source, whether it be from a QuickTime movie, an MP3 file, or a JPEG image. So in this case all we have to do is attempt to get data from a list of well-defined annotations. If our media file does not have a particular item, we just move on to the next. The end result, for any file that is appropriately tagged, is usually a useful synopsis of information:

```
'Add the Annotations section
AddSection("Annotations")

AddAnnotationProperty("Name",
        QTAnnotationsEnum.qtAnnotationFullName)
AddAnnotationProperty("Info",
        QTAnnotationsEnum.qtAnnotationInformation)
AddAnnotationProperty("Description",
        QTAnnotationsEnum.qtAnnotationDescription)
AddAnnotationProperty("Comment",
        QTAnnotationsEnum.qtAnnotationComments)
AddAnnotationProperty("Artist",
        QTAnnotationsEnum.qtAnnotationArtist)
AddAnnotationProperty("Album",
        QTAnnotationsEnum.qtAnnotationAlbum)
AddAnnotationProperty("Genre",
        QTAnnotationsEnum.qtAnnotationGenre)
AddAnnotationProperty("Author",
        QTAnnotationsEnum.qtAnnotationAuthor)
AddAnnotationProperty("Copyright",
        QTAnnotationsEnum.qtAnnotationCopyright)
```

```
AddAnnotationProperty("Software",
          QTAnnotationsEnum.qtAnnotationSoftware)
```

AddAnnotationProperty is another convenient helper routine.

```
'Adds an Annotation property if present
Private Sub AddAnnotationProperty(ByVal propName As String,
          ByVal annotationID As Long)

  Dim val As String

  If IsNothing(m_viewer) Then Exit Sub

  val = m_viewer.GetAnnotation(annotationID)

  If Trim(val) <> "" Then AddProperty(propName, val)

End Sub
```

Instead of accessing m_viewer.Movie.Annotation directly, we have adopted good OOP practice by adding a GetAnnotation function to our MediaViewer so as to encapsulate the specifics of getting an Annotation from the movie.

```
'Gets an Annotation from the movie if present
Public Function GetAnnotation(ByVal annotationID As Long) As String

  Dim val As String = ""
  Try
    val = Me.Movie.Annotation(annotationID)
  Catch e As Exception
    'Ignore error
  End Try

  GetAnnotation = val

End Function
```

With our MediaInspector more or less complete, all that remains is to plumb it in to our main application and see if it works. To incorporate the MediaInspector, we add two routines to our MediaDisplayPanel:

```
'Hide/Show the MediaInspector
Sub MediaInspectorToggle()

  If Not IsMediaInspectorOpen() Then
    m_mediaInspector = New MediaInspector
    m_mediaInspector.Owner = CType(Me.Parent, Form)
    m_mediaInspector.StartPosition = FormStartPosition.Manual
    m_mediaInspector.DesktopLocation =
            New Point(Me.Parent.Left + Me.Parent.Width + 20,
                      Me.Parent.Top)
    m_mediaInspector.Show()
  Else
    m_mediaInspector.Close()
    m_mediaInspector.Dispose()
  End If

End Sub

'Returns TRUE if the MediaInspector is open
Private Function IsMediaInspectorOpen() As Boolean

  Dim bRet As Boolean = True

  If IsNothing(m_mediaInspector) Then
    bRet = False
  Else
    'If the X button on the Inspector was clicked, then the
    'form will be disposed but not necessarily set to Nothing
    'if the garbage collector hasn't come around
    If m_mediaInspector.IsDisposed Then
      bRet = False
    End If
  End If

  Return bRet

End Function
```

MediaInspectorToggle toggles the MediaInspector palette open or closed and is attached to the Media | Info... item off the main menu. Note how our MainForm is made the owner of the MediaInspector after it is created. This ensures that our MediaInspector hangs out closely with our main application form should, for example, we minimize our application or switch to another application. IsMediaInspectorOpen returns True if the MediaInspector is open.

In More Depth

The function IsMediaInspectorOpen turns out to be nontrivial because we have allowed our MediaInspector to have a close box—the small X in its top right-hand corner—making it possible for the MediaInspector to be closed without the MediaDisplayPanel to whom it belongs being aware of it. You might imagine that IsNothing(m_media-Inspector) would be sufficient to determine if the inspector is closed or open. Unhappily though, just because a form is closed, we cannot assume that object references to that form will be set to Nothing. This only happens once the Common Language Runtime (CLR) garbage collector comes along and actually frees the memory used by the form. The useful IsDisposed function determines if our form is one of these zombie objects awaiting the attentions of the garbage collector.

Now that we can open and close our MediaInspector, let's make it a little more useful by actually connecting it to whichever MediaViewer we click on. Since our MediaViewer inherits from the QuickTime Control, we should be able to intercept the control's MouseDownEvent. All we have to do is add a handler for this event in our MediaDisplayPanel after we create a Media-Viewer in MediaDisplayPanel.Load():

```
'Add event handlers
AddHandler mv.MouseDownEvent, AddressOf MediaViewerMouseDown
```

and create a handler routine for the event:

```
'Handles MouseDown event from media viewer
Private Sub MediaViewerMouseDown(ByVal sender As Object, ByVal e As
            AxQTOControlLib._IQTControlEvents_MouseDownEvent)

  Dim mv As MediaViewer

  'Cast sender object to a MediaViewer
  mv = CType(sender, MediaViewer)

  'Select the viewer
  SelectMediaViewer(mv)
```

```
'Load the MediaInspector
If IsMediaInspectorOpen() Then m_mediaInspector.SetViewer(mv)
```

```
End Sub
```

Note how we use CType to explicitly convert or *cast* the generic sender object reference to a MediaViewer object reference. This conversion is only possible, of course, because MediaViewer inherits ultimately from Object.

Note for C++ Developers

CType is essentially equivalent to the __try_cast managed C++ extension—a dynamic_cast that throws an exception if it fails.

So that we know which MediaViewer the MediaInspector refers to, I have added a SelectMediaViewer routine to the MediaDisplayPanel class. This simply highlights the selected MediaViewer by altering its border color. Once the MediaViewer is selected, we pass the MediaInspector a reference to the selected MediaViewer using its SetViewer method.

A Tooltip

Finally, a little icing on the cake: we'll add a tooltip containing the most useful metadata and have it appear when you simply move the mouse over a MediaViewer, as illustrated in the examples shown in Figure 7.9.

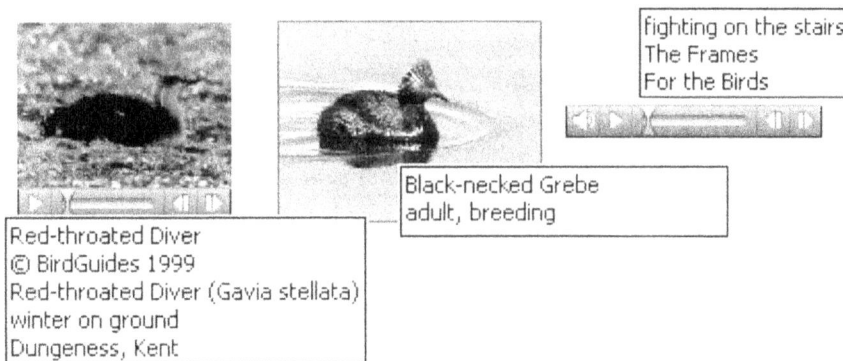

Figure 7.9 Typical tooltips for movie, image, and MP3 files.

Windows Forms comes to the rescue once again with its `ToolTip` component. We just add one to our `MediaDisplayPanel` by declaring a member
variable

```
Private m_viewerTooltip As ToolTip
```

and then create our `ToolTip` object in `MediaDisplayPanel.New`

```
m_viewerTooltip = New ToolTip
```

and, finally, in the Load method of `MediaDisplayPanel`, we tell the tooltip
what to display when the mouse rolls over a `MediaViewer`:

```
'Set tooltip for the viewer
m_viewerTooltip.SetToolTip(mv, mv.GetTooltipInfo())
```

Adding the `GetTooltipInfo` function to our `MediaViewer` class lets us
define exactly what should be displayed in the tooltip:

```
'Returns info for the MediaViewer tooltip
Public Function GetTooltipInfo() As String

  Dim nSaveImageIndex As Integer
  Dim strInfo As String = ""

  AppendAnnotation(strInfo,
          QTAnnotationsEnum.qtAnnotationComments)
  AppendAnnotation(strInfo,
          QTAnnotationsEnum.qtAnnotationInformation)
  AppendAnnotation(strInfo,
          QTAnnotationsEnum.qtAnnotationFullName)
  AppendAnnotation(strInfo,
          QTAnnotationsEnum.qtAnnotationArtist)
  AppendAnnotation(strInfo,
          QTAnnotationsEnum.qtAnnotationAlbum)
  AppendAnnotation(strInfo,
          QTAnnotationsEnum.qtAnnotationDescription)
  AppendAnnotation(strInfo,
          QTAnnotationsEnum.qtAnnotationCopyright)

  Return strInfo
```

```
End Function

'Appends Annotation to line-delimited info string if item exists
Private Sub AppendAnnotation(ByRef info As String,
            ByVal annotationID As Long)

  Dim val As String = GetAnnotation(annotationID)
  If val = "" Then Exit Sub

  If info <> "" Then info += vbCrLf
  info += val

End Sub
```

And that's it: a very useful tooltip facility for very little effort indeed. If you have iTunes, or other music collection software, go point the Media Browser at a couple of folders of music files and you'll appreciate the tooltip!

Summary

The completed Media Browser application *MediaBrowserVB/Complete*, shown in Figure 7.10, may be found at

www.skylark.ie/qt4.net/Samples

Of course, we could add lots more to our Media Browser, for example

- Ability to double-click on a `MediaViewer` to open it full size in a separate window
- Ability to edit any annotation in the `MediaInspector` and save it back to the media file
- Facility to drag-and-drop media files into the `MediaDisplayPanel`

No doubt you can think of still more features. Hopefully, the approach that I've used in this chapter will give you the confidence to extend and adapt this simple Media Browser into something really useful.

Looking back on what we've achieved in this chapter, I'm sure you'll agree that leveraging the .NET Framework in conjunction with the Quick-Time Control is an impressive way of rapidly building feature-rich QuickTime-based applications.

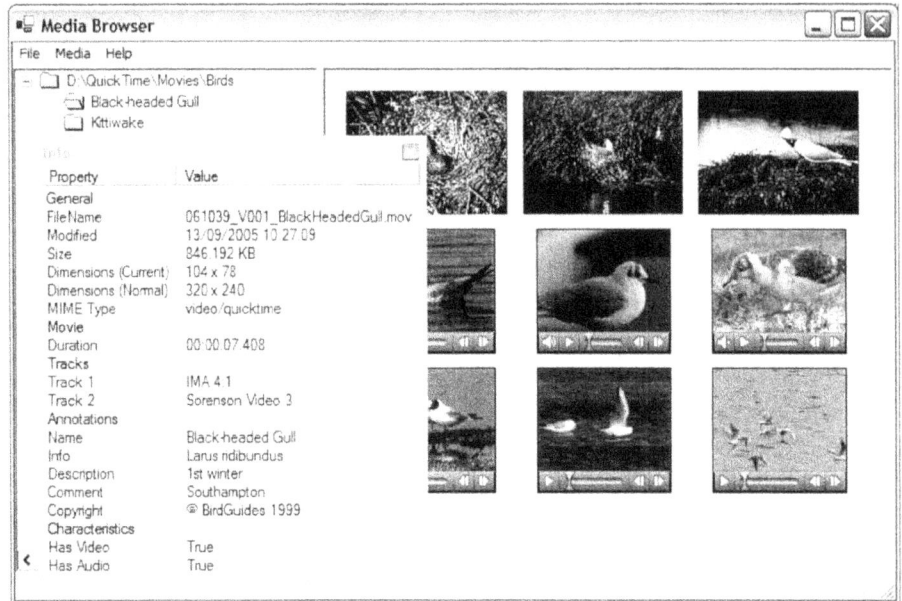

Figure 7.10 Completed Media Browser.

Using a RAD environment does not exempt us from the need to design and plan our applications carefully. If anything, it encourages us to be more rigorous in the application of good OOP principles since the underlying .NET Framework is so thoroughly object-based from the ground up. Not only that, but the existence of so many rich Windows Forms components frees us from a lot of the tedium often associated with developing UI-based applications. Instead, we have been able to concentrate most of our energies on the application itself and our QuickTime-specific code.

Scripting QuickTime Player

Introduction

Incredible though it might seem to the more cynical among us, computers were indeed conceived to make our lives easier—in particular by relieving us of the drudgery associated with repetitive manual tasks. Perversely though, as computers and software have become more powerful, the drudgery element hasn't exactly faded into extinction; it's just evolved into a more complex form. Anyone involved in media production will attest to this.

Dedicated applications often handle a specific task—such as color-correcting a video clip—wonderfully well. If you must perform this task over and over again, though, the shine quickly fades as it turns into a chore. A complex production workflow may involve the use of several such applications to process and integrate the various media elements that are combined into the finished piece of content. Content producers are always on the lookout for any means of automating some or all of these tasks that eat up so much of their time.

Sample scripts for this chapter are available at

www.skylark.ie/qt4.net/Samples/WSH/

Scripting QuickTime on the Mac

The Mac has traditionally been the choice of professionals involved in content production, and this has mainly been driven by the quality and sophistication of the applications available on the Apple platform. But another not insignificant factor has been the ease with which parts—or even all—of the production process could be automated using the easy-to-use and mature scripting environment that is AppleScript. Eschewing the syntactical complexity of traditional programming languages, AppleScript is a more natural —almost English-like—scripting language and as such, has particular appeal for those who have little or no programming background but are nevertheless anxious to get the job done.

But a scripting language isn't a lot of use on its own; to be truly useful, the applications that we want to automate need to be scriptable. We need a way to dispatch commands to the application and to retrieve data from its logical objects—in short, the application must support a scripting interface. With AppleScript a relatively mature technology, there is no want of Mac applications exposing such a scripting interface. Scrolling down the long list of scriptable OS X applications, you will come across such industry stalwarts as Adobe Acrobat, Macromedia Freehand, Adobe Illustrator, Microsoft Excel, Adobe Photoshop, and QuarkXpress. And, of course, tucked into this list along with many of Apple's own applications is QuickTime Player.

You can get a flavor of QuickTime Player scripting from the following self-explanatory script:

```
tell application "QuickTime Player"
  activate
  open file "Myrtle:Users:john:Movies:wedding.mov"
  tell movie 1
    set the selection start to 3000
    set the selection end to 5000
    cut
  end tell
end tell
```

The scripting dictionary of QuickTime Player is quite rich, allowing you to do lots of interesting things with the player application itself and with the movies that it can open.

At this point you may well interject: that's all fine and well, but what about Windows? Is there an equivalent to AppleScript on the Windows platform? Let's find out.

Windows Scripting Host

Windows does indeed sport a scripting platform to rival AppleScript, and it comes with a decidedly more grown-up—and predictably less catchy—name: *Windows Scripting Host* (WSH). Glamorous it may not be but Windows Scripting Host comes with big ambitions: not content with supporting a single scripting language, it boasts an agnostic framework that claims to be language independent. As bundled with Windows (98, 2000, and XP), WSH comes with a choice of two scripting languages, VBScript and JScript. VBScript is the scripting version of Visual Basic and is easy to learn and use, albeit without the natural-language flavor of AppleScript. JScript is Microsoft's implementation of the ECMAScript language, better known as JavaScript. Syntactically closer to C++ and Java, JScript tends to be the preferred scripting language of developers already familiar with those languages. With third-party add-ons, WSH can also host other scripting languages such as TCL, Perl, Python, and Rexx.

Windows Scripting Host 5.6

All the examples in this chapter are based on Windows Scripting Host 5.6, which comes pre-installed with Windows XP. If you are using Windows 98, Me, 2000, or NT4, then you should make sure to install WSH 5.6 (or later), which you can download from *http://msdn.microsoft.com/scripting.*

The potential of the WSH environment becomes apparent when you realize that, with the aid of a simple function—`WScript.CreateObject`—a script can create any of the hundreds of COM components that are registered on the system. For example, `Scripting.FileSystemObject` is a very handy utility component for working with files and folders.

As a quick WSH warm-up, here's an example of how the `FileSystemObject` object can be used in a very simple script to obtain the size of a folder. This is what it looks like—first in VBScript

```
' GetFolderSize.vbs
Dim fso, fldr
Set fso = WScript.CreateObject("Scripting.FileSystemObject")
Set fldr = fso.GetFolder("D:\QuickTime\Movies")
If Not (fldr Is Nothing) Then
  WScript.Echo(fldr.Path + " contains " + CStr(fldr.Size) + " bytes")
End If
```

and now in JScript:

```
// GetFolderSize.js
var fso = WScript.CreateObject("Scripting.FileSystemObject");
var fldr = fso.GetFolder("D:\\QuickTime\\Movies");
if (fldr)
  WScript.Echo(fldr.Path + " contains " + fldr.Size + " bytes");
```

Apart from the obvious syntax differences, the code is remarkably similar—especially the way in which the COM objects are used. The WScript object is always available within a WSH script and provides useful support for creating COM objects and for handling input and output, as well as other utility functions.

A WSH script is usually saved in a text file: JScript script files use the *.js* file extension while VBScript should be saved into a *.vbs* file. Once we have a script file—for example, *GetFolderSize.js*—running the script is as simple as double-clicking on the file on the desktop or in Windows Explorer. Windows will invoke *wscript.exe* to run the script for us. The result, for *GetFolderSize.js*, is

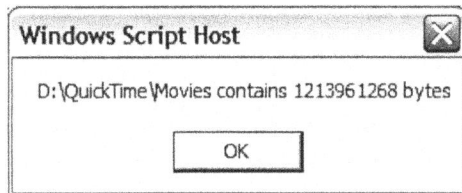

Scripts can also be run from within the Command window as *command line* scripts, this time using *cscript.exe*. In this instance, making sure first to change directories to the folder containing the script file *GetFolderSize.js*, we can enter at the command prompt

```
cscript GetFolderSize.js
```

and the result this time will be

```
D:\QT4.NET\Samples\WSH>cscript GetFolderSize.js
Microsoft (R) Windows Script Host Version 5.6
Copyright (C) Microsoft Corporation 1996-2001. All rights reserved.

D:\QuickTime\Movies contains 1213961268 bytes

D:\QT4.NET\Samples\WSH>
```

What Is the Command Window?

The Command window is a special window into which you can directly type commands for the Windows operating system and from which you can run batch files or scripts. It is an essential tool for developers, systems administrators, and anyone else who either needs to—or prefers to—access the operating system directly rather than through its graphical user interface (GUI).

The quickest way to invoke the Command window is to select Run... from the Start menu, enter cmd, and click OK. A typical Command window is shown in Figure 8.1.

For Mac users, the Command window is the equivalent of Terminal on OS X.

Tip If you use the Command window regularly, it is a good idea to change its font and color to something less primitive looking and more legible. To do this, right-click in the title bar of the Command window and choose Properties.

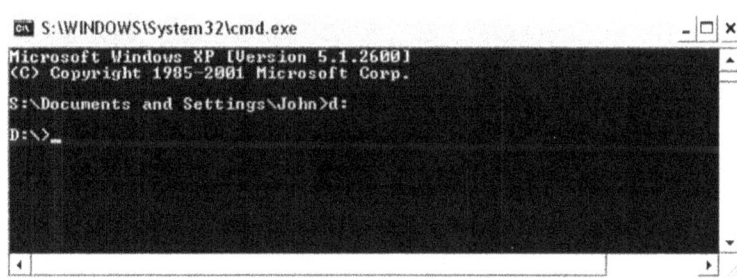

Figure 8.1   The Command window.

COM (Automation) Server

So far in this book, the COM components that we have encountered—such as the QuickTime Control or even the Scripting.FileSystemObject—have all been instantiated *within* the host application, be it a Visual Basic .NET or C# executable or, in the case of WSH, *wscript.exe* or *cscript.exe.* These are *in-process* objects, living out their brief lives within the single process that is the running host application.

But it is also possible to access COM objects that reside in another process or application running on the same computer or even, perhaps, running on a remote networked computer. For this to be possible, an application must choose to expose *itself* as a COM object, available to other COM-aware applications. Any application that exposes a public COM interface in this way is known as a *COM Automation server,* or simply a *COM server.*

If a client application wants to use functionality exposed by a particular COM server (another application), it will attempt to create an instance of that server's public COM interface. It does this using the programmatic identifier (ProgID) that the COM server will have registered with the system. If the COM server is already running, the client will get back a reference to the running application. If not, the server application will be launched, and then a reference to it will be returned. Either way, the COM object returned to the client is an *out-of-process* COM object, since it refers to an object that resides in another process.

The COM interface exposed by a COM server is its public face, so to speak. It will expose selected application functionality and may reveal an internal COM object model of the application and of the documents that the application currently holds open.

All this may sound rather complicated and is really best understood by way of an example. The Microsoft Office suite of applications—Word, Excel, PowerPoint, Access, and others—are all popular COM servers. The ProgID for Word is Word.Application and scripting it is straightforward. Here's a script that will open a document and display the number of words in it:

```
// Open a document and count the words
var wordApp = WScript.CreateObject("Word.Application");
if (wordApp)
{
  wordApp.Visible = true;
  wordApp.Documents.Open("UserGuide.doc");
  WScript.Echo("Words: " + wordApp.ActiveDocument.Characters.Count);
  wordApp.Quit();
}
```

Notice that the application object—wordApp—has child objects: in this case Documents, the collection of open documents, and ActiveDocument, the current active document. Drilling down through the COM object hierarchy, we are able to access the Characters collection of the document and get its Count property.

Just for interest, here's the equivalent AppleScript script:

```
tell application "Microsoft Word"
  activate
  open file "UserGuide.doc"
  display dialog "Words: " & (count each word in window 1)
  quit
end tell
```

It should be obvious that the COM server on Windows is the analog of the scriptable application on the Mac. And, if we can script QuickTime Player on the Mac, surely it ought to be possible to script QuickTime Player on Windows as a COM server.

QuickTime Player: A COM Server

Sure enough, as of QuickTime 7.0.2, QuickTime Player on Windows has opened its stall for business as a COM server, happily offering its services to any COM client that cares to create an instance of

```
QuickTimePlayerLib.QuickTimePlayerApp.
```

Opening and Playing a Movie

It only takes a few lines of code to launch Player and open a movie:

```
var qtPlayerApp = WScript.CreateObject(
          "QuickTimePlayerLib.QuickTimePlayerApp");

if (qtPlayerApp != null)
{
  var qtPlayer = qtPlayerApp.Players(1);

  if (qtPlayer)
    qtPlayer.OpenURL("d:\\QuickTime\\Movies\\sample.mov");
}
```

The COM class that "wraps" the QuickTime Player application and exposes it for scripting is `QuickTimePlayerApp`, of which `qtPlayerApp` is an instance. Creating an object of this class will launch QuickTime Player if it is not already running.

The `QTControl` property of `qtPlayerApp` is where the fun starts—it returns an object of type `QTControl` or, in other words, the instance of the Quick-Time Control that is in use by the QuickTime Player window. Just as we've done many times in earlier chapters, we can obtain the `QTMovie` object via the control's `Movie` property. Suddenly the entire QuickTime Object Model is exposed and available for the scripting developer just as if we had instantiated a QuickTime Control in our own application.

To play the movie, we need only add one more line

```
qtPlayer.QTControl.Movie.Play();
```

and to list the format for each track of the movie:

```
var mov = qtPlayer.QTControl.Movie;

if (mov)
{
  var s = "";
  for (var i=1; i<=mov.Tracks.Count; i++)
  {
    if (s != "") s += "\n";
    s += "Track " + i + ": " + mov.Tracks(i).Format;
  }
  WScript.Echo(s);
}
```

The QuickTime Player Object Model

The QuickTime Player object model (Figure 8.2) shows the core classes in the QuickTime Player object library as well as the relationship that exists between QuickTime Player and the QuickTime Object Model that we first met in Chapter 4. At the root is the `QuickTimePlayerApp` class, which can be considered to encapsulate the entire QuickTime Player application. This class has a `Quit` method that has the same effect as selecting File | Exit in QuickTime Player. To check it out, launch QuickTime Player manually and open several new player windows. This rather pointless script will connect

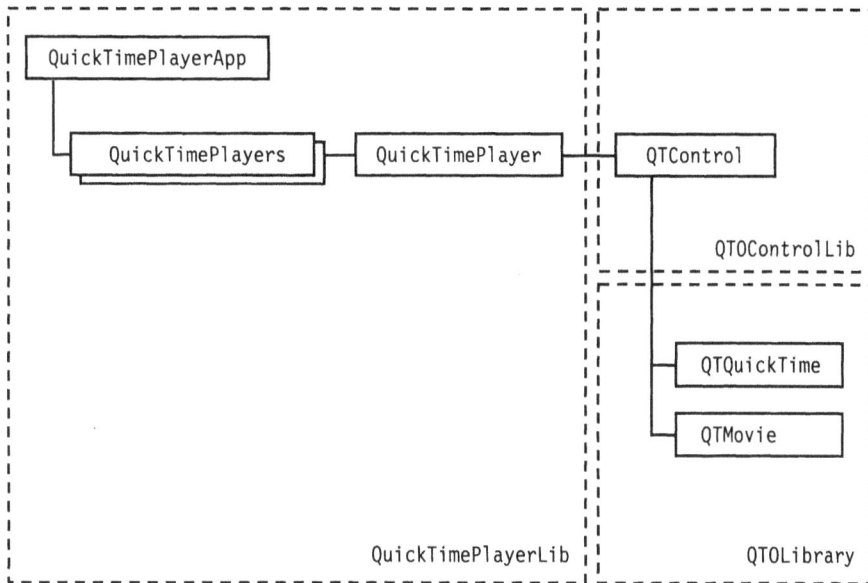

Figure 8.2 The QuickTime Player object model.

to the currently running QuickTime Player application and promptly pulls the plug on it:

```
// Quit QuickTime Player
var qtPlayerApp = WScript.CreateObject(
          "QuickTimePlayerLib.QuickTimePlayerApp");

if (qtPlayerApp != null)
  qtPlayerApp.Quit();
```

Of considerably greater interest is the Players property of the application: this returns the QuickTimePlayers collection, which is a collection of the player windows that happen to be open at this moment in time. Each item in the QuickTimePlayers collection is an instance of the QuickTimePlayer class and wraps a QuickTime Player window. Manipulating the window is possible using the various properties and methods of this class. In essence, the QuickTime Player window is just a fancy wrapper around a QuickTime Control. The QuickTimePlayer class has a QTControl property that returns a reference to its QuickTime Control. This is our gateway to the movie itself and to the other QuickTime objects that we have become familiar with.

Working with Players

If you launch QuickTime Player manually again, this time opening several movies in different windows, and run the following script, you will find that the player windows are listed in the order in which you opened them.

```
var qtPlayerApp = WScript.CreateObject(
            "QuickTimePlayerLib.QuickTimePlayerApp");

if (qtPlayerApp != null)
{
  var s = "";
  for (var i=1; i<=qtPlayerApp.Players.Count; i++)
  {
    var qtPlayer = qtPlayerApp.Players(i);
    if (s != "") s += "\n";
    s += "Player " + i + ": " + qtPlayer.QTControl.URL;
  }
  WScript.Echo(s);
}
```

Close a player window or open a new window and run the script again. The result should be different.

Opening a movie under script control in a QuickTime Player window can be accomplished in two ways. If we have an existing player window, as is always the case when QuickTime Player is first launched, then we can use the OpenURL method of QuickTimePlayer:

```
var qtPlayer = qtPlayerApp.Players(1);

if (qtPlayer)
  qtPlayer.OpenURL("d:\\QuickTime\\Movies\\sample.mov");
```

Or we can add a new empty player window:

```
qtPlayerApp.Players.Add();

var qtPlayer = qtPlayerApp.Players(qtPlayerApp.Players.Count);

if (qtPlayer)
  qtPlayer.OpenURL("d:\\QuickTime\\Movies\\sample.mov");
```

For convenience the Add method can take an optional URL parameter, which opens a new window and loads a movie all in one go:

```
qtPlayerApp.Players.Add("d:\\QuickTime\\Movies\\sample.mov");
```

Once we have a QuickTimePlayer object, we can do quite a lot with it. If opening several movies, it is often useful to be able to organize them on the screen:

```
// Cascade player windows
var qtPlayerApp = WScript.CreateObject(
            "QuickTimePlayerLib.QuickTimePlayerApp");

if (qtPlayerApp == null) WScript.Quit();

var x = 50;
var y = 50;
var dx = 50;
var dy = 50;

for (var i=1; i<=qtPlayerApp.Players.Count; i++)
{
  var qtPlayer = qtPlayerApp.Players(i);

  qtPlayer.Move(x, y);

  x += dx;
  y += dy;
}
```

As well as moving the player window, you can Activate it (i.e., bring it to the front) or Close it.

The QuickTimePlayer method that provides the most scope for experimentation is DoMenu. Exactly as it states, DoMenu will execute one of the menu items in the QuickTime Player menus.

We can open a movie and then display it full screen:

```
qtPlayer.OpenURL("d:\\QuickTime\\Movies\\sample.mov");
qtPlayer.DoMenu("View", "Full Screen");
qtPlayer.QTControl.Movie.Play();
```

The first parameter for DoMenu is the name of the menu—in this case, "View". The second parameter is the name of a menu item in that menu—"Full Screen". The optional third parameter allows you to specify a submenu item. You'll get the idea when you try

```
qtPlayer.DoMenu("Window", "Favorites", "Show Favorites");
```

The beauty of DoMenu is that it allows us to automate many of the manual procedures that can be carried out using the QuickTime Player menus. Of particular interest are those menu items that reside in the Edit menu. You will recall from Chapter 6 that simple cut, copy, and paste type operations allow us to do some quite sophisticated production tasks. With DoMenu, we don't even need to know anything about the QuickTime Control, since the basic editing functions are available at the player window level.

QuickTime Player Pro

If you want to get the most out of QuickTime Player scripting, especially with DoMenu, then you will need to shell out for the Pro version of QuickTime. Visit

www.apple.com/quicktime/pro/win.html

A Movie Builder Script

To give you an idea of what can be achieved, let's look at a more complex script, this time using QuickTime Player automation in conjunction with the Windows Scripting library to build a composite movie from a folder of movies.

First, we launch player and open a second player window into which we will assemble the new movie:

```
// BuildMovieSimple.js : create a movie from a folder of movies
var qtPlayerApp = WScript.CreateObject("QuickTimePlayerLib.
          QuickTimePlayerApp");

var sourcePath = "D:\\Movies\\Birds\\Kittiwake";
var destFile = "D:\\Movies\\Exported\\NewMovie.mov";

if (qtPlayerApp != null)
{
  var qtPlayerSrc = qtPlayerApp.Players(1);
```

```
  qtPlayerApp.Players.Add();
  var qtPlayerDest = qtPlayerApp.Players(qtPlayerApp.Players.Count);
  qtPlayerDest.Visible = true;
}
```

At this point we have a source player (qtPlayerSrc) in which we can open movies and copy them to the clipboard plus a destination player (qtPlayerDest) into which we can paste each movie. The FileSystemObject comes in handy to obtain the Files collection of the source folder. Using a JScript Enumerator, we can iterate over the source movies, copying each to the clipboard using the "Copy" menu item of qtPlayerSrc and pasting them into the destination movie using the "Paste" menu item of qtPlayerDest.

```
if ((qtPlayerSrc == null) || (qtPlayerDest == null)) WScript.Quit();

var fso = WScript.CreateObject("Scripting.FileSystemObject");
var fldr = fso.GetFolder(sourcePath);

// Regular expression to match file extension
var re = new RegExp(".mov$", "i");

// Iterate over the source files
var fc = new Enumerator(fldr.Files);
for (; !fc.atEnd(); fc.moveNext())
{
  // Filter by file extension
  if (!re.test(fc.item().Name)
    continue;

  // Open the movie
  qtPlayerSrc.OpenURL(fc.item());

  // Paste into destination movie
  qtPlayerSrc.DoMenu("Edit", "Select All");
  qtPlayerSrc.DoMenu("Edit", "Copy");
  qtPlayerDest.DoMenu("Edit", "Paste");
}

qtPlayerDest.DoMenu("Edit", "Select None");
```

When iterating over a folder of files, there is always the possibility of encountering the odd file of a type that we're not interested in—for example, the cache file of an image browser. In the preceding code, we use a regular expression (".mov$" meaning any string that ends with ".mov") that we test against each file name. If the test fails, then we `continue` to the next file.

Having assembled a movie, it would be sensible to save it, but this is where the limitations of DoMenu become apparent. Yes, we can call

```
qtPlayerDest.DoMenu("File", "Save As…");
```

but all we get is QuickTime Player's *Save A File* dialog box: our automation has suddenly run into a brick wall. But all is not lost; this is the time to reach down for the movie object (QTControl.Movie) and use its `Save` or `SaveSelf-Contained` method directly:

```
var mov = qtPlayerDest.QTControl.Movie;

if (mov)
  mov.SaveSelfContained(destFile);
```

Now that we have our hands on the movie (QTMovie) object, there's really no limit to what we can get up to behind QuickTime Player's back. Borrowing from our *MovieBuilder* sample in Chapter 6, let's see if we can superimpose a logo:

```
// From BuildMovieWithLogo.js

// Start with the destination movie
var movDest = qtPlayerDest.QTControl.Movie;

var logoFile = "D:\\QuickTime\\Movies\\Birds\\Logo.png";

if (movDest)
{
  // Open the logo graphic in a new player window
  qtPlayerApp.Players.Add();
  var qtPlayerLogo = qtPlayerApp.Players(qtPlayerApp.Players.Count);
  qtPlayerLogo.Visible = true;

  qtPlayerLogo.OpenURL(logoFile);
```

```
  // Copy the logo into the destination movie
  if (qtPlayerLogo.QTControl.Movie)
  {
    qtPlayerLogo.QTControl.Movie.Copy();

    movDest.SelectAll();
    movDest.AddScaled();
    movDest.Time = 0;

    var trkLogo = movDest.Tracks(movDest.Tracks.Count);

    // Adjust logo position and transfer mode
    if (trkLogo)
    {
      trkLogo.Left = movDest.Right - trkLogo.Width - 10;
      trkLogo.Top = 10;

      // Define enumeration constant
      var qtTransferModeStraightAlphaBlend = 260;

      trkLogo.TransferMode = qtTransferModeStraightAlphaBlend;
      trkLogo.OperationColor = "32768, 32768, 32768";
      trkLogo.HighQualityMode = true;
    }
  }

  // Tidy up
  qtPlayerSrc.Close();
  qtPlayerLogo.Close();
  qtPlayerDest.DoMenu("Edit", "Select None");

  // Save the new movie
  movDest.SaveSelfContained(destFile);
  WScript.Echo("New movie created of duration: " + movDest.Duration);
}
```

This employs exactly the same technique as was used in Chapter 6; that is, AddScaled is used to paste the logo into the destination movie as a new video track superimposed on the movie. The position and transfer mode of this logo track are then adjusted.

Notice that we had to explicitly define the `qtTransferModeStraight-AlphaBlend` constant since JScript cannot directly use the enumerated constants that are defined in the `QTOLibrary` type library. Later in this chapter we will find a way to address this frustrating limitation.

Batch Export from the Command Line

In a busy production environment, we really don't want to have to mess around with editing hard-coded paths in our script files, or even with having to double-click on the script files to run them. Ideally, we would like to be able to run frequently used scripts from the command line, passing a few arguments, and have the script tell us when it's done.

Movie export is a common repetitive task that lends itself to batch processing. Taking a batch of media files in one format, we export them to a different format or even to several different formats—perhaps for delivery on diverse platforms such as DVD, the Web, or mobile devices, such as a PDA, smartphone, or video iPod.

Let's consider a batch export script that takes a source folder of media files and exports them, using a specified QuickTime exporter, to a destination folder. The script needs to run from the command line and takes four arguments:

1. The path to the source folder

2. The path to the destination folder

3. The type of exporter to use (e.g., AVI, QuickTime Movie, DV Stream)

4. The file extension for the exported files (e.g., avi, mov, dv)

Exporter Types

The definitive list of available exporter types for any movie or track can be obtained from its `PotentialExporters` property. However, for convenience I've listed, in Appendix C, most of the standard exporter types available with QuickTime Pro.

A typical call would be

```
cscript BatchExport.js D:\Movies\Source D:\Movies\Dest "DV Stream" dv
```

In other words, we would like to take all the movies in *D:\Movies\Source* and export them one at a time using the QuickTime *"DV Stream"* exporter to similarly named files—but with the *"dv"* file extension—that we will put in *D:\Movies\Dest.*

Tip Command line arguments that contain one or more spaces should always be enclosed in double quotes so that they are interpreted as a single argument.

Capturing the arguments from the command line is the raison d'être of the WScript object's Arguments collection. It contains one item for every white-space–delimited argument on the command line. The first part of our batch export script involves getting the arguments followed by the tedious, but necessary, task of validating them:

```js
// BatchExport.js
var sourcePath, destPath, exporterType, exportFileExtension;

// Get script arguments
if (WScript.Arguments.Length >= 4)
{
  sourcePath = WScript.Arguments(0);
  destPath = WScript.Arguments(1);
  exporterType = WScript.Arguments(2);
  exportFileExtension = WScript.Arguments(3);
}

// Sanity check arguments
var fso = WScript.CreateObject("Scripting.FileSystemObject");

var e = "";

if (!fso.FolderExists(sourcePath))
  e += "Source path does not exist : " + "[" + sourcePath + "]\n";

if (!fso.FolderExists(destPath))
  e += "Destination path does not exist : " + "[" + destPath + "]\n";

if (exporterType == undefined)
  e += "No exporter type supplied!\n";

if (exportFileExtension == undefined)
  e += "No exporter file extension supplied!\n";

if (e != "")
{
```

```
    WScript.Echo(e);
    WScript.Echo("Usage:");
    WScript.Echo("cscript BatchExport.js <sourcePath>, <destPath>,
            <exporterType>, <exportFileExtension>");
    WScript.Quit();
}
```

Now that we have our parameters all lined up, the next task is to launch QuickTime Player and set ourselves up with a QTExporter object that we will need to process the movies.

```
// Launch QuickTime Player
var qtPlayerApp = WScript.CreateObject(
            "QuickTimePlayerLib.QuickTimePlayerApp");

if (qtPlayerApp == null)
{
  WScript.Echo("Unable to launch QuickTime Player!");
  WScript.Quit();
}

var qtPlayerSrc = qtPlayerApp.Players(1);

if (qtPlayerSrc == null)
  WScript.Quit();

// Set up the exporter and have it configured
var qt = qtPlayerSrc.QTControl.QuickTime;
qt.Exporters.Add();
var exp = qt.Exporters(1);

if (exp)
{
  exp.TypeName = exporterType;
  exp.ShowSettingsDialog();
}
```

Our QTExporter object is obtained, as we learned in Chapter 5, by first getting hold of the Exporters collection from QTControl.QuickTime and then adding an exporter. Once we have the exporter, we can set its TypeName to the exporter type specified on the command line. Finally, before the export process begins, the Exporter Settings Dialog is opened so that the exporter options can be configured once for the batch.

At this point the process of iterating over the source files can begin.

```javascript
var fldr = fso.GetFolder(sourcePath);

// Regular expression to match file extension
var re = new RegExp(".mov$", "i");

// Iterate over the source files
var fc = new Enumerator(fldr.Files);
for (; !fc.atEnd(); fc.moveNext())
{
  var f = fc.item().Name;

  // Filter by file extension
  if (!re.test(f))
    continue;

  try
  {
    // Open the movie and export it
    qtPlayerSrc.OpenURL(fc.item());

    var mov = qtPlayerSrc.QTControl.Movie;
    if (mov)
    {
      exp.SetDataSource(mov);

      // Strip file extension and compose new file name
      f = f.replace(/\.[^\.]*$/, "");
      var fDest = destPath + "\\" + f + "." + exportFileExtension;

      exp.DestinationFileName = fDest;
      exp.BeginExport();

      WScript.Echo("Exported: " + fDest);
    }
  }
```

```
  catch (err)
  {
    WScript.Echo("Error Exporting: " + fc.item());
  }

}

// Tidy up
qtPlayerSrc.Close();
```

The code that is concerned with opening the source file and exporting it is protected within a `try...catch` block; thus, should an exception occur with a particular rogue file, it does not cause the whole script to fail.

Regular expressions come in handy in all sorts of places. As well as using a regular expression to filter the source files by file extension, a regular expression is also used in the JScript `replace` function to strip the file extension off the source movie file name so that it can be replaced with export-FileExtension to create the destination file name.

```
// Strip file extension and compose new file name
f = f.replace(/\.[^\.]*$/, "");
var fDest = destPath + "\\" + f + "." + exportFileExtension;
```

While this batch script is concerned with exporting media files, the processing code could, of course, easily be adapted to carry out other useful tasks on a bunch of movies, such as entering a copyright notice as an annotation, adding in a sound track, checking format and size, and so on.

Event Handlers

Now that we are getting more adventurous with our QuickTime Player scripts, we begin to wonder if it might even be possible to intercept events from the QuickTime Control. One or two extra lines of code and an event handler is all it takes.

First we need to connect the outgoing events of the QuickTime Control to our script:

```
WScript.ConnectObject(qtPlayer.QTControl, "QTControl_");
```

All we need now are some event handlers:

```
// SizeChanged event handler
function QTControl_SizeChanged(width, height)
{
  WScript.Echo("SizeChanged: " + width + "," + height);
}


// StatusUpdate event handler
function QTControl_StatusUpdate(statusCodeType, statusCode,
          statusMessage)
{
  WScript.Echo("StatusUpdate: " + statusCodeType + ","
          + statusCode + "," + statusMessage);
}
```

The name of each event handler function must begin with the same prefix as we specified in the second parameter of ConnectObject—in this case "QTControl_".

Before adding these event handlers to a simple command line script that opens a movie, we need to do one more important thing: make sure our script stays running long enough to catch the events! Whenever we run a script, it executes all the code in the script and then, having gotten its work done, the script just quits—it doesn't hang around for any after-hours frivolity. The crudest way to get the script to stay running is to add something like the following at the bottom of the script:

```
WScript.Sleep(10000);
```

This instructs the script to hang around for 10 seconds before leaving us. This should give us enough time to see the output from our event handlers. Grab the resize handle of the player window and you should get a stream of SizeChanged events.

Here's a typical session:

```
D:\Projects\QTBook\Samples\WSH>cscript
          QTControl_Events.js D:\Movies\sample.mov
Microsoft (R) Windows Script Host Version 5.6
Copyright (C) Microsoft Corporation 1996-2001. All rights reserved.
```

```
SizeChanged: 206,243
StatusUpdate: 0,4099,MovieLoadFinalize
StatusUpdate: 2,100000,
StatusUpdate: 0,4096,URL Changed
StatusUpdate: 2,100000,
SizeChanged: 207,243
SizeChanged: 207,244
SizeChanged: 215,244
SizeChanged: 215,254
SizeChanged: 220,254
SizeChanged: 220,260
SizeChanged: 223,260
SizeChanged: 223,263
SizeChanged: 231,263
SizeChanged: 231,272
StatusUpdate: 0,4096,URL Changed
^C
D:\Projects\QTBook\Samples\WSH>
```

Notice that we were able to terminate the script execution with *Ctrl-C* from the keyboard once we had seen enough.

The events that are really of interest, however, are those QuickTime Events that we discussed in Chapter 5—events such as qtEventRateWill-Change, which notifies us that the movie play rate is about to change. Recall that we must register for those QuickTime Events that we want to be notified of by adding them to the EventListeners collection of the movie.

```
var mov = qtPlayer.QTControl.Movie;

if (mov)
{
  // Register to be notified of Rate change
  mov.EventListeners.Add(qtEventClassStateChange,
          qtEventRateWillChange);
}
```

You will also recall that all QuickTime Events are notified to us through the QTEvent event of the QuickTime Control, and so we need a handler for QTEvent:

```
// QTEvent handler
function QTControl_QTEvent(eventClass,
            eventID, phase, eventObject, cancel)
{
  WScript.Echo("QTEvent: " + eventClass + "," + eventID);
}
```

We can put this all to good use now with a script that launches QuickTime Player, loads a movie that we specify on the command line, plays it through, and then quits. This is only possible if we can determine when the movie has stopped playing so that we can close it and exit Player. Here's the complete script:

```
// LoadPlayAndQuit.js

var fileName;

// qtEvent constants
var qtEventClassStateChange = 0x73746174;
var qtEventRateWillChange   = 0x72617465;
var qtEventParamMovieRate   = 0x72617465;

// Get the filename
if (WScript.Arguments.Length > 0)
  fileName = WScript.Arguments(0);
else
  fileName = "d:\\QuickTime\\Movies\\sample.mov";

// Launch QuickTime Player
var qtPlayerApp = WScript.CreateObject(
            "QuickTimePlayerLib.QuickTimePlayerApp");

var movieStopped = false;

if (qtPlayerApp == null) WScript.Quit();

var qtPlayer = qtPlayerApp.Players(1);
```

```
        if (qtPlayer)
        {
          // Connect this script to events from QTControl
          WScript.ConnectObject(qtPlayer.QTControl, "QTControl_");

          qtPlayer.OpenURL(fileName);

          var mov = qtPlayer.QTControl.Movie;

          if (mov)
          {
            // Register to be notified of Rate change
            mov.EventListeners.Add(qtEventClassStateChange,
                    qtEventRateWillChange);

            mov.Play();
          }
        }

        // Wait for movie to finish playing
        while (!movieStopped)
        {
          WScript.Sleep(100);
        }

        // Quit QuickTime Player and exit the script
        qtPlayerApp.Quit();

        WScript.Quit();

        // QTEvent handler
        function QTControl_QTEvent(eventClass, eventID,
                    phase, eventObject, cancel)
        {
          switch (eventID)
          {
            case qtEventRateWillChange:
              var rate = eventObject.GetParam(qtEventParamMovieRate);
              if (rate == 0.0)
                movieStopped = true;
          }
        }
```

This time we keep the script going by running a while loop that polls a movieStopped flag every 100 milliseconds. Just before we Play the movie, we register for qtEventRateWillChange so that we will be notified whenever the play rate changes. When that happens, our event handler—QTControl_QTEvent—is called and in it we get the qtEventParamMovieRate parameter. If it equals zero, the movie must have stopped playing, and it's time to bail out by setting movieStopped to true.

Again, we have had to explicitly define the qtEvent constants that we have used due to the lack of support in JScript for enumerated constants. (See the section "Windows Scripting File (.wsf) Format" later in this chapter for a better solution.)

Script Droplets

Script users on the Mac have a particular weakness for AppleScript droplets. A *droplet* is a script onto which you can drag and drop one or more files or folders. The script will then proceed to do something to every file or folder. So, for example, you might have a HalfScale droplet onto which you can drop a folder; each movie in the folder is then opened and scaled by 50 percent. No fewer than 40 QuickTime Player droplets are listed at *www.apple.com/applescript/quicktime/*.

Windows Scripting users needn't feel left out—creating droplets from our scripts is a cinch. In fact, we've already done it! Open a second Windows Explorer window, browse to some movies, and then drag a single movie file and drop it onto the *LoadPlayAndQuit.js* script file that we have just written. The movie will be opened just as if we had passed it as an argument on the command line.

In fact, any script that can take a list of files or folders as arguments on the command line can also have those same files or folders dropped onto it. In both cases the list of files and folders ends up in the WScript.Arguments collection.

With the addition of just a couple of extra lines of code the *Load-PlayAndQuit.js* script can easily turn into a useful *load movie and play it full screen* droplet. Immediately before we play the movie, we invoke the Quick-Time Player's "Full Screen" menu item:

```
qtPlayer.DoMenu("View", "Full Screen");
mov.Play();
```

and, to ensure an orderly shutdown, we set the movie back to normal size before we quit:

```
// Quit QuickTime Player and exit the script
qtPlayer.DoMenu("View", "Normal Size");
WScript.Sleep(100);
qtPlayerApp.Quit();
```

The WScript.Sleep(100) gives Player a little time to compose itself before we kill it.

Finally, here is a useful droplet that can be used to set the copyright annotation of every movie that is dropped on it. It's a script that can easily be adapted to do almost anything we like to a batch of movies:

```
// SetMoviesCopyright.js
//
// Drop a list of movies onto this script

var qtAnnotationCopyright = 0x63707274;

// Get script arguments
if (WScript.Arguments.Length == 0)
{
  WScript.Echo("You must drop at least one file onto this script!");
  WScript.Quit();
}

// Launch QuickTime Player
var qtPlayerApp = WScript.CreateObject(
            "QuickTimePlayerLib.QuickTimePlayerApp");

if (qtPlayerApp == null)
{
  WScript.Echo("Unable to launch QuickTime Player!");
  WScript.Quit();
}

var qtPlayer = qtPlayerApp.Players(1);

if (qtPlayer == null)
  WScript.Quit();

// Regular expression to match file extension
var re = new RegExp(".mov$", "i");
```

```
// Iterate over the source files
var n = 0;
for (var i = 0; i < WScript.Arguments.Length; i++)
{
  var f = WScript.Arguments(i);

  // Filter by file extension
  if (!re.test(f))
    continue;

  try
  {
    qtPlayer.OpenURL(f);
    var mov = qtPlayer.QTControl.Movie;
    if (mov)
    {
      mov.Annotation(qtAnnotationCopyright)
        = "© 2005 Red Rooster Productions";
      mov.Save();
      n++;
    }
  }
  catch (err)
  {
    WScript.Echo("ERROR: " + f);
  }
}

// Tidy up
qtPlayer.Close();

WScript.Echo("Copyright successfully added to " + n + " movies!");
```

Windows Scripting File (.wsf) Format

If your script frequently references the various QuickTime constants such as
the qtEvent or qtAnnotation IDs, you can avoid the tedium of having to
define these constants by packaging your script in a proper Windows Script
File (.wsf). You can then explicitly reference the QTOLibrary and QTOControl-
Lib typelibs so that all the enumerated constants are available to your script.

A script in the .wsf format looks like this:

```
<job>

  <!-- Import typelibs -->
  <reference guid="{29866AED-1E14-417D-BA0F-1A2BE6F5A19E}" />
          <!-- QTOLibrary -->
  <reference guid="{7B92F833-027D-402B-BFF9-A67697366F4E}" />
          <!-- QTOControlLib -->

  <script language="JScript">

// -- Script starts here --
var qtPlayerApp = WScript.CreateObject(
          "QuickTimePlayerLib.QuickTimePlayerApp");

if (qtPlayerApp != null)
{
  var qtPlayer = qtPlayerApp.Players(1);

  if (qtPlayer)
    qtPlayer.OpenURL("d:\\QuickTime\\Movies\\sample.mov");
}
// -- Script ends here --

  </script>

</job>
```

Scripts packaged in the .wsf format behave exactly as if they were .js or .vbs files.

A bonus is that you can also *include* other .js script files, and use functions defined in them, just as you might in a web page:

```
<script language="JScript" src="QTUtilityScripts.js" />
```

If so inclined, you can even mix scripts in different languages in the same .wsf file, calling functions in one language from another (with some caveats, of course!):

```
<!-- This script requires ActivePerl to be installed -->
<script language="PerlScript">
  $WScript->Echo("Hello world!");
</script>
```

Summary

You should now be well equipped to experiment with writing your own scripts to automate QuickTime Player and to harness the power of the underlying QuickTime Object Model that it exposes. Many of the Quick-Time production tasks that used to be the preserve of scripters using Apple-Script on the Mac can now be accomplished just as easily on Windows.

Don't forget either, that your scripts can automate other applications in conjunction with QuickTime Player, making it possible to interchange data between other applications and the QuickTime movies that you are working with.

9

QuickTime Meets Office

*QuickTime Development in
Microsoft Excel and Access*

Introduction

When it comes to Windows applications that bare their inner souls to be scripted—or automated—the Microsoft Office family of applications arguably tops the pile. Word, Excel, Outlook, Access, PowerPoint—even Visio and Publisher—all sport deep and extensive object models exposing everything from the formula in a spreadsheet cell to the individual characters in a Word document or the properties of a field in a database table. Most of the Office applications can act as COM automation servers under the control of external scripts, just as we have done with QuickTime Player in Chapter 8.

Not only that, but Office applications also feature a powerful internal programming language known as Visual Basic for Applications (VBA). Armed with the object model for an application, with its access to the logical objects and UI elements of a spreadsheet or Word document, a VBA script developer can very quickly pull together impressive mini-applications that come in the guise of an Excel or Word document. VBA is a full-featured programming language that is almost indistinguishable from Visual Basic 6.

But where Visual Basic enjoys the open spaces of its own forms and a toolbox full of controls with which to populate them, in a typical Office application VBA is restricted to using the current document window or form as its playing field. And as for controls, there is a limited set of standard UI controls that can be placed on this window, such as a button, text field, or list box. These are available from the *Control Toolbox*—accessible via View | Toolbars | Control Toolbox in any Office application.

Nestling in the lower right-hand corner of the Control Toolbox is a button whose icon, disquietingly reminiscent of a political symbol, displays a crossed hammer and wrench. Click on this More Controls button and you will be presented with a long list of all the COM controls that are registered on the system. Close to the top of the list, you should find the *Apple Quick-Time Control 2.0*.

But I'm jumping ahead: suffice it to say that it is possible to use the Quick-Time Control—to some extent anyhow—in any of the Office applications that support ActiveX/COM control hosting. Whether a QuickTime Control ensconced between the paragraphs of prose in your Word document can conceivably serve any useful purpose is admittedly a rather moot point. However, drop the same control onto an Excel worksheet or Access form, and interesting possibilities begin to emerge, as we shall see.

Fortunately, the applications in the Office suite share much in common. If we learn how to add a QuickTime Control to a document or form in one Office application, the procedure is usually very similar in the others. In this chapter we concentrate on those two Office heavyweights that are likely to be of most interest to anyone whose task it is to manage or produce Quick-Time content: Microsoft Excel and Microsoft Access.

Note The samples in this chapter are all based on Office 2003. If you are using an earlier version of Office, it should be possible to get the samples working—with perhaps a few differences here and there—since ActiveX support has not changed significantly in Office 2003.

Excel

For all its curiosity value, a spreadsheet that can play a movie in among its rows and columns of figures is unlikely to have you jumping up excitedly and exclaiming "That is *just* what I need!" But we'll persevere, you never know—perhaps it might come in handy after all.

Adding the QuickTime Control

Having launched Excel and created a new blank workbook, the launch pad for adding the QuickTime Control, as mentioned earlier, is the Control Toolbox (View | Toolbars | Control Toolbox). Clicking on the More Controls button presents us with a list of controls from which we can select the Apple QuickTime Control as shown in Figure 9.1.

As soon as you select the QuickTime Control, the worksheet will flip into Design Mode—the Design Mode button in the top-left corner of the Control Toolbox is highlighted—and the cursor will change to a crosshair. Click and drag the mouse anywhere on the sheet to place the QuickTime Control. Then right-click on the new control and select Properties to bring up the Properties palette for the control. Clicking on the Custom property button will display the Property Pages for the QuickTime Control, and within this dialog we can select a movie to be loaded into the control. Alternatively you can just enter the full path and name of a movie directly into the URL property field in the Properties palette.

After dismissing the Properties palette, toggle the mode button in the top-left corner of the Control Toolbox once again, this time to switch out of Design Mode. The movie should now load and will be overlaid on top of the worksheet cells (Figure 9.2), with the QuickTime Control resizing itself to fit the movie. Double-click on the movie or click on the Play button in the movie controller bar, and the movie should indeed play.

Figure 9.1 Adding the QuickTime Control from the Control Toolbox.

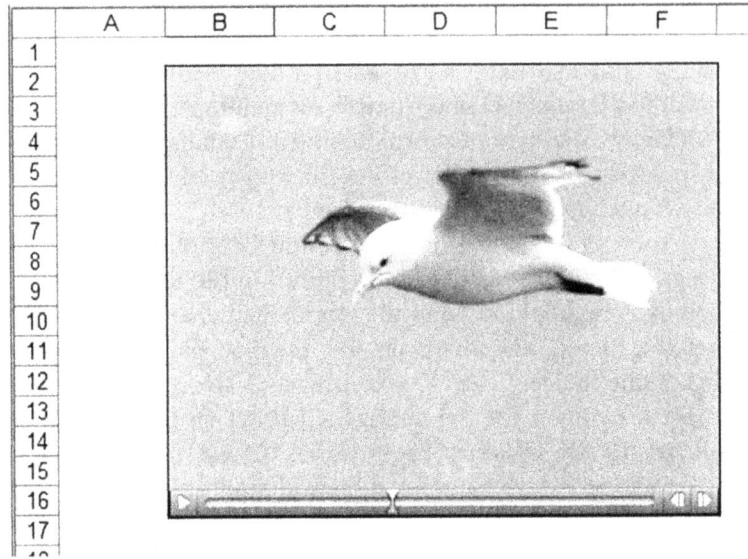

Figure 9.2 QuickTime Control in an Excel spreadsheet.

You can now save the worksheet, close it, and reopen it. Once you have escaped the clutches of Office security (see ActiveX and Macro Security in the next section), the spreadsheet will open and this time the movie will be loaded straight away.

What has happened here is that the URL property, being a *persistent* property of the QuickTime Control, has had its value saved in the document. As soon as the QuickTime Control is loaded, any persistent property values are retrieved from the document and applied to the control once more, with the result that the movie is loaded immediately. Other persistent properties of the QuickTime Control include BackColor, BorderColor, MovieController-Visible, and Sizing.

ActiveX and Macro Security

VBA scripts—confusingly referred to as Macros—are often disabled by default in your Office application. You won't even get a warning when you open a document containing a script: the script code simply won't work and it can be maddeningly difficult to figure out why. To get your scripts working, you should open Tools | Macro | Security... and select the Medium option as shown in Figure 9.3. Even with the Medium setting, you will still

Figure 9.3 Macro Security setting to enable VBA scripts.

be prompted with a Security Warning when you open a document containing any scripts. You should select the Enable Macros button.

Whenever you load an Office 2003 document that contains an ActiveX control, you are likely to be confronted with a message something like this:

> This application is about to initialize ActiveX controls that might be unsafe.
> If you trust the source of this document, select Yes and the control will be
> initialized using your document settings.

If you want to be able to use a control such as the QuickTime Control in your document, then you should click Yes.

All this fuss is regrettably necessary. Office documents containing all sorts of vile scripts are out there in force, and one is very likely to end up in your browser or email inbox at some point. Microsoft has, somewhat belatedly, gone to great lengths to put hurdles in front of such scripts. Unfortunately, for anyone genuinely wanting to use ActiveX controls or scripts in their documents, all this security baggage can be a bit of a headache.

Adding a Play/Stop Cell

Having gotten a movie to open in our worksheet, the logical next step is to add a Play button. Rather than going down the predictable route of using a Command Button control from the Control Toolbox, let's be more adventurous and see if we can get a worksheet cell to act as a Play/Stop button. Picking a free cell somewhere on our sheet, we change its background color to light blue and give it an outline border before—optimistically—entering the word *Play* into it. At least it now looks like a button—getting it to act like a button is maybe not so simple.

This is the point where we must resort to a VBA script. All scriptable Office applications have a VBA code editor that can be invoked using Tools | Macro | Visual Basic Editor or Alt-F11. On the left (usually), you will find the Project Explorer window listing all of the available high-level scriptable objects—in this case the workbook and its worksheets. Double-clicking on Sheet1 opens the code module associated with Sheet1. This will look instantly familiar to anyone who has programmed with Visual Basic.

Selecting Worksheet in the left-hand drop-down list at the top of the code editor, we can browse through the worksheet events in the right-hand list. Unfortunately, there is no such thing as an event that is triggered when you click on a cell: the closest we can get is the SelectionChange event, which occurs whenever the current selection of cells changes. If you click on a cell that is not currently selected, then it becomes the selection, and so SelectionChange will fire, simulating a click event. The only problem is that if you want to have SelectionChange fire when you click on a cell the second time, you must first select another cell elsewhere.

Picking SelectionChange from the right-hand drop-down list, the event handler prototype is inserted into the code module:

```
Private Sub Worksheet_SelectionChange(ByVal Target As Range)


End Sub
```

To work out which cell has been selected, we must decode the Target event parameter. Assuming that the cell destined to be our Play/Stop button is B19, our Play/Stop "button" handler looks like this:

```
Private Sub Worksheet_SelectionChange(ByVal Target As Range)

  If Target.Address = Range("B19").Address Then

    If Not (QTControl1.Movie Is Nothing) Then

      If QTControl1.Movie.Rate = 0 Then
        QTControl1.Movie.Play
      Else
        QTControl1.Movie.Stop
      End If

    End If

    Range("B20").Select

  End If

End Sub
```

Notice that we use Range("B20").Select at the end of our handler to select another (neutral) cell so that we will always get a SelectionChange event if we click on Play/Stop a second time. The *QTControl_Basic.xls* sample is available from

www.skylark.ie/qt4.net/Samples/Office

Having satisfied our curiosity about playing a movie in a spreadsheet, let's move quickly to a more useful application of QuickTime in Excel.

Movie Inspector

Working with multiple QuickTime movies—a frequent production require-ment—often involves lists of movies containing data about the movies and perhaps annotations that need to be added to the movies. For this type of data—to be viewed or edited in a tabular format—Excel is often the first port of call, and so this begs the question, Can we put our new-found ability to open QuickTime movies in Excel to good use in a production scenario where we're dealing with large numbers of movies?

The Movie Inspector is a spreadsheet that allows us to select a folder of movies and fill a column with the file names of the movies in the folder. Selecting a cell that contains the file name of a movie will open the movie and populate the spreadsheet with detailed information about the movie. As before, we employ cells to act as buttons. The completed Movie Inspector is shown in Figure 9.4 with the key cells and cell ranges identified in the accompanying Table 9.1.

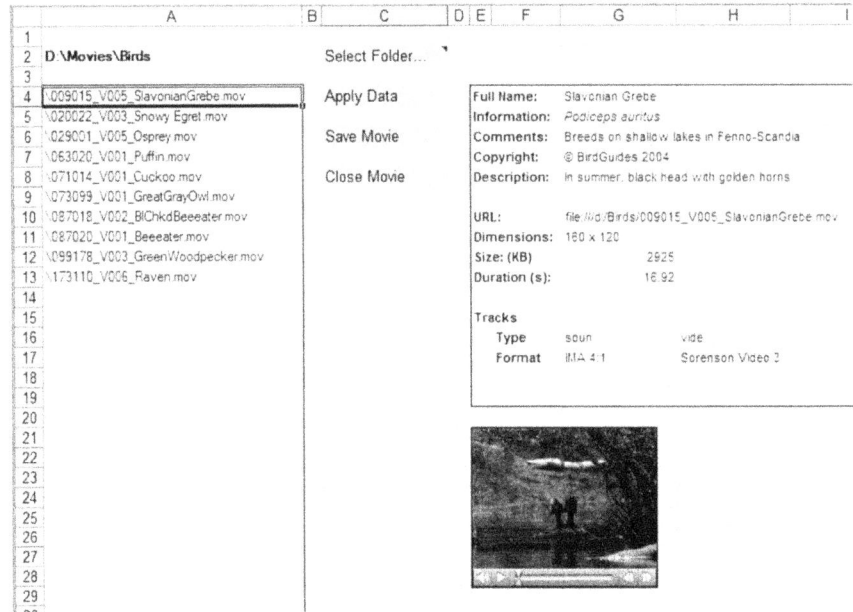

Figure 9.4 Movie Inspector in Microsoft Excel.

Table 9.1 Key cell ranges in Movie Inspector

Function	Cell Range
Movies folder path	A2
List of movie files	A4:An
Select Folder button	C2
Apply Data button	C4
Save Movie button	C6
Close Movie button	C8
Annotations	G4:G8
Other info	G10:G13
Tracks details	G16:n17

From a VBA script point of view, most of the action will be concentrated in the worksheet SelectionChange event handler since all clicks on our 'button' cells, as well as clicks on any of the listed files, end up routed through this handler. Before getting down to the nitty-gritty of this event handler, it's worth pausing to define some constants to represent the rows and columns of the key cell ranges in our worksheet (see Table 9.1). Using these will simplify our subsequent code and spare us the indignity of having to alter hard-coded values if we happen to add a row here or remove a column there.

```
Option Explicit

Const kDataCol = 7
Const kDataRow = 4
Const kFilesCol = 1
Const kFilesRow = 4
Const kPathCol = 1
Const kPathRow = 2
Const kCommandsCol = 3
Const kCommandsRow = 2
```

Note how the columns have integer designations (1 = A, B = 2, etc.) rather than letters. Also, Option Explicit at the top of a code module forces us to explicitly define all variables: it is good discipline to insist on this at the top of every VBA module.

Now for the SelectionChange event handler, which is presented here in outline, with the detailed code removed for clarity:

```
Private Sub Worksheet_SelectionChange(ByVal Target As Range)

    Dim fileName As String
    Dim rootPath As String

    Select Case Target.Column

      Case kFilesCol    'Select a file name

      Case kCommandsCol   'Select a button

        Select Case Target.row

          Case kCommandsRow + 0:    'Select Folder
```

```
                 Case kCommandsRow + 2:    'Apply Movie data

                 Case kCommandsRow + 4:    'Save Movie

                 Case kCommandsRow + 6:    'Close Movie

            End Select

         End Select

   End Sub
```

You will see how the row and column constants that we defined earlier are compared with Target.Column and Target.Row to identify the particular cell that has been selected and to determine the subsequent action. Turning now to the detailed implementation, we start with Select Folder:

```
Case kCommandsRow + 0:    'Select Folder

   Dim objShell, objFolder, objFolderItem

   Set objShell = CreateObject("Shell.Application")
   Set objFolder = objShell.BrowseForFolder(
           0, "Choose Movies Folder:", 0)

   If objFolder Is Nothing Then Exit Sub

   Set objFolderItem = objFolder.Items.Item

   rootPath = objFolderItem.path

   Me.Cells(kPathRow, kFilesCol) = rootPath

   GetListOfFiles rootPath
```

Using the Windows Shell object Shell.Application, we open a standard folder browse dialog. Once a path is selected, this is passed to GetListOf-Files:

```
Private Sub GetListOfFiles(rootPath As String)
```

```
    On Error GoTo ErrorHandler
    Me.Range(Me.Cells(kFilesRow, kFilesCol),
            Me.Cells(kFilesRow + 1000, kFilesCol)).ClearContents

    Application.Cursor = xlWait
    AddFiles rootPath, rootPath, kFilesRow
    Application.Cursor = xlDefault

    Exit Sub

ErrorHandler:
    Application.Cursor = xlDefault
    MsgBox "*** ERROR ***: " + Hex(Err.Number) + ": " +
            Err.Description + vbCrLf

End Sub
```

GetListOfFiles first clears the list of files in column A (kFilesCol) and then calls AddFiles for the root path that we selected:

```
Private Sub AddFiles(rootPath As String, path As String,
            ByRef row As Integer)

    Dim fso As New Scripting.FileSystemObject
    Dim fldrPath As Scripting.Folder
    Dim fldr As Scripting.Folder
    Dim fil As Scripting.File
    Dim f As String

    On Error GoTo ErrorHandler

    Set fldrPath = fso.GetFolder(path)

    For Each fil In fldrPath.Files
        f = fldrPath.path + "\" + fil.Name
        If Len(f) > Len(rootPath) Then
                f = Mid(f, Len(rootPath) + 1) 'Strip root path
        End If
        Me.Cells(row, kFilesCol) = f
        row = row + 1
    Next fil
```

```
    For Each fldr In fldrPath.SubFolders
      AddFiles rootPath, fldr.path, row
    Next fldr

    Exit Sub

ErrorHandler:
    MsgBox "*** ERROR ***: " + Hex(Err.Number) + ": " +
            Err.Description + vbCrLf

End Sub
```

AddFiles adds each file that it finds in the path to the kFilesCol work-sheet column. It then proceeds to recursively call itself for each subfolder so that we end up with a list of all the files in our selected folder and any nested subfolders that it contains. So as not to unduly clutter our worksheet, each file name is stripped of the root path so that it appears in the list of files with a relative path.

Now that we have a list of files, we want to be able to click on any file in the list, have it opened in the QuickTime Control (QTControl1) that we have placed on the worksheet for this purpose, and have the movie data copied into the allocated cells. Here's the relevant code from our SelectionChange event handler:

```
Case kFilesCol   'Select a file name

    If Target.row < kFilesRow Then Exit Sub

    fileName = Me.Cells(Target.row, kFilesCol)
    If fileName = "" Then Exit Sub

    QTControl1.URL = ""

    ClearMovieData

    rootPath = Me.Cells(kPathRow, kPathCol)
    OpenMovie rootPath + fileName
```

The file name is extracted from the target cell that we clicked on, appended to the root path, and then passed to OpenMovie. The function ClearMovieData will clear the range of cells that is to be populated with data about the movie. OpenMovie is not unlike similar functions that we have seen in earlier chapters:

```
Sub OpenMovie(fileName As String)

    On Error GoTo ErrorHandler

    Application.Cursor = xlWait
    QTControl1.ErrorHandling = qtErrorHandlingRaiseException
    QTControl1.URL = fileName
    If Not (QTControl1.Movie Is Nothing) Then
      GetMovieData
    End If
    Application.Cursor = xlDefault

    Exit Sub

ErrorHandler:
    Application.Cursor = xlDefault
    MsgBox "Unable to open movie: " + fileName + vbCrLf +
           "Error: " + Hex(Err.Number)

End Sub
```

Once the movie has been opened successfully, GetMovieData is called to extract data from the movie and its tracks and pop it into the relevant worksheet cells:

```
Private Sub GetMovieData()

    Dim i As Long
    Dim qtu As New QTUtils

    With QTControl1.Movie
      Me.Cells(kDataRow + 0, kDataCol) =
            GetAnnotation(QTControl1.Movie, qtAnnotationFullName)
      Me.Cells(kDataRow + 1, kDataCol) =
            GetAnnotation(QTControl1.Movie, qtAnnotationInformation)
```

```
        Me.Cells(kDataRow + 2, kDataCol) =
                GetAnnotation(QTControl1.Movie, qtAnnotationComments)
        Me.Cells(kDataRow + 3, kDataCol) =
                GetAnnotation(QTControl1.Movie, qtAnnotationCopyright)
        Me.Cells(kDataRow + 4, kDataCol) =
                GetAnnotation(QTControl1.Movie, qtAnnotationDescription)

        Me.Cells(kDataRow + 6, kDataCol) = QTControl1.URL
        Me.Cells(kDataRow + 7, kDataCol) = CStr(.Width) +
                " x " + CStr(.Height)
        Me.Cells(kDataRow + 8, kDataCol) = .Size / 1000
        Me.Cells(kDataRow + 9, kDataCol) = .Duration / .TimeScale

        For i = 0 To .Tracks.Count - 1
            Me.Cells(kDataRow + 12, kDataCol + i) =
                qtu.FourCharCodeToString(.Tracks(i + 1).Type)
            Me.Cells(kDataRow + 13, kDataCol + i) = .Tracks(i + 1).Format
        Next i
    End With

End Sub
```

GetAnnotation is a helper function that returns the value of a movie annotation, or an empty string if the annotation does not exist:

```
Function GetAnnotation(ByRef mov As QTMovie,
            ByVal annotationID As Long) As String

    Dim val As String

    val = ""
    On Error GoTo Bail:
    val = mov.Annotation(annotationID)

Bail:
    GetAnnotation = val
End Function
```

With this we should be able to click on the file name of a movie, image, or sound and have its pertinent details displayed in our worksheet, as shown in Figure 9.4.

Movie Inspector with Annotation Editing

Once you see movie annotations popping into the cells of a spreadsheet, it's not long before you begin to wonder if it might be possible to type something into those cells and have the edited annotations saved back to the movie.

The Apply Data "button" makes this possible, and it is handled in Worksheet_SelectionChange as follows:

```
Case kCommandsRow + 2:     'Apply Movie data

  If QTControl1.URL <> "" Then SetMovieData
```

SetMovieData and its helper routine SetAnnotation are where the action happens:

```
Sub SetMovieData()

  Dim mov As QTMovie

  Set mov = QTControl1.Movie

  SetAnnotation mov, qtAnnotationFullName,
          Me.Cells(kDataRow + 0, kDataCol)
  SetAnnotation mov, qtAnnotationInformation,
          Me.Cells(kDataRow + 1, kDataCol)
  SetAnnotation mov, qtAnnotationComments,
          Me.Cells(kDataRow + 2, kDataCol)
  SetAnnotation mov, qtAnnotationCopyright,
          Me.Cells(kDataRow + 3, kDataCol)
  SetAnnotation mov, qtAnnotationDescription,
          Me.Cells(kDataRow + 4, kDataCol)

End Sub
```

```
Sub SetAnnotation(ByRef mov As QTMovie,
          ByVal annotationID As Long, newVal)

  Dim val As String, curVal As String

  On Error GoTo ErrorHandler

  val = Trim(CStr(newVal))
  curVal = GetAnnotation(mov, annotationID)

  If val <> curVal Then
    If val = "" Then
      mov.RemoveAnnotation annotationID
    Else
      mov.Annotation(annotationID) = val
    End If
  End If

  Exit Sub

ErrorHandler:
  MsgBox "Unable to Save Annotation: " + Hex(Err.Number) + ": " +
  Err.Description + vbCrLf + mov.URL

End Sub
```

Once the movie annotations have been updated, it's time to save the movie using the Save Movie "button," which has a very straightforward implementation:

```
Case kCommandsRow + 4:    'Save Movie

  If QTControl1.URL <> "" Then
    Application.Cursor = xlWait
    SetMovieData
    QTControl1.Movie.Save
    Application.Cursor = xlDefault
  End If
```

At this point you should be able to click on a movie and then edit the annotations in cells G4 to G8. Click on Save Movie and these changes will be permanently saved with the movie. The *Movie_Inspector.xls* sample is available from

www.skylark.ie/qt4.net/Samples/Office

Batch Processing: Movie Annotator

Instead of just opening a single movie and listing its annotations, a VBA script could easily loop through the list of movies, opening each movie in turn and listing its annotations in a single worksheet row per movie as shown in Figure 9.5.

	A	B	C	E	F	G
1						
2	D:\Movies\Birds		Select Folder...			
3					Full Name:	Information:
4	\009015_V005_SlavonianGrebe.mov		Get Annotations		Slavonian Grebe	*Podiceps auritus*
5	\020022_V003_Snowy Egret.mov				Snowy Egret	*Egretta thula*
6	\029001_V005_Osprey.mov		Save Annotations		Osprey	*Pandion haliaetus*
7	\063020_V001_Puffin.mov				Puffin	*Fratercula arctica*
8	\071014_V001_Cuckoo.mov				Cuckoo	*Cuculus canorus*
9	\073099_V001_GreatGrayOwl.mov				Great Gray Owl	*Strix nebulosa*
10	\087018_V002_BlChkdBeeeater.mov				Blue-cheeked Bee-ea	*Merops persicus*
11	\087020_V001_Beeeater.mov				Bee-eater	*Merops apiaster*
12	\099178_V003_GreenWoodpecker.mov				Green Woodpecker	*Picus viridis*
13	\173110_V006_Raven.mov				Raven	*Corvus corax*

Figure 9.5 Movie Annotator in Excel.

Both Get Annotations and Save Annotations "buttons" are implemented using a generic ProcessMovies script that loops through the list of movies and carries out an action on each movie:

```
Private Sub ProcessMovies(action As String)

  Dim mov As QTMovie
  Dim fileName As String, rootPath As String

  On Error GoTo ErrorHandler

  rootPath = Me.Cells(kPathRow, kPathCol)

  QTControl1.ErrorHandling = qtErrorHandlingRaiseException
```

```
      Dim row As Long
      row = kFilesRow
      Do
        fileName = Me.Cells(row, kFilesCol)
        If fileName = "" Then Exit Do

        If OpenMovie(rootPath + fileName) Then

          'Do something with the movie
          Select Case action
            Case "GetAnnotations"
              GetAnnotations QTControl1.Movie, row, kDataCol
            Case "SaveAnnotations"
              SaveAnnotations QTControl1.Movie, row, kDataCol
          End Select

        End If

        row = row + 1

      Loop

      QTControl1.URL = ""

      Exit Sub

  ErrorHandler:
      MsgBox "*** ERROR ***: " + Hex(Err.Number) + ": " +
             Err.Description + vbCrLf

  End Sub
```

For each file in the list, OpenMovie is called returning True if the movie has been successfully opened:

```
Function OpenMovie(fileName As String) As Boolean

  On Error GoTo ErrorHandler

  Dim bRet As Boolean
```

```
  bRet = False
  Application.Cursor = xlWait
  QTControl1.URL = fileName
  bRet = Not (QTControl1.Movie Is Nothing)

ErrorHandler:
  Application.Cursor = xlDefault
  OpenMovie = bRet

End Function
```

If the file was opened successfully in the QuickTime Control, the requested action is carried out on the movie—in this case GetAnnotations or SaveAnnotations:

```
Sub GetAnnotations(ByRef mov As QTMovie, row As Long, col As Long)
  If mov Is Nothing Then Exit Sub
  Me.Cells(row, col + 0) = GetAnnotation(mov, qtAnnotationFullName)
  Me.Cells(row, col + 1) = GetAnnotation( _
          mov, qtAnnotationInformation)
  Me.Cells(row, col + 2) = GetAnnotation(mov, qtAnnotationComments)
  Me.Cells(row, col + 3) = GetAnnotation(mov, qtAnnotationCopyright)
  Me.Cells(row, col + 4) = GetAnnotation( _
          mov, qtAnnotationDescription)
End Sub

Sub SaveAnnotations(ByRef mov As QTMovie, row As Long, col As Long)
  If mov Is Nothing Then Exit Sub
  SetAnnotation mov, qtAnnotationFullName, _
          Me.Cells(row, col + 0).Value
  SetAnnotation mov, qtAnnotationInformation, _
          Me.Cells(row, col + 1).Value
  SetAnnotation mov, qtAnnotationComments, _
          Me.Cells(row, col + 2).Value
  SetAnnotation mov, qtAnnotationCopyright, _
          Me.Cells(row, col + 3).Value
  SetAnnotation mov, qtAnnotationDescription, _
          Me.Cells(row, col + 4).Value
  mov.Save
End Sub
```

With a large number of movies, inserting annotations—such as copyright details—in bulk is easily achieved with the aid of Excel's handy Fill Down facility to "copy down" the copyright notice to the appropriate cell for each movie. Click Save Annotations and the copyright annotation will be rapidly applied to all the movies. If the movies have existing annotations, these may need to be edited or modified, perhaps using a global search and replace. Again, the spreadsheet is an ideal place in which to do this before updating the movies with Save Annotations.

Just as with the batch processing script in Chapter 8, ProcessMovies can be adapted to carry out any number of useful batch operations on the list of movies. In combination with the spreadsheet facilities for tabulating and editing data, this has the potential to be a valuable production tool. The *Movie_Annotator.xls* sample is available from

www.skylark.ie/qt4.net/Samples/Office

Access

While many of us contrive somehow to manage our data in a haphazard assortment of spreadsheets, anyone who really takes data management seriously will turn to a database. And on Windows, at least for desktop purposes, this is very likely to be Microsoft Access.

Movie Display

If our database relates to a collection of content assets—movies, images, sounds—then there is a lot to be said for having the ability to "view" the asset in conjunction with its associated database record. For example, if working in forensics, we might have access to a substantial collection of crime-scene video recordings. A keyword search in our database will retrieve a set of records through which we will then want to browse, ideally with the ability to view each video clip alongside its details on the same database form.

For the purposes of this example, and in deference to sensitive readers, we'll swap the gory crime-scene clips for an avian database comprising just a few bird species records. Each record has an associated video clip whose file name is stored in the FileName field. The entire Species table is shown in Figure 9.6.

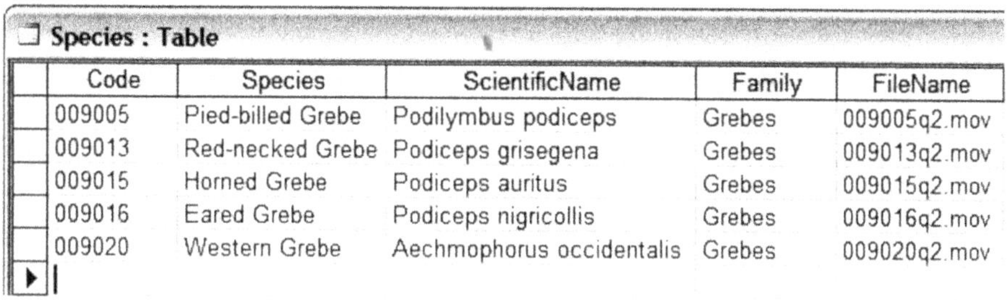

Species : Table

Code	Species	ScientificName	Family	FileName
009005	Pied-billed Grebe	Podilymbus podiceps	Grebes	009005q2.mov
009013	Red-necked Grebe	Podiceps grisegena	Grebes	009013q2.mov
009015	Horned Grebe	Podiceps auritus	Grebes	009015q2.mov
009016	Eared Grebe	Podiceps nigricollis	Grebes	009016q2.mov
009020	Western Grebe	Aechmophorus occidentalis	Grebes	009020q2.mov

Figure 9.6 The Species table.

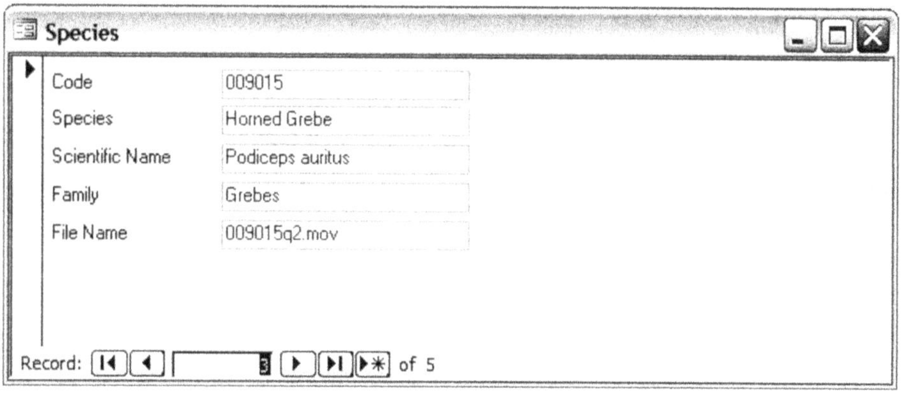

Figure 9.7 Wizard-generated Species form.

Feeding our Species table to the Access Create Form wizard gives us a simple form something like that shown in Figure 9.7. Given that each record contains the file name of a movie, our aim is to have this movie open for us on the right-hand side of this form. To achieve this, we must toggle the form into Design Mode and add a QuickTime Control—using the More Controls button in the Control Toolbox—in exactly the same way as we added the QuickTime Control to our Excel worksheet. Having done this, right-click on the QuickTime Control that has been added to the form, select Properties and the All tab. Along with the familiar QuickTime Control properties, you will notice that the default name given to the control is `QTControl0` (bizarrely—the default name is always `QTControl1` in Excel and other Office applications). This is the name we must use to refer to the control in our VBA script.

Merely plonking a QuickTime Control on the form isn't sufficient, of course; we must add a VBA script to load the control each time a record changes. As with Excel, press Alt-F11 to get into the code editor and locate the Project Explorer. An object with the name Form_Species should be visible and double-clicking on this should open up the code module associated with the form.

The form event we need to handle is Current. This event is triggered whenever a record becomes the current record displayed in the form. The Current event handler to load a movie each time the record changes is simplicity itself:

```
Private Sub Form_Current()

  If Me.Code <> "" Then
    QTControl0.Sizing = qtControlFitsMovie
    QTControl0.URL = "D:\Movies\Grebes\" + Trim(Me.FileName)
  Else
    QTControl0.URL = ""
  End If

End Sub
```

The form object itself is accessible through the object reference Me. Access cleverly supplements the properties of the form with the field names of the database record so that the movie file name can be simply obtained using Me.FileName. Prepending a hard-coded path to the Movies folder, we use the value of Me.FileName to load the QuickTime Control. If the Code field is empty, as will be the case should we add a new record, then the QuickTime Control is unloaded. In practice, of course, this handler could do with some toughening up in the form of an error handler.

Good housekeeping dictates that we clean up after ourselves by unloading the movie when the form is unloaded. This is easily handled in the form's Unload event handler:

```
Private Sub Form_Unload(Cancel As Integer)
  QTControl0.URL = ""
  DoEvents
End Sub
```

QuickTime Event Handling

Harking back momentarily to the crime-scene video clips, our forensic specialist may wish to note down the timecode of certain frames—perhaps the point where the camera focuses in on that crumpled note pinned to the victim's chest or, in our less gruesome avian example, the time when the grebe dives. We'd like the timecode to appear in a field on the form as we drag the movie controller back or forward.

To implement this, we will need to register with the movie for its qtEvent-TimeWillChange event:

```
Private Sub Form_Current()

  If Me.Code <> "" Then
    QTControl0.Sizing = qtControlFitsMovie
    QTControl0.URL = "D:\Movies\Grebes\" + Trim(Me.FileName)

    If Not (QTControl0.Movie Is Nothing) Then
      QTControl0.Movie.EventListeners.Add
            qtEventClassTemporal, qtEventTimeWillChange
    End If

  Else
    QTControl0.URL = ""
  End If
  Me.tbTime = ""

End Sub
```

Next, to display the timecode we add an unbound text field to the form called tbTime, which we can update in the QTEvent handler for our Quick-Time Control as follows:

```
Private Sub QTControl0_QTEvent(ByVal EventClass As Long,
          ByVal EventID As Long, ByVal Phase As Long,
          ByVal EventObject As Object, Cancel As Boolean)

  Dim t As Long
```

```
    If EventID = qtEventTimeWillChange Then
      t = EventObject.GetParam(QTEventObjectParametersEnum.
            qtEventParamMovieTime)
      Me.tbTime = GetTimeCode(QTControl0.Movie, t)
    End If

End Sub
```

Borrowed from the MovieBuilder sample in Chapter 6, GetTimeCode has been slightly adapted for VBA:

```
'Converts movie time to timecode (HH:MM:SS.ttt) format
Private Function GetTimeCode(ByVal mov As QTMovie, ByVal t As Long)

  Dim ss As Long, mm As Long, hh As Long, tt As Long
  Dim dSecs As Double
  Dim totalSecs As Long

  dSecs = t / mov.TimeScale
  totalSecs = Int(dSecs)

  ss = totalSecs Mod 60
  mm = totalSecs \ 60
  hh = mm \ 60
  mm = mm Mod 60
  hh = hh Mod 24

  tt = t - (totalSecs * mov.TimeScale)

  GetTimeCode = Format(hh, "00:") + Format(mm, "00:")
            + Format(ss, "00") + "." + Format(tt, "000")

End Function
```

The final result can be seen in Figure 9.8. Moving to a Species record will open the corresponding video clip on the Species form. Scrubbing the movie controller to any frame in the movie will then update our dynamic Time field. The *SpeciesDatabase_2003.mdb* sample is available from

www.skylark.ie/qt4.net/Samples/Office

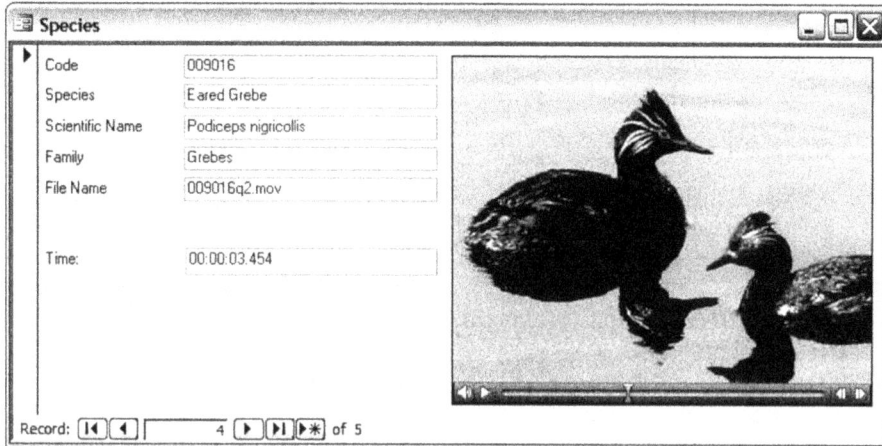

Figure 9.8 Completed Species form in Microsoft Access database.

Summary

Office applications such as Excel and Access can justifiably lay claim to being serious developer tools in their own right. The examples in this chapter really only scratch the surface of what is possible when you bring the capabilities of QuickTime into such COM- and VBA-enabled environments. And we haven't even touched on other more specialized, but equally capable, packages such as Visio and Publisher.

Before attempting development with any of the Office applications, it's well worth taking the time to acquaint yourself with its object model. For obvious reasons, these differ considerably amongst the various applications, but this will help you to zero in on the relevant objects of interest, such as the Workbook object in Excel or the Form in Access. Full details of these object models and lots of other useful developer resources are available from the Microsoft Office Developer Center at *http://msdn.microsoft.com/office/*.

Appendix A:
QuickTime COM
Library Reference

◉ QuickTime Control (QTOControlLib)

Classes

QTControl	QuickTime COM/ActiveX control. Handles opening of movie and interaction with host window.

Enumerations

BorderStylesEnum	Control border options. Default is bsPlain.
QTErrorEventOriginEnum	Origin of the error that triggered an Error event.
QTFullScreenFlagsEnum	Flags to control full-screen display mode. Used with the FullScreenFlags property. Default is qtFullScreenDefaultFlags.
QTFullScreenSizingModeEnum	Sizing options for full-screen display mode. Used with the FullScreenSizing property. Default is qtFullScreenMovieFitsMonitorMaintainAspectRatio.
QTInitializeQTMLFlagsEnum	Flags for QuickTime initialization as used with the QuickTimeInitialize method.
QTOpenMovieFlagsEnum	Flags that govern how a movie is opened. Used with the NewMovieFlags property. Default is qtOpenMovieDefaultFlags.
QTSizingModeEnum	Options for control sizing. Used with the Sizing property. Default is qtControlFitsMovie.
QTStatusCodesEnum	Codes for StatusUpdate events from the control.
QTStatusCodeTypesEnum	Code types for StatusUpdate events from the control.

⏵ QuickTime Object Library (QTOLibrary)

Classes	
CFObject	General-purpose data container class that wraps a Core Foundation object. Used for properties that handle complex data. Can be created with New.
CFObjects	Collection of CFObject.
Error	Holds information about the last error that occurred. Obtained from the Error property of QTMovie or QTQuickTime.
IQTObject	Base interface implemented by many QuickTime objects.
QTChapter	Chapter of a movie.
QTChapters	Collection of chapters within a movie. Returned by the Chapters property of QTMovie.
QTEventListeners	Collection of QuickTime events that are registered for notification with an object. Any QuickTime object that implements IQTObject has a collection of event listeners exposed through its EventListeners property.
QTEventObject	Holds information, including event parameters, about a QuickTime event that is being notified through the QTEvent event.
QTExporter	Provides an export facility to convert a movie or track into a specified format. Wraps a QuickTime exporter component.
QTExporters	Collection of QTExporter objects. Returned by the Exporters property of QTQuickTime.
QTFrequencyMeter	Provides access to data that can be used to display an audio frequency meter while a movie is playing. Returned by the FrequencyMeter property of a movie.
QTHotspot	Hotspot within a QuickTime VR node.
QTHotspots	Collection of hotspots within a QuickTime VR node. Returned by the Hotspots property of QTVRNode.
QTMatrix	A transformation matrix that can be applied to a movie or track via the Matrix property. Can be used to perform rotation, translation, scaling, skewing, or a combination thereof. Can be created with New.
QTMovie	QuickTime movie. Any entity that the QuickTime Control can successfully open is exposed as a QTMovie object through the Movie property of QTControl.

continued

QTQuickTime	Class that wraps QuickTime itself and provides global services such as export and access to QuickTime settings. Returned by the QuickTime property of QTControl. Can be created with New.
QTSettings	Exposes some of the global QuickTime settings that are available in the QuickTime Settings control panel. Returned by the Settings property of QTQuickTime.
QTStream	A media stream within a QuickTime streaming track as served by a streaming server.
QTStreams	Collection of streams within a streaming track. Returned by the Streams property of QTTrack.
QTTrack	Track within a movie.
QTTracks	Collection of tracks within a movie. Each movie will usually have one or more tracks and these are exposed through the Tracks property of QTMovie.
QTUtils	Provides convenient utility functions. Can be created with New.
QTVRNode	Node within a QuickTime VR movie.
QTVRNodes	Collection of nodes within a QuickTime VR movie. Returned by the VRNodes property of QTMovie.

Types

QTEventListener	The EventListeners collection of any QuickTime object comprises items of this data type. Each QTEventListener specifies an event that has been registered for on the object.
QTPOINT	Point data type.
QTRECT	Rectangle data type—e.g., Rectangle property.

Enumerations

CFObjectTypesEnum	Type (CFType) of a CFObject as used with its Type property.
QTAnnotationsEnum	Standard Annotation IDs that can be used with the Annotation property of a QTMovie or QTTrack.
QTConnectionsSpeedsEnum	Options for streaming connection speed as used in ConnectionSpeed property of QTSettings.
QTErrorHandlingOptionsEnum	Determines how QTControl, QTMovie, and QTQuickTime respond to errors. Default is qtErrorHandlingFireErrorEvent.
QTEventClassesEnum QTEventIDsEnum	Classes and IDs for QuickTime events. Used when adding event listeners to a QuickTime object so as to be notified when an event occurs. Returned in QTEvent whenever an event is fired.

continued

QTEventObjectParametersEnum	Event parameters available through the GetParam method of QTEventObject as supplied in the EventObject parameter of the QTEvent event.
QTFindTextFlagsEnum	Flags that can be used with either the QTFindText method or the FindTextFlags property of QTMovie. Default is qtFindTextDefaultFlags.
QTMatrixTypes	Type of transformation represented by a matrix as returned by the Type property of QTMatrix.
QTMovieCharacteristicsEnum	Characteristics of a movie that can be obtained using the HasCharacteristic property of QTMovie.
QTMovieControllerTypesEnum	The type of movie controller bar associated with a movie as returned by the MovieControllerType property.
QTObjectClassesEnum	Each QuickTime object that implements IQTObject has an object class as returned by its ObjectClass property.
QTTrackCharacteristicsEnum	Characteristics of a track that can be obtained using the HasCharacteristic property of QTTrack.
QTTransferModesEnum	Graphics transfer modes that determine how a visual track is combined with the movie when rendered. Use with the TransferMode property of QTTrack. Default is qtTransferModeDitherCopy.

Appendix B:
Additional COM
Host Environments
QuickTime Control Basics in
Other COM Hosts

Visual Basic 6

With its massive existing developer and code base, Visual Basic 6 (VB6) remains a serious developer tool, particularly for in-house projects. If your priority is to get something working quickly, there really is no competition—no need either to wrestle with the .NET Framework, and the runtime is a frugal 1MB.

Suggestions by Microsoft that it would gradually phase out support for Visual Basic 6 were greeted with howls of protest from the substantial VB6 developer community. A reprieve of sorts was granted in the form of VBRun—the official Microsoft Visual Basic 6.0 Resource Center:

http://msdn.microsoft.com/vbrun/

This sample project is available on the website at

www.skylark.ie/qt4.net/Samples/VB6

Getting Started

- Create a new Standard EXE project.
- Choose Project | Components...

- Find *Apple QuickTime Control 2.0*, check the box beside it, and click OK. This should add the QuickTime Control to the VB6 Toolbox. If the Toolbox isn't visible, choose View | Toolbox.

- Select the QuickTime Control icon in the Toolbox. Click and drag on the form to add the control. If all goes well, the control will appear with the QuickTime logo in the center.

- To view the properties of the control, choose View | Properties Window or press F4. You will find that the default name given to the control is QTControl1.

Adding a Load Button

- Revisit Project | Components... and this time add the *Microsoft Common Dialog Control 6.0.*

- From the Toolbox, add a Common Dialog control to the form: CommonDialog1.

- Add a Load button (btnLoad) to the form, double-click to open the code window, and enter the following:

```
Private Sub btnLoad_Click()

    CommonDialog1.ShowOpen
    If CommonDialog1.FileName = "" Then Exit Sub
    QTControl1.URL = CommonDialog1.FileName

End Sub
```

Adding a Play/Stop Button

- Add another button (btnPlayStop) to the form and give it the caption "Play" as shown in Figure B.1. Don't worry: we'll come to "Stop" in a minute!

- Enter the following code:

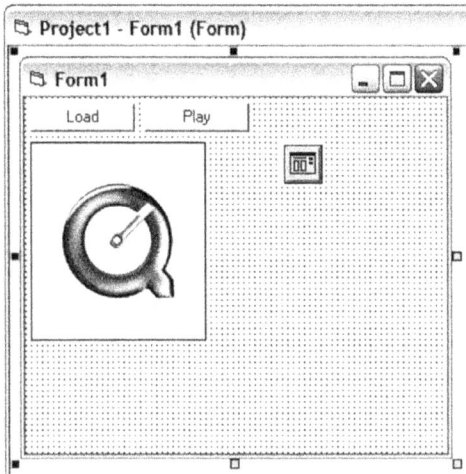

Figure B.1 The QuickTime Control on a Visual Basic 6 form.

```
Private Sub btnPlayStop_Click()

    If QTControl1.Movie Is Nothing Then Exit Sub

    With QTControl1.Movie
        If .Rate > 0 Then
            .Stop
        Else
            .Play
        End If
    End With

End Sub
```

To make the caption of the Play/Stop button context-sensitive, we will need to register for the qtEventRateWillChange QuickTime event. First, though, we must add to our project a reference to the QuickTime Objects library (QTOLibrary) so that we can use the classes and enumerations defined therein. Choose Project | References... and add *Apple QuickTime Library 2.0.*

We can register for qtEventRateWillChange after loading the QuickTime Control:

```
Private Sub btnLoad_Click()

  CommonDialog1.ShowOpen
  If CommonDialog1.FileName = "" Then Exit Sub
  QTControl1.URL = CommonDialog1.FileName

  If QTControl1.Movie Is Nothing Then Exit Sub

  QTControl1.Movie.EventListeners.Add qtEventClassStateChange,
        qtEventRateWillChange

End Sub
```

The QTEvent handler should change the caption of the Play/Stop button each time there is a change in the movie play rate. To create the event handler, choose QTControl1 from the left-hand drop-down list of controls at the top of the Form1 code window, and then choose QTEvent from the list of events available in the right-hand drop-down list. Here's the event handler implementation:

```
Private Sub QTControl1_QTEvent(ByVal EventClass As Long,
        ByVal EventID As Long, ByVal Phase As Long,
        ByVal EventObject As QTOLibrary.IQTEventObject,
        Cancel As Boolean)

  Dim rate As Single

  If EventID = qtEventRateWillChange Then

    rate = EventObject.GetParam(qtEventParamMovieRate)
    If rate > 0 Then
      btnPlayStop.Caption = "Stop"
    Else
      btnPlayStop.Caption = "Play"
    End If

  End If

End Sub
```

Resizing the Form to Fit the Control

A common requirement is for the form to fit the QuickTime Control when a movie of a particular size is loaded. Unlike Windows Forms in the .NET Framework, VB6 forms lack the ClientSize property. Thus, we must resort to using a pair of API-based helper functions to obtain the horizontal and vertical border widths of the form—that is, the difference between the external width and height of the form and the width and height of the client area of the form.

```
Private Declare Function GetSystemMetrics Lib "user32"
          (ByVal nIndex As Long) As Long
Private Const SM_CYCAPTION = 4
Private Const SM_CYFRAME = 33
Private Const SM_CYMENU = 15

Function GetFormExtraWidth()
  GetFormExtraWidth = GetSystemMetrics(SM_CYFRAME) * 2
End Function

Function GetFormExtraHeight()
  GetFormExtraHeight = GetSystemMetrics(SM_CYCAPTION) +
          (GetSystemMetrics(SM_CYFRAME) * 2)
End Function
```

Note that if we happen to have a menu bar across the top of our form, GetFormExtraHeight would become

```
Function GetFormExtraHeight()
  GetFormExtraHeight = GetSystemMetrics(SM_CYCAPTION) +
          GetSystemMetrics(SM_CYMENU) +
          (GetSystemMetrics(SM_CYFRAME) * 2)
End Function
```

To ensure that the form gets resized whenever the control is resized, we intercept the SizeChanged event of the QuickTime Control and compute a new width and height for the form:

```
Private Sub QTControl1_SizeChanged(ByVal Width As Long,
            ByVal Height As Long)

    Dim w As Long, h As Long

    'Ignore if control was resized as a result of form being resized
    If m_bExternalSizeChange Then Exit Sub

    'Resize window to wrap control
    w = (Width + GetFormExtraWidth()) * Screen.TwipsPerPixelX
    h = (Height + GetFormExtraHeight()) * Screen.TwipsPerPixelY

    Me.Move Me.Left, Me.Top, w, h

End Sub
```

Responding to Manual Resize of the Form

Lastly, in this whirlwind guide to using the QuickTime Control in VB6, we will look at what it takes to add support for resizing the movie in response to manual resizing of the form. The starting point, of course, is the Form_Resize event handler that gets called anytime the form is resized. In this routine we resize the control to fit snugly inside the newly resized form. First, though, we must temporarily switch the Sizing mode of the QuickTime Control so that the movie is resized to fit the control. Having resized the control—and consequently the movie—we restore the Sizing mode to what it was:

```
Private Sub Form_Resize()

    Dim oldSizingMode As QTSizingModeEnum
    Dim w As Long, h As Long

    'Lock out SizeChanged handling while we resize the control
    m_bExternalSizeChange = True

    'Movie resized to fit control
    oldSizingMode = QTControl1.Sizing
    QTControl1.Sizing = qtMovieFitsControl
    w = Me.Width - (GetFormExtraWidth() * Screen.TwipsPerPixelX)
    h = Me.Height - (GetFormExtraHeight() * Screen.TwipsPerPixelY)
```

```
QTControl1.Move 0, 0, w, h
QTControl1.Sizing = oldSizingMode

m_bExternalSizeChange = False
```

```
End Sub
```

Note the use of the m_bExternalSizeChange flag here, and in QTControl1_SizeChanged, to ensure that SizeChanged events from the control are ignored while Form_Resize does its thing. A more in-depth discussion of this can be found in the section of Chapter 3 entitled "A Resizeable Window for Simple Player."

Porting Code Samples to Visual Basic 6 or Visual Basic for Applications (VBA)

Adapting the VB.NET code samples in this book to VB6 or VBA shouldn't be particularly difficult if you have a good working knowledge of VB6/VBA. You will of course have to alter any Windows Forms–related code to use VB6 forms and controls. Any delegate-based event handlers in the .NET code will have to be recast in the more traditional VB6 connection point format.

Watch out also for the following common differences in the code itself:

- In VB6/VBA, assignment of object references *must* use the Set keyword:

```
'VB.NET
Dim mov as QTMovie
mov = AxQTControl1.Movie
```

```
'VB6/VBA
Dim mov as QTMovie
Set mov = QTControl1.Movie
```

- In VB6/VBA, you cannot initialize a variable at the same time that you define it:

```
'VB.NET
Dim n as Long = 0
```

```
'VB6/VBA
Dim n as Long
n = 0
```

- String concatenation using the convenient += shortcut is not legal syntax in VB6 or VBA:

```
'VB.NET
Dim msg as String = ""
msg += "this is legal"

'VB6/VBA
Dim msg as String
msg = ""
msg = msg + "this is more long-winded"
```

Delphi

Borland's Delphi is a popular Rapid Application Development (RAD) environment of long standing, and its support for COM components has always been excellent. Current incarnations support C# and C/C++ as well as the traditional Object Pascal–based Delphi programming language.

The following sample is based on Delphi 6 and 7, which remain popular with many developers, not least because Borland captured their hearts with a free (with registration) Personal Edition. The sample code is available from

www.skylark.ie/qt4.net/Samples/Delphi

Getting Started

Before we can use the QuickTime Control in Delphi, we must add it to the Component Palette. To do this

- Choose Component | Import ActiveX Control...

- Select *Apple QuickTime Control 2.0 (Version 1.0)* from the list. *TQTControl* should appear in the list of class names.

- Make sure ActiveX is selected as the Palette page (tab) in which the control will appear.

- Click Install... and, in the Install window, either select an existing package into which the control will be installed or create a new package.

- Click OK, and then Yes when asked if you want to rebuild the package. This will generate Delphi wrappers for the QuickTime Control (QTOControlLib) and QuickTime Objects (QTOLibrary) type libraries.

- Once the package is rebuilt, close the Package window.

- If you choose the ActiveX tab on the Component Palette, the QuickTime Control icon should now be there.

Now the QuickTime Control can be added to a form just as you would any other Delphi control. The default name given to the control when added to a form is QTControl1.

Loading a Movie

Add an Open Dialog control (OpenDialog1) and a Load button (ButtonLoad) to the form (Figure B.2), and we can quickly put the QuickTime Control to work loading a movie:

```
procedure TForm1.ButtonLoadClick(Sender: TObject);
begin

  QTControl1.ErrorHandling := qtErrorHandlingRaiseException;
  if OpenDialog1.Execute then
  begin
    try
      QTControl1.URL := OpenDialog1.FileName;
    except
      on E: Exception do ShowMessage('Unable to load Movie!' +
             #13#10 + E.Message);
    end;
  end;

end;
```

As always, when setting the URL property, it is advisable to guard against a possible load error—in this case using a try...except block.

Unfortunately, when you attempt to load a movie, this may fail with a floating-point exception. This is a known problem with the way Delphi uses the floating-point unit (FPU). Delphi expects the FPU to be in a certain state and when an external library—such as QuickTime or DirectX—alters this state, it can cause an exception on return. If you run into this problem, the easiest work-around is simply to disable floating-point exceptions when you create the form and reenable them when the form is destroyed:

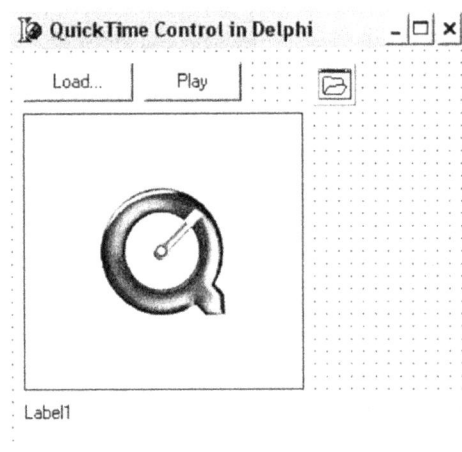

Figure B.2 The QuickTime Control on a Delphi form.

```
var
  Form1:       TForm1;
  Saved8087CW: Word;


...

procedure TForm1.FormCreate(Sender: TObject);
begin
  Saved8087CW := Default8087CW;
  // Disable FPU exceptions
  Set8087CW($133f);
end;

procedure TForm1.FormDestroy(Sender: TObject);
begin
  // Restore FPU exceptions
  Set8087CW(Saved8087CW);
end;
```

Playing the Movie

To play and stop the movie, we can add another Play/Stop button (Button-PlayStop):

```delphi
procedure TForm1.ButtonPlayStopClick(Sender: TObject);
var
  mov: QTMovie;
begin

  mov := QTControl1.Movie;

  if mov <> nil then
  begin
    if (mov.Rate > 0) then
      mov.Stop
    else
      mov.Play(1);
  end
end;
```

But before we can declare a mov variable of type QTMovie, we must add a reference to the QuickTime Objects library (QTOLibrary_TLB) to the uses clause of our form:

```delphi
uses
  Windows, Messages, SysUtils, Variants, Classes, Graphics,
          Controls, Forms,
  Dialogs, StdCtrls, OleCtrls, QTOControlLib_TLB, QTOLibrary_TLB;
```

Note that the reference to the QuickTime Control (QTOControlLib_TLB) was added automatically when we placed a control on the form: we just add QTOLibrary_TLB after it.

Handling QuickTime Events

Enhancing our load procedure to register for notifications when the play rate is about to change is simple:

```delphi
QTControl1.URL := OpenDialog1.FileName;
if (QTControl1.Movie <> nil) then
begin
  QTControl1.Movie.EventListeners.Add(qtEventClassStateChange,
          qtEventRateWillChange, 0, 0);
end;
```

But, for this to be of any use, we must handle the resulting QTEvent events that will be fired by the QuickTime Control. If you locate QTControl1 in the Delphi Object Inspector and click on the Events tab, you should see QTEvent. Double-clicking in the adjacent empty box in the right-hand column should generate a skeleton event handler to which we can add our specific event handling code:

```
procedure TForm1.QTControl1QTEvent(Sender: TObject;
          EventClass, EventID, Phase: Integer;
          const EventObject: IQTEventObject;
          var Cancel: WordBool);
var
  vRate : Variant;
begin

  case EventID of
    qtEventRateWillChange:
      begin

        vRate := EventObject.GetParam(qtEventParamMovieRate);
        Label1.Caption := 'Rate changed: ' + VarToStr(vRate);

        if vRate = 0 then
          ButtonPlayStop.Caption := 'Play'
        else
          ButtonPlayStop.Caption := 'Stop';
        end;

    end;
  end;

end.
```

For qtEventRateWillChange, the rate parameter is extracted from the EventObject and used to set the state of the Play/Stop button.

ATL/WTL

The Active Template Library (ATL) is a suite of lightweight C++ template classes originally released by Microsoft to facilitate the development of COM objects, including ActiveX controls and automation server applications. The existence in ATL of useful window and dialog classes, together with its lightweight wrapper classes for many Windows controls, has led to the adoption of ATL as a popular lightweight alternative to Microsoft Foundation Classes (MFC) for application development. Visual Studio includes a number of ATL Wizards that generate skeleton ATL projects as well as ATL objects such as dialogs and COM components.

The Windows Template Library (WTL) is an extension of ATL that has been released into the public domain by Microsoft under the open-source Common Public License. The SourceForge WTL project continues to be actively updated and can be found at

http://sourceforge.net/projects/wtl/

If your requirement is to develop a Windows C++ application that uses the QuickTime Control, and you are looking for a productive Win32 framework without the overhead of MFC or similar monolithic frameworks, then ATL/WTL is certainly worth a serious look.

This sample project is available on the website at

www.skylark.ie/qt4.net/Samples/ATL

Getting Started

- In Visual Studio .NET, create a new *ATL Project* and call it something—say, *Vireo*.
- When the ATL Project Wizard appears, click on Application Settings as shown in Figure B.3:
  - uncheck Attributed
  - select Executable (EXE) as the server type
  - click Finish to generate a skeleton ATL application

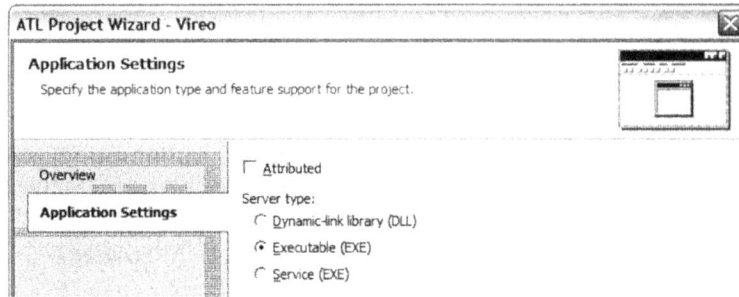

Figure B.3 Application Settings in ATL Project Wizard.

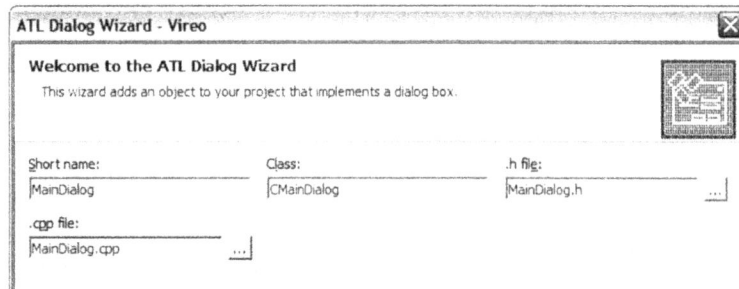

Figure B.4 Using the ATL Dialog Wizard.

Now we'll add the dialog class that we will use to host the QuickTime Control.

- Make sure you have selected the Vireo project in Solution Explorer and choose Project | Add Class...
- Select ATL Dialog from the class templates and click Open to launch the ATL Dialog Wizard (Figure B.4).
- In the Short name field, enter "MainDialog" and click Finish to create a dialog class called CMainDialog.
- Open the dialog in the Resource View—it will be called IDD_MAINDIALOG— and resize it, making it a good deal bigger.

- Open *Vireo.cpp,* which contains the main application module class—CVireoModule—that inherits from CAtlExeModuleT.
  - #include "MainDialog.h"
  - add a global variable m_dlg of type CMainDialog

To open our dialog when the application launches, we override PreMessageLoop and call m_dlg.DoModal(). The completed *Vireo.cpp* follows:

```
// Vireo.cpp : Implementation of WinMain

#include     "stdafx.h"
#include     "resource.h"
#include     "Vireo.h"
#include     "MainDialog.h"

CMainDialog m_dlg;

class CVireoModule : public CAtlExeModuleT< CVireoModule >
{
public :
  DECLARE_LIBID(LIBID_VireoLib)
  DECLARE_REGISTRY_APPID_RESOURCEID(IDR_VIREO,
    "{430FF806-AE25-40F0-87F9-B3C7BC9EE021}")

  HRESULT PreMessageLoop(int nShowCmd)
  {
    HRESULT hr = S_OK;
    hr = CAtlExeModuleT<CVireoModule>::PreMessageLoop(nShowCmd);
    if (FAILED(hr))
      return hr;

    m_dlg.DoModal();

    return S_FALSE;
  }
};

CVireoModule _AtlModule;
```

```
//
extern "C" int WINAPI _tWinMain(HINSTANCE /*hInstance*/,
            HINSTANCE /*hPrevInstance*/, LPTSTR /*lpCmdLine*/,
            int nShowCmd)
{
  return _AtlModule.WinMain(nShowCmd);
}
```

At this point, before we go anywhere near QuickTime, take a moment to build and run the application. The dialog should open, and clicking OK should dismiss it.

Adding the QuickTime Control

Before we can use the QuickTime Control and QuickTime objects in our ATL application, we need to *import* the QTOControlLib and QTOLibrary type libraries. This is most easily done by adding the following imports at the end of *stdafx.h*:

```
// Import QT control and library typelibs
#import "libid:29866AED-1E14-417D-BA0F-1A2BE6F5A19E"
           no_namespace named_guids
#import "libid:7b92f833-027d-402b-bff9-a67697366f4e"
           no_namespace named_guids
```

This will ensure that all the classes, types, and enumerations in these type libraries will be available in our application.

Next we turn our attention to the dialog in which we want to create an instance of the QuickTime Control and load a movie. ATL helps us enormously here by providing the CAxWindow class as a window class specifically for hosting ActiveX controls. We add a member variable to CMainDialog to host the control:

```
CAxWindow m_winAx;
```

There are three steps to the process of instantiating the QuickTime Control:

1. Use CAxWindow::Create to create the host window for the control as a child window of CMainDialog.

2. Create the instance of the QuickTime Control using CAxWindow::Create-ControlEx.

3. Retrieve an interface pointer to IQTControl using CAxWindow::QueryControl so that we can use it to call functions of the QuickTime Control.

All of this can be done in the OnInitDialog function that we have arranged—in our message map in *MainDialog.h*—to be called whenever the dialog has just been created:

```
CAxWindow m_winAx;

LRESULT OnInitDialog(UINT uMsg, WPARAM wParam, LPARAM lParam,
          BOOL& bHandled)
{
  HRESULT               hr = S_OK;
  RECT                  rc;
  LPOLESTR              wszQTControlCLSID = NULL;
  CComPtr<IQTControl>   spQTControl;

  CenterWindow(::GetDesktopWindow());

  GetClientRect(&rc);

  StringFromCLSID(__uuidof(QTControl), &wszQTControlCLSID);

  // Create Ax host window for control
  if (!m_winAx.Create( *this, rc, _T(""),
          WS_CHILD | WS_VISIBLE | WS_CLIPCHILDREN,
          0, IDC_QTCONTROL))
  {
    MessageBox(_T("Unable to create host window for control!"),
            _T("Error"));
    goto bail;
  }

  // Create the control instance
  hr = m_winAx.CreateControlEx(wszQTControlCLSID, 0, 0, 0);
  if (FAILED(hr))
  {
```

```
      MessageBox(__T("Unable to create control!"), __T("Error"));
      goto bail;
   }

   // Get interface pointer to control
   hr = m_winAx.QueryControl(&spQTControl);

   if (spQTControl)
   {
      spQTControl->put_URL(CComBSTR("d:\\quicktime\\movies\\
                                     sample.mov"));
   }

bail:
   return 1;
}
```

IDC_QTCONTROL is the ID that we assign to the QuickTime Control within its parent dialog window. It can be an arbitrary integer but must not clash with the IDs of any other control on the dialog.

Adding a Play/Stop Button

- Open the dialog in the Resource Editor and add a Play button with an ID of IDC_BTN_PLAY.

- In *MainDialog.h* add a Command handler to the CMainDialog message map to direct click events on this button to a handler function, OnClicked-Play().

```
COMMAND_HANDLER(IDC_BTN_PLAY, BN_CLICKED, OnClickedPlay)
```

- Add the button-click handler function to CMainDialog:

```
LRESULT OnClickedPlay(WORD wNotifyCode, WORD wID, HWND hWndCtl,
            BOOL& bHandled)
{
   CComPtr<IQTControl>     spQTControl;
   CComPtr<IQTMovie>       spMovie;
   float                   rate;
```

```
    if (SUCCEEDED( m_winAx.QueryControl(&spQTControl) ))
    {
      spQTControl->get_Movie(&spMovie);

      if (spMovie)
      {
        spMovie->get_Rate(&rate);

        if (rate > 0.0)
          spMovie->Stop();
        else
          spMovie->Play();
      }
    }
    return 0;
}
```

Handling Events from the QuickTime Control

In order to be able to handle events from the QuickTime Control in our ATL dialog class, it must become a connection-point sink for events from the control. Several things are necessary to achieve this:

1. An `IDispEventImpl` interface must be added to `CMainDialog` for the `_IQTControlEvents` dispatch interface of the QuickTime Control.

   ```
   class CMainDialog :
     public CAxDialogImpl<CMainDialog>,
     public IDispEventImpl<IDC_QTCONTROL, CMainDialog,
             &DIID__IQTControlEvents, &LIBID_QTOControlLib, 1, 0>
   ```

2. A sink map must be declared to map events to their respective handlers.

   ```
   BEGIN_SINK_MAP(CMainDialog)
     SINK_ENTRY_EX(IDC_QTCONTROL, DIID__IQTControlEvents, 1,
             OnQTEvent)
     SINK_ENTRY_EX(IDC_QTCONTROL, DIID__IQTControlEvents, 2,
             OnQTControlSizeChanged)
   END_SINK_MAP()
   ```

Notice that the control identifier IDC_QTCONTROL is used both here and in the IDispEventImpl interface declaration.

3. The connection points need to be set up or *advised*. This can be done after the QuickTime Control has been instantiated:

```
// Set up _IQTControlEvents connection point
AdviseSinkMap(this, TRUE);
```

4. The connection point should really be *unadvised* when we close the dialog, and this can be done in a WM_DESTROY handler:

```
LRESULT OnDestroy(UINT uMsg, WPARAM wParam, LPARAM lParam,
            BOOL& bHandled)
{
  //Unadvise the connection points
  AdviseSinkMap(FALSE);
  return 1;
}
```

Don't forget to add WM_DESTROY to the message map in *MainDialog.h:*

```
MESSAGE_HANDLER(WM_DESTROY, OnDestroy)
```

And, of course, we mustn't forget the event handler. It must use the __stdcall calling convention:

```
// Sink handler for SizeChanged event
void __stdcall OnQTControlSizeChanged(long width, long height)
{
  ATLTRACE(_T("CMainDialog::OnQTControlSizeChanged: %d, %d\n"),
          width, height);
}
```

QuickTime Events

To receive QuickTime events, we must register event listeners with the movie. This can easily be done once the movie is loaded:

```
spQTControl->put_URL( CComBSTR("d:\\quicktime\\movies\\
        sample.mov") );

CComPtr<IQTMovie>           spMovie;
CComPtr<IQTEventListeners>  spEventListeners;

spQTControl->get_Movie(&spMovie);

if (spMovie)
{
  spMovie->get_EventListeners(&spEventListeners);
  if (spEventListeners)
    spEventListeners->Add(qtEventClassStateChange,
        qtEventRateWillChange);
}
```

The following QTEvent handler demonstrates how to access the event parameters:

```
// Sink handler for QTEvent event
void __stdcall OnQTEvent(long EventClass, long EventID, long Phase,
        IQTEventObject* EventObject, VARIANT_BOOL* Cancel)
{
  CComVariant var;
  CComPtr<IQTEventObject> event = EventObject;

  switch (EventID)
  {
    case qtEventRateWillChange:

      var = event->GetParam(qtEventParamMovieRate);
      ATLTRACE(_T("Play Rate %f\n"), var.fltVal);
  }
}
```

These brief introductions to using the QuickTime Control in Visual Basic 6, Delphi, and ATL/WTL should provide you with a useful starting point for your own development. With a little bit of effort, many of the code samples in this book can be adapted to any of these development environments.

Appendix C:
QuickTime Exporter Types

Exporter Types

The following is a list of exporter types[1] that are available with QuickTime 7. When using a QTExporter object, the required exporter type name from the first column should be assigned to the TypeName property exactly as shown. For example

```
exp.TypeName = "QuickTime Movie"
exp.TypeName = "DV Stream"
exp.TypeName = "iPod (320x240)"
```

---

1 This list is not intended to be exhaustive.

Movie Exporters

Type Name	Type Code	File Extension	Description
3G	'3gpp'	.3gp	3GPP, 3GPP2, AMC
AVI	'VfW '	.avi	AVI with various compression options
DV Stream	'dvc!'	.dv	DV, DVCPRO (NTSC or PAL)
FLC	'FLC '	.flc	FLC animation format
Hinted Movie	'MooV'	.mov	QuickTime movie with 'hints' added for streaming from a server
Image Sequence	'grex'		Sequence of numbered images in a variety of image formats
iPod (320x240)	'M4V '	.m4v	320 x 240 movie for playback on video iPod (H.264, AAC)
MPEG-4	'mpg4'	.mp4	MPEG-4 with AAC audio compression
QuickTime Media Link	'embd'	.qtl	XML file that contains URL to movie
QuickTime Movie	'MooV'	.mov	QuickTime movie with numerous video and sound compression options

Sound Exporters

Type Name	Type Code	File Extension	Description
AIFF	'AIFF'	.aif	AIFF—Mac audio format
AU	'ULAW'	.au	AU—Sun/Next audio format
Wave	'WAVE'	.wav	WAV—Windows audio format

Image Exporters (Current Frame of Movie)

Type Name	Type Code	File Extension
BMP	'BMPf'	.bmp
JPEG	'JPEG'	.jpg
MacPaint	'PNTG'	.pntg
Photoshop	'8BPS'	.psd
PICT	'PICT'	.pct/.pic
Picture	'PICT'	.pct/.pic
PNG	'PNGf'	.png
QuickTime Image	'qtif'	.qtif
SGI	'.SGI'	.sgi
TGA	'TPIC'	.tga
TIFF	'TIFF'	.tif

Index

A

Access, 288–293
  completed Species, 293
  Create Form wizard, 289
  dynamic Time field, 292
  movie display, 288–290
  QuickTime event handling, 291–293
  Species table, 288, 289
  wizard-generated Species form, 289
  See also Office
Active Template Library (ATL), 311–319
  CAxWindow class, 314–315
  defined, 311
  Dialog Wizard, 312
  event handling, 317–318
  Play/Stop button, adding, 316–317
  Project Wizard, 312
  QuickTime Control, adding, 314–316
  QuickTime events, 318–319
  starting in, 311–314
ActiveX, 272–273
Add method, 172, 182, 249
AddScaled method, 172, 182, 253
AfterSelect event, 220
AIFF, 322
Annotation property, 116, 118, 121, 148
annotations, 115–121
  custom, 119–120
  defined, 115
  dictionary, 121–122, 130
  editing, 283–285
  IDs, 116
  nonstring values, 131
  retrieving, 116–117
  standard, 119
  string, 130
  See also metadata
Annotations dictionary, 128–132
  contents, 128
  iteration over items in, 129–130
AppleScript, 240
applications
  COM-aware, 244
  configuration files, 204
  configuration information, loading, 203
  event-driven, 218
  .NET, 6
  Office, 269
aspect ratio
  altering, 43
  defined, 42
  movies, 42–43
  preserving, 45
  scale and, 43
audience, this book, 8–10
Automation server. *See* COM server
auto play, 52
AutoPlay property, 19, 52, 70
AVI, 322

B

BackColor property, 50, 272
background color, 49–50
    default setting, 50
    relevance, 49
batch export, 90–94
    from command line, 254–258
    script, 254, 255, 258
BCD version format, 84–85
BMP, 323
BorderColor property, 51, 272
borders
    color, 49
    style options, 50
BorderStyle property, 25, 50

C

C#
    adding QTEvent handler in, 98–99
    resources, 12–13
CAxWindow class, 314–315
CFArray, 124–126
    CFObject containing, 126
    creating, 124
CFDictionary, 126–128
    Annotations, 128–132
    CFObject containing, 128
    creating, 126–127
    defined, 126
    PotentialExporters, 133
    QTEvent event parameters, 138
CFObject, 122–144
    array, 124–126
    Boolean, 122
    complex data structures, 132–139
    contents, dumping, 136
    contents, saving to disk, 143
    creation, 122–123
    defined, 122, 296
    dictionary, 126–128, 132

    familiarity, 153
    Number, 122
    persistent, 140–144
    reference, 123
    String, 122
    types, 122
CFObjects collection, 124–128, 296
chapters, 82–83
    adding, 82
    name, 82–83
    start time, 82–83
ClientSize property, 303
clipboard, 172
    copying logos to, 172, 174
    setting Bitmap onto, 191
CLR
    code running under, 6
    defined, 5
    garbage collector, 234
    porting QuickTime to run under, 8
code samples, this book, 10–12
color(s)
    background, 49
    border, 49
    text, 175
COM (Component Object Model), 1, 4–5
    aware applications, 244
    components, 4, 5
    defined, 4
    error codes, 145
    exceptions, 145
    interfaces, 5, 40, 244
    Interop, 6–7, 145
    QuickTime and, 7–8
    standard, 5
    success, 4
    support, 4, 5
COM controls
    COM components vs., 5
    defined, 38
    See also controls
COMException, 146, 147
    HRESULT error code and, 150
    trapping explicitly, 149–150

command line
    arguments, 255
    batch export from, 254–258
Command window (Windows), 243
Common Language Runtime. *See* CLR
Common Public License, 311
COM objects, 244
    creation, 5
    reference, 295–298
    See also objects
complex CFObjects
    data structures, 132–139
    inspecting, 134–138
    See also CFObject
Component Object Model. *See* COM
computer-generated movies, 190
COM server, 243–245
    defined, 244
    example, 244
    Office applications as, 269
    ProgID, 244
    QuickTime Player, 245–267
configuration files, 204
controls
    border options, 50
    child objects of, 58
    information, displaying, 35
    initialization, 24–25
    instances, 40
    memory allocation, 40
    naming, 18, 21
    properties, 18, 19
    Properties palette, 271
    Property Pages, 19
    resizing, 304
    size change, 34
Control Toolbox
    accessing, 269
    Design Mode button, 271
    illustrated, 271
    More Controls button, 289
CopyFrame method, 182
Copy method, 182
Core Foundation, 123

Count property, 73
CreateNewMovieFromImages method, 181, 183
CreateNewMovie method, 159
CType, 235
Current event, 290
Current event handler, 290
CurrentNodeID property, 80
custom annotations, 119–120
Customize Toolbox dialog, 17–18
    COM Components tab, 17
    illustrated, 18
Cut method, 182

D

DeleteSelection method, 182
Delphi, 306–310
    defined, 306
    FPU, 307
    getting started in, 306–307
    handling QuickTime events, 309–310
    movies, loading, 307–308
    movies, playing, 308–309
    Play/Stop button, 308–309
    QuickTime Control, 308
    QuickTime events, handling, 309–310
Design Mode, 271
dictionaries
    CFObject, 126–128
    defined, 126
    potential exporters, 132
digiscoping, 195
DirectoryNavigator class
    configuring, 205
    container, 202
    defined, 200
    population, 207
    SelectRootDirectory event and, 205
DirectoryNavigator object, 196
    AfterSelect event, 220
    MediaDisplayPanel indirect linkage, 220, 221
    MediaDisplayPanel object and, 219–220

Dock property, 203
Document Object Model (DOM), 61, 64, 66
DoMenu, 250, 252
DrawRandomBallFrame function, 192
droplets, 263–265
    defined, 263
    load movie and play it full screen, 263
DumpCFObject, 134–138
    calling, 138
    code, 134–135
    functioning, 13–17
Duration property, 22, 31, 68
DV Stream, 322

E

Edit menu
    illustrated, 156
    implementing, 156–157
    in single event handler, 157
Enabled property, 74
encapsulation, 213
enumerations, 25
    QTOControlLib, 295
    QTOLibrary, 297–298
error handling, 144–152
    I/O and, 152
    .NET Framework facility, 144
    See also exception handling
ErrorHandling property, 145
error messages, 146
event classes
    qtEventClassApplicationRequest, 103
    qtEventClassProgress, 103
    qtEventClassSpatial, 102
    qtEventClassStateChange, 102–103
    qtEventClassTemporal, 103
event handlers
    catch-all, 146
    Current, 290
    defined, 34
    delegate, 99
    function names, 259

Load, 190
QTEvent, 97–99
QuickTime Player, 258–263
Resize, 218, 228
SelectedIndexChanged, 164, 166–167
SelectionChange, 277–278, 280
Sink, 319
SizeChanged, 34, 46–48, 259
StatusUpdate, 54, 259
Unload, 290
WM_DESTROY, 318
event listeners, registration, 318
EventListeners collection, 111, 260
event parameters, 99–105
    accessing, 101
    QTEvent, 100
events, 95–114
    AfterSelect, 220
    ATL and, 318–319
    class, 96
    Current, 290
    event model, 98
    handling, 96–105
    ID, 96
    Media Browser application, 199
    notifications, 96, 100, 260
    OnBeforeExpand, 207–208
    processing, 139
    QTEvent, 97
    qtEventAudioBalanceDidChange, 102
    qtEventAudioMuteDidChange, 102
    qtEventAudioVolumeDidChange, 102
    qtEventChapterListDidChange, 102
    qtEventCloseWindowRequest, 103
    qtEventCurrentChapterDidChange, 102
    qtEventEnterFullScreenRequest, 103
    qtEventExitFullScreenRequest, 103
    qtEventExportProgress, 103
    qtEventGetNextURLRequest, 103
    qtEventLinkToURLRequest, 103
    qtEventLoadStateDidChange, 102
    qtEventMovieDidChange, 102
    qtEventMovieSelectionDidChange, 102,
        164

qtEventMovieWasEdited, 103, 111
qtEventRateWillChange, 96, 101, 102, 110, 260
qtEventShowMessageStringRequest, 103
qtEventShowStatusStringRequest, 103
qtEventSizeDidChange, 102
qtEventTimeWillChange, 103
registration, 96, 260
SelectedIndexChanged, 163
SelectionChange, 274, 275
SelectRootDirectory, 205
SizeChanged, 34–35, 47–48, 95, 303, 305
StatusUpdate, 54, 259
Events Demo, 105–114
defined, 105
illustrated, 106
Excel
batch processing, 285–288
Movie Annotator, 285–288
Movie Inspector, 275–283
Movie Inspector with annotation editing, 283–285
Play/Stop cell, 274–275
QuickTime Control, adding, 271–272
QuickTime Control, illustrated, 272
See also Office
exception handlers, 146
adding, 146
error messages with, 149
exceptions
COM, 145
defined, 30
in lower-level routines, 152
MediaViewer load, 212
.NET, 145, 146
unhandled, 29
ExpectedFrameRate property, 78
exporters, 86–94
3G, 322
AIFF, 322
AU, 322
AVI, 322
BMP, 323
configuration, 90

data source, 90
DV Stream, 322
FLC, 322
Hinted Movie, 322
image, 323
Image Sequence, 322
iPod, 322
JPEG, 323
MacPaint, 323
movie, 322
MPEG-4, 322
options, 257
Photoshop, 323
PICT, 323
Picture, 323
PNG, 323
potential, 94, 132, 133
QuickTime Image, 323
QuickTime Media Link, 322
QuickTime Movie, 322
settings, saving, 143–144
SGI, 323
sound, 322
TGA, 323
TIFF, 323
types, 254–258, 321–323
Wave, 322
Exporters collection, 256
Exporter Settings dialog, 143–144, 257
exporting
batch, 90–94
with Export dialog, 88–89
with Export Settings dialog, 90
movies, 194
Export progress dialog, 89

F

file extensions
for exporter types, 322–323
JScript/VBScript, 242
stripping, 258

File menu
  Export menu item, 151, 162
  illustrated, 159
  New Movie menu item, 160
  Open Folder menu item, 219
  Open Movie menu item, 26
  Save As menu item, 158, 162
  Save menu item, 158
  Select Source Folder menu item, 161
File Open dialog, 26, 183
Files collection, 251
FileSystemObject object, 241
Final Cut Pro, 155
FLC, 322
floating-point unit (FPU), 307
Form1_Load subroutine, 25
forms
  automatically sizing, 34–35
  Delphi, 308
  loaded, 40
  manual resize, 304–305
  resizing, to fit control, 303–304
FourCharCode, 75–77
frame rate, 166
FrameRate property, 78
frames
  adding, 191
  drawing, 190, 192
FullPath property, 207
FullScreenEndKeyCode property, 53
FullScreenFlags property, 53
full-screen mode
  configuring, 53–54
  display, 52–54
  exit, 53
  multiple monitors, 53
  sizing, 53
FullScreenMonitorNumber property, 53
full-screen movies, 33
FullScreen property, 33, 52
FullScreenSizing property, 53, 54

functions
  ClearMovieData, 281
  DrawRandomBallFrame, 192
  GetAnnotation, 117, 232, 282
  GetMovieSelectionInfo, 165
  GetTimeCode, 165–166
  GetTooltipInfo, 236
  Hex, 75
  IsDisposed, 234
  IsMediaInspectorOpen, 234
  LoadMovie, 106
  OnInitDialog, 315
  OpenMovie, 281
  StringToFourCharCode, 76

G

GDI+
  creating movies with, 189–192
  defined, 189
  potential movie frame generation with, 192
GetAnnotation function, 117, 232, 282
GetMovieSelectionInfo function, 165
GetParam method, 101, 138–139
GetTimeCode function, 165–166
GetTooltipInfo function, 236
GoToChapter method, 83
graphics, pasting in movie, 190

H

Hello World!
  movie, 16
  Play button, 21
  See also QTHelloWorld
Hex function, 75
Hinted Movie, 322
hotspots, 81–82
HRESULT error code, 150, 151
Human Body object model, 62, 63

I

image exporters, 322
images
    creating movies from, 181–183
    JPEG, 231
    tooltips, 235
    Windows Forms class for displaying, 213
Image Sequence, 322
iMovie, 155
Indeo codec, 85
information
    configuration, loading, 203
    control, displaying, 34–35
    movie, getting, 30–31
    movie selection, current, 165
    tooltip, 236
inheritance, 213
initialization
    of controls, 24–25
    QuickTime, 55–58
InsertEmptySegment method, 182
InsertSegment method, 168, 182
Interop Assembly, 39
iPod, 322
IsDisposed function, 234
IsMediaInspectorOpen function, 234
IsQuickTimeAvailable property, 58
IsVRMovie property, 79
Item property, 72

J–K

JPEG
    as image exporter type, 323
    images, 231
JScript, 5, 242
    enumerated constants and, 254, 263
    file extension, 242
    replace function, 258
    See also Windows Scripting Host

L

LabVIEW, 8
language setting, 85
Load button, 105, 106, 300
Load event handler, 190
loading
    application configuration information, 203
    controls, 55
    defined, 55
    errors, handling, 57
    movies, 41–42, 307–308
    QuickTime, 55–58
    time, disguising, 56
LoadMovie function, 106
Location property, 218
logos
    copying to clipboard, 172, 174
    graphics transfer mode, 186
    overlay illustration, 173
    SMIL and, 186
    track, position/transfer mode, 253
    See also overlays
LoopIsPalindrome property, 71
Loop property, 71

M

MacErrors.h, 151
MacPaint, 323
macro security, 272–273
MainForm
    defined, 202
    FolderBrowserDialog component, 219
    Form1_Load routine, 210
    loading, wrapping, 203
    menu events, 204
    mnuOpen_Click event handler, 219
    resizing, 218
    See also Media Browser
managed code, 6
Matrix property, 296

Media Browser
 adding to, 237
 bare bones, 201–204
 bare bones illustration, 202
 based on `PictureBox` control, 222
 completed, 238
 core functionality, 197
 defined, 196
 design decisions, 196–199
 design visualization, 197–199
 directory browsing, 204–208
 directory navigator, 196
 `DirectoryNavigator` object, 196, 200
 as event-driven application, 218
 file types, limiting, 209
 `MediaBrowser` object, 197, 200
 media display, 208–212
 `MediaDisplayPanel` object, 196, 197, 200
 Media Inspector, 225–235
 `MediaInspector` object, 197, 201
 media viewer, 212–215
 `MediaViewer` object, 197, 200
 objects, 196–197
 objects and base classes, 201
 principal events, 199
 QuickTime Control, adding, 221–224
 tooltips, 235–237
 website, 237
`MediaBrowser.ini`, 204, 209
 code, 204
 `FileExtensions` setting, 209, 224
`MediaBrowser` object, 197, 200
`MediaDisplayPanel` class
 `MediaViewer` object loading/positioning,
  213
 `SelectMediaViewer` routine, 235
`MediaDisplayPanel` object, 196, 197
 adding `MediaViewer` objects to, 212
 container, 202
 defined, 200
 `DirectoryNavigator` indirect linkage, 220,
  221
 `DirectoryNavigator` object and, 219–220
 resizing, 218

 skeleton classes, 202
Media Inspector, 225–235
`MediaInspector` object, 197
 defined, 201
 as floating palette, 225–226
 functionality, 225
 incorporating, 232–233
 instances, 225
 `ListView` in, 228, 229
 palette, toggling, 233
media keys
 defined, 85
 permanently adding, 85
 unlocking with, 85–86
`MediaViewer` class, 212
 abstract, 212
 code, 222–223
 encapsulation, 213
 inheritance, 213
 private code, 212
 starter, 214
`MediaViewer` objects, 197
 creating, 210–212
 defined, 200
 fixed-size, 215
 instances, 208
 keeping in order, 215–218
 laying out, 208, 215
 load exceptions, 212
 loading, 208, 213
 maximum number in single row, 216–217
 `PictureBox`-based, 214
 positioning, 213
 positioning parameters, 216
 single-pixel border, 215
 sizing, 215
 spatial order, 215
metadata, 114–122
 defined, 30, 115
 format, 115
 image with, 114
 in MPEG files, 120–121
 track, 119
 See also annotations

methods
 Add, 172, 182, 249
 AddScaled, 172, 182, 253
 Copy, 182
 CopyFrame, 182
 CreateNewMovie, 159
 CreateNewMovieFromImages, 181, 183
 Cut, 182
 DeleteSelection, 182
 drop-down list, 22
 GetParam, 101, 138
 GetParams, 138
 GoToChapter, 83
 InsertEmptySegment, 182
 InsertSegment, 168, 182
 OpenURL, 248
 Paste, 182, 191
 Play, 22, 29, 30, 67
 QuickTimeInitialize, 55, 56, 57
 QuickTimePlayer, 249
 QuickTimeTerminate, 55, 56
 Quit, 246
 ReplaceSelection, 182
 Rewind, 29, 67, 170
 Save, 193, 252
 SaveSelfContained, 193, 252
 ScaleSegment, 182
 SetDataSource, 87
 SetExtensions, 210
 SetScale method, 32–33
 SetSelection, 69, 70
 SetViewer, 228, 235
 ShowAboutBox, 35
 ShowExportDialog, 88
 Step, 67
 Stop, 67
 TrimToSelection, 182
 Undo, 182
Microsoft. *See* Access; Excel; Office
MIMEType property, 224, 230
Movie Annotator, 285–288
Movie Builder, 160–181
 defined, 160
 image folder selection, 181

 interface, 161–162
 interface illustration, 161
 sample, 161
movie controller, 51–52
 defined, 51
 height, 52
 illustration, 51
 Play button, 271
 scrubbing, 292
 turning on/off, 52
 uses, 51
 visible, 224
MovieControllerVisible property, 19, 272
movie exporters, 322
Movie Inspector, 275–285
 with annotation editing, 283–285
 defined, 276
 illustrated, 276
 key cell ranges, 276
Movie property, 22, 28
movies, 40–54
 aspect ratio, 42–43
 auto play, 52
 build routine, 169–170
 closing, 26–28
 computer-generated, 190
 controller bar, 163
 controlling, 28–30
 creating, with GDI, 189–192
 creating from images, 181–183
 defined, 40–41
 empty, creating, 114
 exporting, 162
 frame rate, 166
 full-screen, 33
 information, getting, 30–31
 loading, 41–42
 new, creating, 159–160
 new, saving, 193–194
 nonlinear, 78
 opening, 26–28, 245–246
 overlays, 171–174
 playback control, 67–68
 playback settings, 70–71

movies (*continued*)
  playing, 245–246, 308–309
  rewinding, 67
  saves, unnecessary, 164
  saving, 158–159, 162, 170
  scaling, 32–33, 42–43
  segments, copying to QTMovie object, 168
  size change, knowing, 34
  sizing, 44–45
  SMIL, 183–189
  source folder, 91
  stopping, 67
  stop playing determination, 261–262
  subtitling, 175–181
  time scale, 68–69
  tooltips, 235
  unlocking, 85–86
  VR, 78–82
movie selections
  appending, 169
  duration, 168
  information, current, 165
  playing, 69–70
  start/end, 164
  start time, 168
movie time, 68–69
MP3 files, tooltips, 235
MPEG
  file metadata, 120–121
  MPEG-4, 322

N

Name property, 18
.NET, 1, 5–6
  adding QTEvent handler in, 97–98
  applications, 6
  exceptions, 145, 146
  QuickTime and, 7–8
  resources, 12–13
  runtime, 6
.NET Framework, 5
  COM support, 39

error-handling facility, 144
Windows Forms, 200
nodes, 79–81
  defined, 79
  hotspots, 81–82
nonlinear movies, 78

O

object models, 62–64
  COM, 62–63
  DOM, 61, 64
  Human Body, 62, 63
  .NET, 63–64
  QuickTime, 64–94
  QuickTime Player, 246–247
object-oriented programming (OOP), 196
objects
  COM, 244, 295–298
  DirectoryNavigator, 196, 200
  FileSystemObject, 241
  MediaBrowser, 197, 200
  MediaDisplayPanel, 196, 197, 200
  MediaInspector, 197, 201
  MediaViewer, 197, 200
  MenuItem, 157
  QTChapter, 83
  QTControl, 66
  QTExporter, 87, 90, 194
  QTHotspot, 81, 296
  QTMovie, 66, 79, 116
  QTQuickTime, 66, 83–85
  QTSettings, 85–86
  QTStream, 77, 78
  QTTrack, 72, 116
  QTUtils, 75–76
  QTVRNodes, 79
  sender, 235
  ToolTip, 236
  TreeNode, 205, 206
  TreeView, 204, 205
  WScript, 242, 255

Office
    Access, 288–293
    applications, 269
    applications as COM servers, 269
    Excel, 270–288
    QuickTime and, 269–293
OnBeforeExpand event, 207–208
OnInitDialog function, 315
Open dialog, 20
Open File dialog, 144
OpenFileDialog control, 26–27
Open Movie dialog, 105
OpenMovie function, 281
OpenURL method, 248
overlays
    adding, 171–174
    code, 174
    copying to clipboard, 172
    illustrated, 173
    rendering operation, 173
    tracks, 172

P

Paste method, 182, 191
persistent CFObjects, 140–144
persistent properties, 272
Photoshop, 323
PICT, 323
PictureBox control, 222
Picture exporter type, 323
Play button, 21, 23
players
    destination, 251
    DoMenu, 250
    empty windows, adding, 248
    new windows, opening, 249
    source, 251
    windows, closing, 248
    windows, moving, 249
    working with, 248–250
    See also QuickTime Player
Players property, 247

Play method, 22, 29, 30, 67
PlaySelectionOnly property, 69
Play/Stop button
    ATL, 316–317
    Delphi, 308–309
    VB6, 300–302
    VB.Net, 107
PNG, 323
PositionMediaViewers routine, 218
potential exporters, 94
    CFDictionary, 133
    in dictionary, 132
    See also exporters
PotentialExporters property, 94
ProcessMovies script, 285–286
programmatic identifiers (ProgIDs), 244
properties
    Annotation, 116, 118, 121, 148
    AutoPlay, 19, 52, 70
    BackColor, 50, 272
    BorderColor, 51, 272
    BorderStyle, 25, 50
    ClientSize, 303
    Count, 73
    CurrentNodeID, 80
    Dock, 203
    drop-down list, 22
    Duration, 22, 31, 68
    Enabled, 74
    ErrorHandling, 145
    ExpectedFrameRate, 78
    Filter, 27
    FrameRate, 78
    FullPath, 207
    FullScreen, 33, 52
    FullScreenSizing, 53, 54
    Hotspots, 81
    IsQuickTimeAvailable, 58
    IsVRMovie, 79
    Item, 72
    Location, 218
    Loop, 71
    LoopIsPalindrome, 71
    Matrix, 296

properties (*continued*)
 MIMEType, 224, 230
 Movie, 22, 28
 MovieControllerVisible, 19, 272
 Name, 18
 persistent, 272
 Players, 247
 PlaySelectionOnly, 69
 PotentialExporters, 94
 QTControl, 246, 247
 QuickTime, 83
 Settings, 85
 Sizing, 44–45, 272
 Streams, 77, 78
 Time, 68
 Tracks, 72
 TransferMode, 173
 Type, 122
 TypeName, 321
 URL, 19, 20, 41, 42, 271, 272
 VersionAsString, 84
 viewing, 300
 VRNodes, 79
 Width, 22
 XML, 140
Properties palette, 271
Properties window (Visual Studio)
 Annotations tab, 30–31
 opening, 18
property inspectors, 225
Property Pages
 accessing, 20
 defined, 19
 dialog, 20
 opening, 271
 support, 19

Q

QTChapter object, 83, 296
QTChapters collection, 82, 296
qtControlFitsMovie, 46, 48, 52
QTControl object, 66, 295

QTControl property, 246, 247
qtEventAudioVolume events, 102
qtEventClassApplicationRequest events, 103
qtEventClassProgress event, 103
qtEventClassSpatial events, 102
qtEventClassStateChange events, 102–103
qtEventClassTemporal events, 103
QTEvent event, 97
 constants, 263
 parameters, 100
QTEvent handler, 97–99, 260–261, 291
 in C#, 98–99
 dedicated, 111
 implementation, 302
 sharing, 111–113
 in VB.NET, 97
QTEventListeners collection, 296
qtEventMovieSelectionDidChange event, 164
qtEventMovieWasEdited event, 111
QTEventObject class, 296
qtEventRateWillChange event, 260
 defined, 110
 qtEventParamMovieRate parameter, 101
 registration, 96, 110, 263
QTExporter object, 87, 90, 194, 256
 defined, 296
 obtaining, 256
 TypeName property, 321
 using, 321
QTExporters collection, 86, 296
QTFrequencyMeter class, 296
QTHelloWorld, 17
QTHotspot object, 81, 296
QTHotspots collection, 296
QTMatrix class, 296
QTMovie object, 116
 copying movie segments to, 168
 defined, 66, 296
 edit capabilities summary, 181, 182
 properties for VR navigation, 79
 source, 168
QTOControl.dll, 38
QTOControlLib, 295
 classes, 295

enumerations, 295
namespace, 49
QTOLibrary, 296–298
  classes, 296–297
  enumerations, 297–298
  types, 297
QTOLibrary.dll, 38
QTQuickTime object, 66, 83–85
  availability, 83
  defined, 66, 297
  programmatic access, 85
QTSettings object, 85–86
  defined, 297
  obtaining, 85
QTStream object, 77, 78, 297
QTStreams collection, 77, 297
QTTrack object, 72, 116
  defined, 297
  *n*th, 72
QTTracks collection, 72, 297
QTUtils object, 75–76, 297
QTVRNode object, 297
QTVRNodes collection, 79, 297
QuickTime
  API, 2, 13
  availability, 58
  capacities, 3
  COM and, 7–8
  configuring, 57–58
  developer perspective, 3
  events, 95–114
  initializing, 55–58
  language setting, 85
  metadata, 114–121
  .NET and, 7–8
  Office and, 269–293
  resources, 13
  scripting on Mac, 239–240
  services, 21
  settings, 85–86
  text importer, 179
  version dialog, 16
  version display, 83–84
  why?, 2–3
QuickTime Control, 4, 15–36
  About box, 36
  adding, 221–224
  adding, in ATL, 314–316
  adding to Access form, 289
  adding to Delphi form, 307, 308
  adding to Excel worksheet, 271–272
  adding to VB6 form, 300, 301
  adding to VB.Net form, 18
  adding to Visual Studio Toolbox, 17
  buttons, 105
  as COM control, 8
  defined, 38
  dynamic link libraries, 38
  Error Handling mode, 117
  in Excel spreadsheet, 272
  hosted in container window, 39
  loading, 55
  persistent properties, 272
  properties, 18, 19
  Property Pages, 271
  resizing, 271
  using, 37–59
QuickTime for Windows, 2–3
QuickTimeInitialize method, 55
  in configuration, 57
  error code, 57
  using, 56
QuickTime Kit (QTKit), 7
QuickTime Media Link, 322
QuickTime Object Model, 64–94
  defined, 64
  illustrated, 65
  summary, 94
QuickTime Player
  COM server, 245–267
  event handlers, 258–263
  launching, 245, 246, 248
  Movie Info, 226
  object model, 246–247
  on Windows, 9
  opening movies, 245–246
  playing movies, 245–246
  Present Movie... option, 33

QuickTime Player (*continued*)
    Pro version, 156, 250
    Save A File dialog, 252
    scripting, 239–267
    window, 247
QuickTimePlayerApp class, 246
QuickTimePlayer class, 247
QuickTimePlayers collection, 247
QuickTime property, 59, 83
QuickTimeTerminate method, 55, 56
Quit method, 246

R

Rapid Application Development (RAD)
    bare bones assembly, 201
    development tools, 8
    technologies, 10
regular expression, 251, 252, 257, 258, 264
ReplaceSelection method, 182
resizeable windows, 46–49
Resize event handler, 218, 228
resources
    C#, 12–13
    .NET, 12–13
    QuickTime, 13
    Visual Basic, 12–13
    Windows scripting, 13

S

Save button, 109
Save File dialog, 144
Save method, 193, 252
SaveMovie routine, 109–110
SaveSelfContained method, 193, 252
saving movies, 158–159, 162, 170
    export, 194
    new, 193–194
    with Save method, 193
    as self-contained, 193–194
ScaleSegment method, 182

scaling
    aspect ratio and, 43
    defined, 42
    movies, 32–33, 42–43
    text tracks, 179–180
    track length, 172
    X/Y axes and, 42
scripting, 239–267
    example, 240
    language, 240
    See also AppleScript; Windows Scripting
        Host (WSH)
scripts
    batch export, 254, 255, 258
    droplets, 263–265
    mixing, in different languages, 266
    ProcessMovies, 285–286
    stop-playing determination, 261–262
    VBA, 272
    in .wsf format, 265–267
    WSH, 242
security, macro, 272–273
Security Warning, 273
SelectedIndexChanged event, 163
SelectedIndexChanged handler, 164, 166–167
SelectionChange event, 274, 275
SelectionChange event handler, 277–278, 280
sender object, 235
SetDataSource method, 87
SetExtensions method, 210
SetScale method, 32–33
SetSelection method, 69, 70
Settings property, 85
SetViewer method, 228, 235
SGI, 323
ShowAboutBox method, 35
ShowExportDialog method, 88
Simple Player
    adding export feature, 89
    construction, 23–35
    Edit menu, 156–157, 160
    File menu, 26, 151, 159
    Help menu, 35
    illustrated, 24

menus, 24
Movie menu, 29
with new empty movie, 160
Open Movie dialog, 28
resizeable window, 24, 46–49
Sink handler, 319
SizeChanged event, 34–35, 47–48, 95, 303, 305
Sizing property, 44–45
   defined, 44
   option illustration, 44
   options, 44–45
   as persistent property, 272
SMIL, 183–189
   defined, 184
   description, importing, 184
   description code, 188–189
   descriptions, 189
   document illustration, 185
   document sections, 184
   extensions, 186
   <head> section, 184
   <layout> section, 184–185
   <par> element, 187
   QuickTime implementation, 189
   <region> element, 185
   <seg> element, 185
   sequences, playback performances, 189
   <text> element, 187
   tutorials, 184
   URL location, 185
   <video> element, 185
   as W3C recommendation, 184
Sorenson codec, 85, 86
sound exporters, 322
Step methods, 67
Stop button, 89
streams, 77–78
Streams property, 77, 78
StringToFourCharCode function, 76
subtitles
   adding, 175–181
   illustrated, 180
   movies, copying, 176, 179

overlaying, 187
text descriptor, 175–176
text track, 175
timecode, 177
track, adding, 176
translucent effect, 180
Synchronized Multimedia Integration Language. *See* SMIL
System.NullReferenceException, 147

T

text
   color, 175
   font, 175
   importer, 179
   size, 175
text descriptor
   beginning, 175
   data specifier, 187
   defined, 175
   example, 175
   format documentation, 176
   generating, 176
   generation code, 177
   illustrated, 178
   MIME type, 187
   See also subtitles
text tracks
   adding, 176
   defined, 175
   formatting, 180
   illustrated, 176, 179
   position, 180
   scaling, 179–180
   See also subtitles
TGA, 323
3G, 322
TIFF, 323
timecode, 166, 177
Time property, 68, 69
time scale, 68–69, 166
ToolTip object, 236

tooltips, 235–237
 illustrated, 235
 information, 236
tracks
 default transfer mode, 173
 defined, 71
 disabling, 74
 enabling, 74
 iterating, 72–74
 length, scaling, 172
 metadata, 119
 multiple, 72
 overlays, 172
 positioning, 74
 text, 175
 VR movies, 79
Tracks property, 72
TransferMode property, 173
TreeNode object, 205, 206
TreeView object, 204, 205
 OnBeforeExpand event, 207–208
 populating, 205
TrimToSelection method, 182
TypeName property, 321
Type property, 122

U

UNC (Universal Naming Convention) path,
 41
Undo method, 182
Unload event handler, 290
URL property, 19, 20, 41, 42, 271, 272

V

VBScript, 241
 file extension, 242
 WSH in, 5
VersionAsString property, 84
Visual Basic, 3–4
 for GUI application development, 4

release, 3
resources, 12–13
 See also Visual Basic 6 (VB6)
Visual Basic 6 (VB6), 299–306
 form, manually resizing, 304–305
 form, resizing, 303–304
 Load button, adding, 300
 object references assignment, 305
 Play/Stop button, adding, 300–302
 porting code samples to, 305–306
 QuickTime Control in, 301
 starting with, 299–300
 string concatenation, 306
 support, 299
 Toolbox, 300
 variable initialization, 305
Visual Basic for Applications (VBA), 269
 porting code samples to, 305–306
 scripts, 272
 string concatenation, 306
 variable initialization, 305
Visual Studio
 environment, coding in, 21
 Intellisense, 22
 Properties window, 18, 19
Visual Studio Toolbox
 adding QuickTime Control to, 17
 Windows Forms tab, 21
VR movies, 78–82
 hotspots, 81–82
 nodes, 79–81
 tracks, 79
 See also movies
VRNodes property, 79

W

Wave, 322
Width property, 22
Windows
 Command window, 243
 Scripting File (.wsf) format, 265–267
 scripting resources, 13

Windows Forms
    class for displaying images, 213
    defined, 200
    ToolTip component, 236
    TreeView control, 204
Windows Scripting Host (WSH), 5, 241–245
    defined, 241
    potential, 241
    version 5.6, 241
    See also scripting; WSH scripts
Windows Template Library (WTL), 311
WM_DESTROY handler, 318
WScript object, 242, 255
.wsf format, 265–267
WSH scripts
    running, 242
    save format, 242
    See also Windows Scripting Host (WSH)

X–Z

XML
    file, loading CFObjects from, 143
    parsers, 142
    string representation, 140
XML property, 140

www.ingramcontent.com/pod-product-compliance
Lightning Source LLC
Chambersburg PA
CBHW080905220326
41598CB00034B/5484